DATE DUE			
Oct 2 '72			
Nov 8 '74			
3 '76			
May 16 '77			
May 22 78			
May 22 78			
Mar 10 80			
Dec 12 '80			

Interfaith Marriages: *Who and Why*

Interfaith Marriages:

Who and Why

by

Paul H. Besanceney, S.J.

COLLEGE & UNIVERSITY PRESS · *Publishers*

NEW HAVEN, CONN.

MANUFACTURED IN THE UNITED STATES OF AMERICA BY
UNITED PRINTING SERVICES, INC.
NEW HAVEN, CONN.

TO MY PARENTS

Preface

FOR WHOM HAS THIS BOOK BEEN WRITTEN? It is directed mainly to three classes of people: to clergymen, to marriage counselors, and to social scientists. Professionals of the first two categories frequently must answer the questions of parents and of young people who are considering an interfaith marriage. This book will help them to put their advice into a larger context that is factual. Social scientists, on the other hand, have long found that the factors involved in mate selection bring into focus a great variety of topics which are central to their interests. I have taken some care, particularly in the notes, to specify improved methods for handling these rather complicated data and also to indicate some points of contact with recent theoretical statements.

Among the roles played by the writer of this book are those of priest and social scientist. The former role prompts me to be a guardian of religious values and traditions; the latter role requires that I be an objective observer of social reality. Since understanding must precede action of any sort, I find these roles quite compatible in everyday life. However, they are distinct and one cannot exercise them simultaneously in the same breath. My role as priest had much to do with my interest in the subject matter of interfaith marriages, but my investigation of the subject as related in this book is that of a social scientist. Particularly for the sake of my fellow clergymen, I must be very clear on this point. Otherwise, some will be surprised and indignant that I refrain from pleading for any form of action in this book. The value judgments of others on this subject have been examined here at length—but not my own.

Let me say something now about the title of this book, which is at the same time as simple and as descriptive as I could make it. "Interfaith Marriages—Who and Why" states, first of all, that we are concerned here with marriages between two people of different religious preferences. The "Who" in the title focuses our attention on the distinctive social characteristics of those who marry across religious lines, rather than considering their behavior within the marriage relationship. The "Why" is meant to suggest not "causes" in any inevitable sense, nor "motives" within psychological consciousness; rather, it calls attention to some *social situations* associated with the decision to enter into an interfaith marriage.

The work could be subtitled "With Data on Marriages of Protestants and Catholics in the Detroit Area" to describe the limitations of the new empirical findings presented here. Some aspects of these data are interesting and surprising. However, I do not feel that this fact alone would justify the publication of this book. It is mainly because I have thoroughly researched all the available literature written by social scientists on this subject that I feel motivated to share my evaluation of it.

The topic is certainly of practical importance. Such a book as this, which focuses on the circumstances of Protestants and Catholics who intermarry, has not so far appeared. It seems to me that it has long been needed and, in view of the spreading Protestant-Catholic dialogue, is particularly timely now. If (as is hoped) the writing of this book contributes to a more realistic discussion of the topic of interfaith marriages among Protestants and Catholics, the effort will have been well rewarded. This book should help to prepare the subject for dialogue.

The author is sincerely grateful to the many friends and associates who have helped with the research and writing of this book. It is impossible to acknowledge all of them by name because the book went through several stages and was so long in preparation. However, a few must be singled out for special thanks. At the Survey Research Center of the University of Michigan my friend John C. Scott was particularly helpful as Director of the Detroit Area Study. Dr. Jay Artis of Michigan State University was generous and kind in consenting to read and comment on two different versions of this study. I am also grateful to three other professional sociologists who read the final version and offered valuable criticisms: Dr. Hyman Rodman (Merrill-Palmer Institute), John L. Thomas, S.J. (Cambridge Center for Social Studies), and Joseph P. Fitzpatrick, S.J. (Fordham University). Their comments helped to make this a more valuable book, but of course the author must accept responsibility for the deficiencies which are still to be found in it. I wish to acknowledge also the careful and patient work of my typist for the final manuscript, Miss Helen Dougherty. Finally, I am grateful to the many fellow Jesuits who made available to me the time and facilities without which this pleasant work on the context of interfaith marriages could not have been completed.

PAUL H. BESANCENEY, S.J.

John Carroll University
February 9, 1969

Contents

List of Tables

Interfaith Marriages: *Who and Why*

I

Genesis of a Book

THIS IS A BOOK about interfaith marriages. The viewpoint and method are those of a social scientist. It is also a book with a history of its own. Perhaps the best way for the reader to be introduced to the content of what is between these two covers is to learn how it came to be what it is.

Three Stages

The writer's interest in interfaith marriages as an object of sociological study began in the spring of 1959 when he participated as a graduate student in the annual survey by the Detroit Area Study at the University of Michigan. What was learned in this stage of interest and the two to follow will presently be described in brief. Moving on to Michigan State University, the writer added the samples of several other annual surveys from the Detroit Area Study for secondary analysis and narrowed the focus of the study to factors associated with the actual choice of a marriage partner. The concept of social control and related ideas provided a theoretical framework for the data at this stage. In the present third stage, the Detroit samples have been modified somewhat. But, more importantly, the Detroit findings have been integrated with, and subordinated to, a fuller investigation of the whole subject of the decision to cross religious lines in marriage.

When one approaches a subject for the first time, the tendency is to assume that it is a simple matter that can be described and explained in all its aspects. During the writer's first stage of interest in the topic, interfaith marriages were treated as though they could stand by themselves without relation to any other type of marriage. And it seemed that one could both describe the distinctive background characteristics of those who had intermarried and also discover the ways in which their behavior *after* marriage differed from that of couples who were always religiously homogeneous. At this stage, too, little thought was given to how one might explain what was happening by some general principles; straightforward description seemed to be enough.[1]

However, in spite of this simplistic approach, the writer did learn in this first stage a few things about handling this kind of data. For instance, it was evident that Catholics and Protestants as a whole were numerous enough in the Detroit sample to allow for analysis by cross-tabulations, but that the Jews, the Orthodox Christians, and those with no religious preference were too small in number to be so analyzed. Nonwhites were also eliminated from the sample because there were too few Catholics in this category for interfaith marriages to reach a sizable number and because the taboo on racial intermarriage would distort the rest of the data on interfaith unions.

Secondly, the writer saw that, even restricting the data to the marriages of Protestants and Catholics, he would need to make a double comparison throughout: one between Protestants who were in a mixed marriage and those who were not, and another comparison between Catholics who were in a mixed marriage and those who were not.

A third discovery at this time was that one must be very clear whether one is counting married *couples* or married *individuals* when reporting intermarriage rates. For instance, in the data used from the 1959 survey, it was found that of all marriages involving Catholics, 36 per cent were mixed marriages, even though only 22 per cent of the married white Catholics were partners in these marriages. The reason for the different percentages is simply that it takes two Catholics to make a nonmixed marriage but only one to contribute toward a mixed marriage.[2]

Fourthly, one of the most significant decisions made in this study was arrived at during this first stage. This was the decision to define an interfaith marriage as one in which the two partners had been raised (socialized) in different major religious traditions. It was possible to do this because both present and previous religious preferences were ascertained for all the respondents and their spouses. Hence, for our purposes, both convert-marriages and permanently mixed marriages are included in the category of interfaith marriages. The importance of this decision will become evident later.

In the second stage of involvement in this topic, the writer was able to add the Detroit Area Study samples of 1955 and 1958 to that of 1959, yielding a combined sample of 1,470 marriages. Furthermore, a small subsample of 185 marriages taken in 1962 became available and was useful in answering several questions about interfaith marriages.[3]

At the same time, an extensive reading program was undertaken in which a search was made for all the factors associated with mate selection, as found in the writings of social scientists. A total of 254 references were examined. From this search the writer arrived at the conclusion that interfaith marriages could best be described as deviations from an endogamous norm because of the absence or ineffectiveness of social control on the part of actors most directly concerned, namely, the family and church of the newlyweds. As we shall see, many researchers have approached the subject of mate selection in these terms. However, the Manhattan study done by Jerold S. Heiss must be acknowledged as having had considerable influence on the writer at this point.

Heiss says that his theory of intermarriage assumes that:

> the ultimate source of barriers to interfaith marriage in American society lie [*sic*] in the family of orientation and formal religious organizations. . . . If, in the case of an intermarried respondent, it can be shown that these sources did not produce effective barriers to intermarriage, we will consider the marriage to be explained.

He sets down six general hypotheses to test this theory, one of which was not substantiated. In general, the intermarried are characterized by:

> (a) non-religious parents, (b) greater dissatisfaction with parents when young, (c) greater early family strife, (d) less early family integration, and (e) greater emancipation from parents at time of marriage.[4]

The Catholic data, he found, supported these five hypotheses. The support was less extensive in the Protestant data and still less in the Jewish.

Before analyzing the new data from the Detroit area, the writer therefore found it desirable to read all that he could find on the subjects of social norms, institutions, social control, and various explanations of deviant behavior, in order to understand better the phenomenon of intermarriage against an endogamous rule. By this time it must be clear to the reader why the distinctive attitudes and behavior of those who have already entered an interfaith marriage were not also investigated at this time. Although we cannot answer such questions as "Is it good or not?" or "Are they happy or not?" we have at least restricted our investigation to manageable proportions. Perhaps the other questions can be taken up at a later time.

After a lapse of two years, the writer found himself involved for the third time in the study of this topic. A new search was undertaken for writings on mate selection and on all aspects of social control as these related to interfaith marriages. By now the total of references examined had reached neary 600. It is to cull the best from this mass of sociological literature, to put it into order, and to focus it particularly on the interfaith marriages of Protestants and Catholics that this book has been written.

In going over the Detroit data at this time, the writer decided to remove eighty cases from the total of 1,470 marriages, producing a new total of 1,390 marriages. It was felt that these eighty cases had been classified earlier on the basis of inadequate information about the respondents. However, the writer also used this occasion to develop several new tables and to introduce some refinements into the handling of the data in other tables. In this book, which represents the third stage of the writer's involvement in this subject, these Detroit data will be inserted where it seems appropriate in the discussion of the entire flow of research and theorizing on this subject.

Looking Ahead

The order of treatment in the chapters below will, it is hoped, be found to be a logical one. We shall first consider the subject of mate selection in ways that do not assume the operation of social norms. This will prepare the

way for discussing in Chapter III the various types of intermarriage (other than religious) which are viewed as deviations from some of the social norms attached to the choosing
of a marriage partner. In Chapter IV the main topic, interfaith marriages, will be introduced by critically examining
sources of this type of data, the various ways of presenting
rates and ratios of intermarriage, and the empirical findings regarding rates of interfaith marriages among the three
principal religious groups in our society (Protestant, Catholic,
and Jewish). Chapter V will describe some social characteristics found to be related to intermarriage.

The concept of social control (and related sociological
ideas) will be explored in Chapter VI as a way of explaining
the phenomenon of interfaith marriages. In Chapter VII we
shall backtrack a little bit by bringing evidence to support
our assumption that there is a norm of religious endogamy
in the United States; in the same chapter the trends toward
urbanization and industrialization, as well as the forces of
secularism and individualism, will be shown to conflict with
this norm. The agents of social control which are expected
to operate in support of religious endogamy will be examined
empirically in Chapter VIII. A frequently used sociological
concept, anomia (normlessness), will be discussed in Chapter
IX as a way of explaining deviations from an endogamous
norm, and some applications of it will be empirically tested.

In Chapter X, the final one, we shall try to pull things
together by summarizing the principal conclusions and insights
which our research has led us to. There will also be a
review of recent developments, particularly in the ecumenical
movement, and an effort to project what influence these will
have on the occurrence of interfaith marriages.

Appendix A is an important part of the book for any
reader trained in social sciences. It describes the ecological
setting, the methodology, and the operational definitions of
the dependent variable. It is recommended that any reader
who is not anxious to avoid technical matters read Appendix
A before proceeding to Chapter II.

II

Social Scientists Look at Marriage Selection

THE TERM "MARRIAGE SELECTION" or "mate selection" seems to have been borrowed by sociologists from the biologists and eugenicists.[1] However, studies which ask the questions, "Who marries whom?—and why?" i.e., marriage selection, have during this century become one of the characteristic interests of sociologists. In fact, after a thorough search for journal articles concerned in some way with marriage selection, I can state confidently that the two outstanding sociological journals in this country, *American Sociological Review* and *American Journal of Sociology,* rank first and second in the number of articles published on this subject during this century. Let us see how these social scientists have approached the subject.

Marriage Rates: To Be or Not to Be? How Soon?

Every married person has at least implicitly made two decisions: first, to marry rather than not to marry; then, to marry a particular person with given characteristics. The first decision is logically prior, so we shall give some attention to it first. It can be related only indirectly to the occurrence of interfaith marriages. However, both decisions examined generally help to provide a context for our principal topic.

The *Population Bulletin* of June, 1961, gives an excellent analysis of marriage rates for many countries in the world.[2] In this issue it can be observed that since 1920 the United States has had the highest and Ireland the lowest marriage rates of Western countries. However, it is difficult to say much more than that about national gross marriage rates because their fluctuations are due to so many factors: periods of war or depression, relative size of the marriage-age population, etc.

Few social scientists have said much about those people who do not marry at all. William Ogburn, using United States Census data for 1920 and 1930, stated that "about 10 per cent reach old age without having married."[3] Paul Popenoe observed that during the first half of this century in the United States, the trend has been for fewer people to remain permanently unmarried, with the exception of the highly educated women.[4]

Although a decision to postpone marriage is not as drastic as the decision to forego it for the duration of one's life, postponements do have their impact in determining what proportion of the total population will be in the married state at any given time. This factor of age at marriage has, in fact, been widely studied. Again the best overall data on this point are provided by the *Population Bulletin*. In the United States, from 1890 to 1960, the median age at first marriage fell for men from 26.1 to 22.8 years, for women from 22.0 to 20.3 years.[5] The greatest drop occurred between 1940 and 1950 for both men and women, with no change in the following decade. However, this decline was matched or surpassed between 1930 and 1950 by most countries with comparable data.[6] Furthermore, in the latest census years, in no recorded country did men marry at an earlier age than in the United States, except in India. However, our women do not marry as young as they do in the recorded countries of Africa, most of Latin America, and half of the Asian countries.[7] No doubt there are many factors at work here, but I would guess that our high standard of living (with installment plans), together with the widespread practice of birth control, make marriage relatively less difficult to support for American men.

One reason, in fact, for considering in the same section of this chapter both the overall rates of marriage and age at marriage is that many studies combine the two when reporting what factors are found to be associated with them. For instance, besides the well-known fact that women tend to marry earlier than men, we are told that women teachers have a low marriage rate, except at forty years or over.[8]

Similarly, the rural-urban differences are reported both as rates of marriage and as age at marriage: Farm brides (not grooms) marry about one year earlier, at least in Wisconsin, than nonfarm brides.[9] Besides, even women who migrate from rural to urban areas find that their marriage rate goes down, contrary to the case for most categories of mobile people.[10] Looking at national survey data for marriages between 1947 and 1954, Paul Glick discovered that the median age at first marriage is a rather high 24.5 for men and 21.2 for women in urban areas.[11]

It is not surprising to learn that dropouts from high school and college, whether male or female, tend to marry younger than those who graduate. However, it is worth noting that highly educated people are more likely now to marry early, compared to their former practice.[12] By contrast, economic depressions make for later marriages.[13]

One of the recurring factors affecting marriage rates is an unbalanced sex ratio in a local population. Joseph Greenberg made a study of the marital status in all cities in this country with a population of 50,000 or more. He discovered, not very surprisingly, that the higher the sex ratio (male to female) of an American city, "the greater its percentage of married women and the smaller its percentage of married men."[14]

To sum up, countries have their distinctive marriage rates, as do groups or categories within a nation. The trend in recent decades has been for marriage rates to go up while age at marriage has been going down. Some of the important factors influencing marriage rates and age at marriage are sex ratio, education, and urban residence.

Should we expect such findings to have any connection with interfaith marriages? Not directly. However, there may well be some pressure on individuals to select marriage partners across religious lines if they find themselves at a disadvantage in the marriage market because of an unfavorable sex ratio locally, or if urban residence or higher education (for women) puts them at a disadvantage.

Still, one would have to be cautious about predicting a trend toward more intermarriage on the basis of any one of these variables. For instance, the increasing urbanization of our society (or of any religious groups within it) might lead one to expect lower marriage rates (and more pressure to intermarry); but the fact is, as we have seen, that the overall marriage rate has gone up with earlier marriages.

Homogamy: Like Marries Like

When biologists study mate selection, as they have done, their subject matter does not prompt them to be concerned with social norms or social control. The sociologist is concerned with these aspects, and we shall take up that concern in the next chapter. Then we shall see that the difference between homogamy and endogamy is that the latter involves a social norm. However, since some students have focused on homogamy as a pattern of "like marries like," whether or not a social norm is involved, let us do the same for now.[15]

To my knowledge, not much has been discovered to indicate strong homogamy in strictly biological characteristics, except in age relationships. Burgess and Wallin, using data from 1,000 engaged couples, found some homogamy in height, weight, health, and "physical attractiveness." They also tested for homogamy of psychological traits and discovered that the positive correlation between the scores of these couples on the Thurstone Neurotic Inventory was .25, and on a self-rating scale of twenty-three personality traits it was only .13.[16] In these aspects "like marries like" is a small truth. There is somewhat more evidence for homogamy in intellectual abilities. The same authors, reviewing earlier studies, said that "These studies, using standardized tests, gave an unweighted average husband-wife correlation of approximately .55."[17]

Age relationships are a special case of homogamy in biological characteristics. It is an everyday observation in our society that the husband is generally just a little older than the wife, but it is interesting to learn to what extent this is true. The best study of this factor seems to be that of Glick and Landau, based on a sample of 25,000 households by the United States Census Bureau, 1948. They found that the "average" wife was 2.8 years younger than her husband; 78 per cent were younger than their husbands, 12 per cent were older, 10 per cent were of the same age.[18]

Socioeconomic characteristics have sometimes been treated in studies as just another basis for assortative mating. (In later chapters we shall see that some of these are also objects of a rule of endogamy.) As one example of such a characteristic we can mention the level of education. Hollingshead found in New Haven, 1948, that for two generations there was a tendency at all levels to marry someone of comparable education. This tendency was strongest for Jews, weakest for Catholics.[19]

More than a decade ago the idea of homogamy in mate selection was given practical expression in a "Personal Acquaintance Service" in California.[20] In more recent years this has developed into something of a fad on college campuses—computer-matched dating. However, this is based not only on similar background characteristics but also on similar attitudes and values.

At this time we can confirm in general the observation made by Reuben Hill, after reviewing 150 studies, that, in the case of most of the characteristics studied, "people tend to marry people like themselves rather than opposites."[21] To the extent that this is generally true, then we would expect to find a tendency toward homogamy according to religious affiliations, even if we did not find evidence that this is also a social norm.

Heterogamy: Complementarity of Needs

Now we turn to the opposite of homogamy, namely, heterogamy, for not in all respects does it seem to be true that "like marries like.". "Opposites attract" may still be a dictum with some truth in it when one is talking about mate selection. Anderson noted, as early as 1938, that "the sole concrete evidence for heterogamy involves personality traits; but the accumulated recent data appear to demonstrate that similarity prevails here as well."[22] Let us see.

Two articles by Anselm Strauss and the later work by Robert Winch are remarkably similar to each other, but the latter does not seem to have been aware of Strauss' earlier discussion. At least he did not remember to acknowledge it among his sources. Strauss compared the temperamental traits of one's mate and one's father and/or mother. He found that "three temperamental traits had coefficients averaging over .55 for both sexes (mate—both parents): (1)

gets over anger easily, (2) self-confident, and (3) sense of duty."[23] Using the same sample and turning to the question of personality needs, he observes: "Personality needs are a direct outgrowth of early childhood affectional relationships with one or both parents"—or, later, with other associates; "the mate fills either the same needs for the individual as were previously filled by a parent, or he fills those needs that a parent left unsatisfied."[24]

Robert Winch, in collaboration with Thomas and Virginia Ktsanes, wrote an article some years later called "The Theory of Complementary Needs in Mate-Selection: An Analytic and Descriptive Study."[25] In the following year they published four more articles on the same subject,[26] finally culminating in Winch's book, *Mate Selection: A Study of Complementary Needs.*[27] The theory represents, therefore, a great expenditure of energy. Let us see what it says, especially as represented in the final version, the book.

Winch first takes note of earlier evidence for homogamy in mate selection, including homogamy of psychological characteristics. But, taking his lead partly from Freud's observation that narcissistic (self-loving) persons tend to mate with anaclitic (dependent) persons, he then states his principal thesis as follows:

> Hence it would seem that mate-selection should follow a principle of homogamy with respect to interests and attitudes. It seems almost as self-evident, on the other hand, that complementariness of motivation (e.g., dominance in one and submissiveness in the spouse, nurturance in one and receptivity in the other) would maximize gratification at the motivational level and hence that on the level of such needs mate-selection should follow a principle of complementariness.[28]

Without in any way abandoning the Freudians' interpretation of love, Winch makes use of H. A. Murray's definition of "need": a tension which, when reduced, is experienced as pleasure. In infancy these needs are mainly biological, but in maturity the social aspects become dominant. The author selects some points in the total picture of child development which he thinks give rise to needs which the individual will later seek to gratify in the marital relationship. Starting with Murray's list of needs and general traits, he and his collaborators compiled a list of twelve needs and three "general traits" to cover "the emotional and motivational elements" involved in mate-selection.[29] They then "hypothesized for every one of our fifteen variables that a person high with respect to that variable would select a mate who was low on that variable." Hence the central hypothesis: *"In mate-selection the need-pattern of each spouse will be complementary rather than similar to the other spouse."*[30]

The types of complementariness and other details of the theory need not concern us here. It is disappointing to discover, however, that the authors were able to test their elaborate theory on no more than *twenty-five* couples, all undergraduates at Northwestern University, married two years and childless. Winch's conclusion was that the data generally supported the hypothesis: The degree of association was low, but significant.

The initial reactions to Winch's theory were rather negative. However, some have tried to put it to an empirical test. Bowerman and Day, using a design which was not a close replication of that of Winch, arrived at conclusions contrary to the theory.[31] Schellenberg and Bee undertook to reconcile the conflicting results above by analyzing new data from 64 recently married couples and 36 pre-married couples. Contrary to Winch's theory, the results tended slightly in the direction of homogamy; i.e., 73 per cent of the married couples and 61 per cent of the pre-married showed *positive* associations of need patterns. "The main difference in data-gathering procedure is that in the present study scores are derived directly from a standardized personality inventory, while Winch's data are based upon ratings made by investigators after interviews."[32]

Kerckhoff and Davis later published another test of this theory.[33] Their subjects were 94 college couples who were seriously considering marriage. The methodology was objective and reported very carefully. In October, 1959, all couples filled out questionnaires separately from each other. The sample was divided into two approximately equal groups: those with "long-term" association (going together eighteen months or more) and those with "short-term" association (less than eighteen months). In May, 1960, each subject was sent another short questionnaire, to establish particularly whether they felt they were nearer to, or farther from, being a "permanent couple." Fifty-six couples thought they were nearer, 38 couples thought they were the same or farther apart.

The general hypothesis that the degree of value consensus is positively related to progress toward a permanent union found support in the data, significant at the .05 level of probability or better. The three measured types of complementarity were in the predicted direction, but their tendency toward a positive relationship with progress toward a permanent union was not statistically significant. The effect of the control variable, length of association, had not been predicted; but the analysis showed an interesting pattern. The direction of relationships remains the same, but for the short-term couples only value consensus is significantly related to progress toward a permanent union, not need-complementarity. On the other hand, for long-term couples the opposite is true: Two of three measures of need-complementarity are significantly related to progress toward a permanent union, but value consensus is not. The authors' *ex post facto* interpretation of their data is this:

> A series of "filtering factors" operate in mate selection at different stages of the selection process. Our data generally support the idea that social status variables (class, religion, etc.) operate in the early stages, consensus on values somewhat later, and need complementarity still later. Our interpretation of the delay in the operation of the complementarity factor is that such personality linkages are often precluded by the unrealistic idealization of the loved one in the early stages of courtship.[34]

In summary, the validity of the theory of complementarity of needs is still very much in question. It has been tested only on small college groups selected without systematic randomization, by researchers who had varying measures of "complementarity," with results which do not consistently support the theory. Although Kerckhoff and Davis seem to have saved the theory by their concept of "filtering factors," it seems to me that Winch must be disappointed in their findings. If the relationship between need-complementarity and a permanent union holds *only* for long-term couples, this means that "love," as Winch understands it, is a factor in mate-selection only after eighteen months or more of association. If he holds this position, he may have to fight it out with Hollywood.

How would mate-selection on the basis of complementary needs, if true, affect our rates of interfaith marriages? As Kerckhoff and Davis have shown, there need not be any direct influence at all, if religion as a social factor and complementary needs operate at different stages in the courtship process. We can probably assume that all religious groups contain some persons of the opposite sex who could satisfy the psychological needs of a given individual mate-seeker. However, if complementary needs or any other individualistic motivation is the overriding consideration, then there would not be much room for the influence of religious endogamy as a social norm.

Residential Propinquity

The theory of complementary needs is a relatively recent contribution to the study of mate-selection. However, one of the earliest hypotheses to be extensively investigated concerning this subject was that marriage partners would tend to have relatively close residences just prior to the marriage. Perhaps this is an example of sociologists belaboring the obvious. The writer was recently told of a young couple in Michigan who were planning to be married. In the course of their plans the husband-to-be moved to Florida. After a few months he wrote back that he wanted to call it off because he was going to marry another girl. The disappointed Michigan girl showed her frustration by asking, "What does she have that I don't have?" The reply came from Florida, "Nothing, except that she has it *here!*" However, granted that there is much "common sense" to the hypothesis, it is still of interest to discover to what extent and under what conditions it is verified in reality, and to see what theoretical meaning it has.

James Bossard gave the initial impetus to this line of research with his study of the distance between residences of couples shown on five thousand marriage license applications in Philadelphia in 1931. He found that one-third of all couples lived within five blocks or less of each other, and "the percentage of marriages decreased steadily and markedly as the distance between residences of the contracting parties increased."[35]

During the ensuing thirty-five years, interest in this approach to the study of mate selection has not lagged. The hypothesis is still being explored in rural American settings,[36] in other cultures,[37] and through more sophisticated mathematical analysis.[38]

However, it seems to me that Katz and Hill have expressed the best middle-range theory to date for putting order into the many ecological and sociological factors which have been shown to play a part in influencing marriage choices. After reviewing fourteen studies of residential propinquity previously published, they arrive at a synthesis which they call a *"norm-interaction"* theory, of which the basic assumptions are the following:

1. That marriage is normative.
2. That, within normative fields of eligibles, the probability of marriage varies directly with the probability of interaction.
3. That the probability of interaction is proportional to the ratio of opportunities at a given distance over intervening opportunities.[39]

The assumptions just stated are synthesized from *two* theories which these authors have drawn (not discovered simply) from the studies which they reviewed. The first of these two more primitive theories they call the *"norm-segregation* theory." This is more central to the question of interfaith marriages, and we shall come back to it in the next chapter. The second theory, which enters into their synthesis, they have characterized as "the *interaction-time-cost theory.*" Since this is more immediately rooted in residential propinquity, we shall pause to consider it here.

Katz and Hill state the basic assumptions of the *"interaction-time-cost theory"* as follows:

1. The marriage decision follows upon a period of courtship interaction. The greater the potential amount of courtship interaction, the higher will be the probability of marital choice.

2. The amount of potential interaction is inversely related to a time-cost function; the greater the cost, the less the potential interaction.

3. The time-cost function is directly related to distance.[40]

Not only does this formulation make use of the basic sociological concept of interaction and the "cost theory" approach widely used in behavioral sciences, but it also helps to explain some specific findings in the studies of residential propinquity. First there are the data from Allentown, Pennsylvania, which show that "the so-called upper classes are consistently less affected by residential propinquity in their choice of marriage partners than are the so-called lower classes."[41] In Columbus, Ohio, "the lower the occupational position, the greater the degree of residential propinquity found."[42] And in Madison, Wisconsin, most brides and grooms resided within twelve blocks of each other just before marriage, "the grooms who resided nearest their brides being semi- and unskilled workers."[43] Therefore, it seems that Katz and Hill are on the right track in including the cost factor in their theory.

*   *   *   *   *

The topics introduced in this chapter have helped to prepare the way for a discussion of interfaith marriages. We saw that sociologists have taken their ideas of mate selection or marriage selection from the biologists. They concerned themselves first with the fundamental questions of rates of marriage and age at marriage in given populations. They have also used a biological perspective in exploring the truth of the commonplace dicta that "like marries like" and "opposites attract." These are referred to scientifically as homogamy and heterogamy (complementarity of needs being a special case of the latter). The evidence indicates a pattern of homogamy in almost all respects.

The continuing interest in residential propinquity as a factor in the selection of marriage partners is another application of a basically biological model, for it is usually recognized as the business of ecology (human or otherwise) to examine the relationship of organisms to distances in their environment. However, we have seen that Katz and Hill used the rationality of economics to interpret such data in their "interaction-time-cost theory."

It seems to me that one could not sensibly study the subject of interfaith marriages without examining it in the total context of mate selection. Therefore, we have spent some time in this chapter in trying to reconstruct that context, which is largely biological, through the studies undertaken by sociologists on marriage rates, age at marriage, homogamy, heterogamy, complementarity of needs, and residential propinquity. Now we are ready to turn to a perspective which is more properly sociological, namely, that of the social norms which tend to regulate the individual's selection of a marriage partner.

III

Endogamy and Types of Intermarriage

FROM THE POINT OF VIEW of a group or category of people within society there are two fundamental and contrasting rules which may be laid down to regulate the choice of a marriage partner for its members. One rule tells them to marry outside the group; the other says to marry within the group or category. The former norm is called by social scientists, exogamy; the latter is called endogamy. In societies which have unilineal kinship systems, a rule of exogamy is generally found to be functional. In economically advanced societies, with their bilateral kinship system, the only rule of exogamy which generally persists is the taboo on incest.[1]

A rule of endogamy is much more commonly expressed in modern societies (although it need be no more modern than a clan). *Endogamy* has been defined by Kingsley Davis as "marriage into a class of persons of which I also am a member." For him *intermarriage* is a term which is always to be used with reference to endogamy as: "the violation of, or deviation from, an endogamous rule."[2] These are the definitions here accepted.

There are several types of groups or categories in our society which promote a rule of endogamy more or less vigorously (and which nevertheless witness a certain rate of intermarriage in these terms). The endogamous categories are race, religion, ethnic group, and class; and intermarriage can be observed in each of these cases. In this chapter we shall consider first of all some studies which encompass several types of intermarriage. Then we shall see what has been discovered about racial, ethnic, and class intermarriage. Since social classes are by definition stratified, we shall need to introduce with class endogamy the notions of hypergamy and hypogamy. The subject of religious intermarriage and its principal subtypes in our country will be reserved for the next chapter, since it is the principal focus of this book.

Intermarriage in General

In the preceding chapter we presented the first of two primitive theories which Katz and Hill synthesized into their "norm-interaction theory," and we left the second of these hanging in mid-air. Now it is time to drop the other shoe. The assumptions of their second primitive theory, which they call the "*norm-segregation*" theory, are these:

1. *The marriage decision is normative.* That is, the right to free choice is limited by cultural considerations. Every individual selector, according to the particular cultural group with which he identifies, has a *field of eligibles* of the opposite sex from among whom he selects his marital partner. . . .
2. *Cultural groups that form fields of eligibles tend to be residentially segregated.* It follows then that through the mechanism of segregation normative marriages would tend to cluster at low residential propinquity distances.[3]

The norm referred to is, of course, one of endogamy. And it is through segregated neighborhood patterns that parents seek to minimize the occurrence of intermarriage on the part of their children.

Earlier writers on the subject of intermarriage considered in general did not formalize a theory this well, but they did certainly recognize the normative principle which was being violated in intermarriage. The pioneering study in this country was carried out by Drachsler in New York City, in which he analyzed about 80,000 marriage certificates. He clearly understands intermarriage to be a violation of group norms, as in this passage:

Intermarriage, as such, is perhaps the severest test of group cohesion. Individuals who freely pass in marriage from one ethnic circle into another are not under the spell of an intense cultural or racial consciousness. Consequently, the greater the number of mixed marriages the weaker, broadly speaking, the group solidarity. Moreover, such a test as this is quantitative.[4]

The relationship between the various forms of intermarriage, particularly ethnic and religious, has long been a topic of some interest in this country where assimilation of immigrants (frequently confused with amalgamation) became part of the national creed. Perhaps the most frequently cited article comparing ethnic and religious intermarriage rates was titled "Single or Triple Melting Pot?" by Ruby Jo Kennedy (nee Reeves).[5] However, some six or seven years before this article was published, the Andersons had each pointed out the emergence of religious pluralism in our society. In reviewing earlier studies of mate selection, C. Arnold Anderson observed that "ethnic, economic, and religious boundaries between groups are often coterminous; but when they diverge, the religious are usually strongest."[6] Elin L. Anderson, in an excellent study of assimilation in Burlington, Vermont, said:

> It was found that for a considerable number of Burlingtonians social horizons are bounded by the barriers which separate the three main religious groups, Catholic, Protestant, and Jewish. Throughout, this was more true of the women than of the men.[7]

Since the Jews were not numerous in Burlington, the data concerned mainly the other two groups. Of these the author concluded that, "Americanization is being accomplished, but only within two separate camps."[8] Nelson also noted the same in rural Minnesota a year before Kennedy's article: "It is noteworthy that . . . intermarriage between religious groups is markedly less than among nationalities."[9] If the observation of religious pluralism was not original with Ruby Jo Kennedy, the descriptive term "triple melting pot" apparently was; and she demonstrated the salience of religious ties over ethnic ties by analyzing thousands of cases from the marriage license bureau of New Haven, Connecticut.[10]

The outstanding work on intermarriage in general is Barron's *People Who Intermarry*.[11] Although his own data collection in Derby, Connecticut, was not very extensive, his review of earlier studies seems to be quite exhaustive. He was concerned with the causes and patterns in the three principal types of intermarriage: racial, ethnic, and religious. Like the present book, his did not enter into the question of the consequences of intermarriage. His summary chapter on the "Socio-logical Factors of Intermarriage" leaves something to be desired, particularly when he groups geographical propin-quity and cultural similarity (i.e., the "closeness" of different ethnic groups to each other, as reflected in similar customs and values) under the single heading of "propinquity." However, the total work is well done and we shall have many occasions to cite it in the pages that follow.

A recent book on this subject by Albert I. Gordon has much to commend it.[12] He includes the consequences of interfaith marriages (the principal type of intermarriage that concerns him) in the scope of this book, for which he draws on his thirty-five years experience as a rabbi and his in-depth interviews with seventeen couples who had intermarried. He presents numerous position statements from clergymen of various denominations. Best of all, he obtained expressions of attitudes on intermarriage from over 5,000 students at forty universities and colleges of various types around the country. His tables are fascinating and will enter into our discussion in later chapters. In his treatment of the factors affecting the rate of intermarriage it seems to me that he is somewhat too sweeping and impressionistic. He freely ac-knowledges that he has a point of view (opposed to inter-marriage) and does not hesitate to express it. One cannot quarrel with such candor, and his fresh data are certainly worth examining.

These few pages were designed to acquaint the reader with the principal works written on intermarriage in general. Other important references will be reserved for the sections which treat of the more specific topics with which they chiefly deal. Now let us turn to the first of our principal types of intermarriage: racial.

Racial Intermarriage

What is racial intermarriage? Our answer to this question depends, of course, on our definition of *race*, and there is not very much agreement on this even among the experts. We will be content to follow the usage of more recent authors, who have stressed the *social* significance of race,

which has been built on its biological base. Race is therefore understood as: "the way members of a society classify
each other by physical characteristics."[13]

Negro-white intermarriage in the United States has taken
place at a very low rate. This is not surprising, considering
the long history of Negro slavery in this country, the long
struggle for abolition, and the fact that twenty-eight of the
states prohibited intermarriage as late as 1958—with punish-
ments as high as $1,000 fine and/or ten years in prison.[14]
We do not yet know the effect of the Loving vs. Commonwealth of Virginia decision of the U.S. Supreme Court declaring
such laws unconstitutional, as of June 12, 1967.

Our information about the rates on Negro-white marriages
is, consequently, rather spotty. Although not very recent, the
data given by Wirth and Goldhamer are probably the most
extensive on this subject. They show from other studies that
Negro-white intermarriage in this country reached its peak
in Boston for a short period after 1900, when the rate was
13.6 per 100 Negro marriages. Their own data for Boston,
1914-1938, and New York State (excluding New York City),
1916-1937, show rates from 3.1 to 5.2 in Boston, 1.7 to 4.8
in New York. Of course, these rates, if reported as per 100
marriages involving *whites,* would be very much lower
because the Negro population in these places was then so
small, proportionately.[15] Even the native-born Negroes of New
York City, 1908-1912, had a rate of intermarriage of only
1.08 per 100 marriages.[16]

More recent data from Philadelphia,[17] from Indiana,[18] and
from Washington, D.C.[19] do not estimate a *rate* of Negro-
white intermarriage but simply present a certain number of
them which the author has been able to identify. From Los
Angeles County we have more definite information. In 1948
the State Supreme Court of California declared that state's
anti-miscegenation law unconstitutional. From that time until
1959, valuable data on this subject became available. (After
1959, racial identities were no longer included in the application for a marriage license in California; hence rates of
racial intermarriage are unknown for these years.) Burma
analyzed these and found that marriages between whites and
those of other races constituted .5 per cent of *all* marriages in
1948 and that they increased little until 1957 (.9%), 1958

(1.2%), and 1959 (1.6%); Negro-white marriages make up about one-third of these intermarriages.[20]

That is about all that can be said so far about the rates of Negro-white intermarriage in the United States. Even less is known about the intermarriage rates of other nonwhites in the United States. The best information again comes from Los Angeles. Panunzio reported for the years 1924-1933 (when Filipinos were added to Japanese, Chinese, and Negroes on the list of those prohibited from marrying whites) that less than 3 per cent of the marriages were interracial—mostly involving Mexicans, Filipinos, and American Indians.[21] During the years 1948-1959 in Los Angeles, less than 1 per cent of the marriages were between whites and those of other races, in a county whose population is about 10 per cent nonwhite.[22] The whites (Anglo or Mexican) most often married (after Negroes) Filipinos, Japanese, or Chinese—in that order. In Washington, D.C., most of the interracial marriages which Sister Annella Lynn discovered were between whites and Filipinos, with the Chinese-white match being a weak second.[23] A recent article on the Puerto Ricans in New York City stated that it was useless to try to analyze their marriages on a racial basis because the Puerto Ricans overwhelmingly identify themselves as white, although other Americans might classify nearly half of them as nonwhites.[24]

Before we turn our attention outside the continental United States, let us take note of some interracial marriages that took place centuries ago among whites, free Negroes, and American Indians, giving rise to settlements which are now referred to as "tri-racial isolates" or "mixed blood racial islands." Located in the East and South of the country, they go back to colonial days. Price estimated that in the eastern United States there are from 50,000 to 100,000 such persons in groups of less than 100 to about 18,000.[25] An example of such a group in the South would be the Sabines of Louisiana (1,371 of them in 1940) who still retain the French language.[26] After the early racial mixing, all such groups became quite endogamous, as evidenced by the recurrence of a relatively small number of surnames. One of the most intensely studied of these groups is the Brandywines of southern Maryland. Harte traced the court records of the six "core" Brandywine names back to the late seventeenth century and found that the Brandywine population existed "as an isolate group from the late eighteenth century onward."[27] The remaining ten family names were added through intermarriage sometime later than 1870. There is now a general trend toward more out-marriages, especially in the smaller communities and in the urban areas.[28]

The study of interracial marriages has probably nowhere been carried on so extensively as in Hawaii, where racial endogamy has certainly not been a social norm. Ever since a small number of white men settled in Hawaii about 1790 and married the daughters of the chiefs, it has been unwise to speak publicly against interracial marriages in the Islands. The two most comprehensive records of this mixing were published by Romanzo Adams[29] and Andrew W. Lind.[30] In addition, the University of Hawaii has published since 1935 a journal called *Social Process in Hawaii*, which contains numerous articles on the interracial marriages of the Islands. Although the Japanese in Hawaii were nearly 38 per cent of the population in 1930 and they intermarried less than any other group, intermarriage rates have not declined, the general rate in 1945-1954 being 28.4 per cent of all marriages.[31]

Information about interracial marriages in other parts of the world is quite rare in English sources. We have case studies in the Panama Canal Zone[32] and in the Philippines.[33] The situation in Latin America is better known as representing a class society rather than a caste society, particularly in Brazil. Brazilians identify race on the basis of physical appearance, rather than ethnic origin. Furthermore, to show their attitude toward color and class, they have a proverb that says: "A rich Negro is a white man, and a poor white is a Negro."[34] Hence we are told that in Bahia, Brazil, "marriages cross race lines more often than class lines."[35] On the other hand, Lowrie found that in the industrialized southern State of São Paulo the racial prejudice and intermarriage patterns were more like the United States than like the rest of Brazil.[36] Should this be borne out, it would *reverse* the pattern of the United States, where more signs of racial prejudice are found in areas in which the concentration of Negroes is highest.

Now we have reviewed as much as we can the patterns of racial intermarriage in the United States and in the rest of the world. Before moving on to another topic, let us examine some of the factors which are said to account for the variations in these rates. Almost every one of the sources which we have quoted above on racial intermarriages attributes importance to their positive relationship to a high sex ratio of males to females among the immigrant groups who have come to explore for jobs and wealth. For instance, until 1900 in Hawaii the sex ratio among foreigners did not get below 299.0 to 100.[37] And in the United States in 1930 there were 40,904 Filipino males compared to 1,640 females; conversely, 76.7 per cent of the Filipino women were married, compared to 18.1 per cent of the males.[38] With rare exceptions, this imbalance is found in first-generation immigrant groups; consequently, it is their men who intermarry with the women of the native population. However, John Burma feels that this factor can be overrated and that not more than 40 per cent of intermarriages in Los Angeles could be accounted for on this basis.[39] As another indication of the stiff competition for brides that the immigrant men must face, there is evidence at least from Los Angeles and Hawaii that Caucasian men who intermarry racially are older than those who do not; i.e., it takes longer on the average for them to find a bride.[40]

It is quite certain that a high sex ratio in immigrant groups (especially racial) stimulates interracial marriages, and that it is generally foreign males (older than the average for grooms) who participate in these marriages. Other relationships have been suggested for interracial marriages, but the evidence for them is slight and it does not seem worth while to review them here.[41]

In this section on racial intermarriage, we have focused on rates of Negro-white marriages in the continental United States, then on intermarriages between whites and other non-whites, and finally on the tri-racial isolates. The more extensive racial intermarriage in Hawaii, Brazil, and other localities was reviewed. The high ratio of males to females among immigrants and its concomitant out-marriage by males at a late average age were underscored. Most observers agree with Davis and Merton that we have basically a racial caste system in this country, at least as far as American Negroes are concerned, which is reflected in the very low rates of racial intermarriage.[42] The two indications of a breakdown in this rigidity so far are the tiny but rapidly increasing rates of intermarriage in Los Angeles in 1958-1959 and the inclusion of Hawaii as a State of the Union. We can expect the movement for the civil rights of Negroes to have its influence on increasing these rates eventually. We should not expect this to come about very rapidly.[43]

Ethnic Intermarriage

As in the discussion on race, we find in the concept "ethnic group" a variable of great importance but one which is also difficult to define to everyone's satisfaction. However, we will adopt the following description of an ethnic group:

> . . . a collection of people considered both by themselves and by other people to have in common one or more of the following characteristics: (a) religion, (b) racial origin (as indicated by identifiable physical characteristics), (c) national origin, or (d) language and cultural traditions. A consequence of this definition is that it is possible to divide the population of the United States into ethnic groups in any one of a number of different ways. A second consequence is that most individuals in the United States are members of several different ethnic groups. . . . It is a hopeless task to specify the boundaries of any ethnic group exactly.[44]

It follows, therefore, that racial and religious intermarriages are merely special types of ethnic intermarriage, as understood here. However, their distinctive aspects and their importance in the literature make it desirable to talk about them apart from other types of ethnic intermarriage. Our focus in this section will therefore be on national origin and language and cultural traditions as constituting self-conscious and recognizable groups. The term is commonly used in this more narrow sense. Avoiding the comparable term "minority group" also makes it possible for us to include the following dominant types in our society as ethnic groups, singly or in combination: whites, Protestants, the English-speaking, Anglo-Saxons. It will be found, however, that authors do not always accept national origin as an adequate description of a specific ethnic group: e.g., Canadians are French or English Canadians; Russian nationals may be Polish or Jewish ethnics; Swedes, Norwegians, and Danes are sometimes grouped as Scandinavians. Even though the term "ethnic intermarriage" has itself also received various operational definitions, we shall not take time to discuss these in detail here.[45]

Those who have studied the behavior of immigrants quickly become aware that, besides interethnic marriage, there is such a phenomenon as intergenerational or internativity marriage. In other words, whether or not an immigrant marries someone of different ethnic origin, he may marry someone who is also an immigrant, or who is the child of immigrants, or who is the child of native-born Americans. Bessie Wessel developed a numerical system for labeling such marriages, which we shall follow here to the extent that it is practical: 1-1 refers to a marriage in which both parties are first-generation Americans, i.e., foreign-born; 2-2 refers to a marriage in which both parties are second-generation Americans, or native-born of foreign parentage; 3-3 refers to a marriage in which both parties are at least third-generation Americans, i.e., native-born of native parentage, whatever the ethnic derivation— also called "Old Americans." If the marriage partners belong to different American generations, the first number belongs to the male, the second to the female, as: 2-1, 1-2, 2-3, 3-2, 3-1, 1-3.[46]

Bossard seems to be the only researcher who restricted his attention to this type of marriage, ignoring interethnic marriages. In upstate New York, 1936, he discovered that 62 per cent of the marriages were between partners of the same generation in America, distributed as follows: 39.0 per cent were 3-3 marriages; 19.9 per cent were 2-2 marriages; 3.2 per cent were 1-1 marriages. The other 37.8 per cent were "internativity" marriages, distributed as follows: 26.5 per cent were 3-2 or 2-3 marriages; 6.6 per cent were 2-1 or 1-2 marriages; 4.7 per cent were 3-1 or 1-3 marriages.[47]

Because, as we have seen, there are so many ways to "slice the pie," i.e., to define categories and analyze data, it is very difficult to find results in one study which are comparable with those in another, as far as ethnic inter-marriage is concerned.[48] It seems more reasonable simply to spare the reader the boredom of a series of statistics which can scarcely be interpreted outside the context of each specific study. We are probably safe in accepting the conclusion of Milton Barron, after reviewing many studies, that "all other factors being equal, it was found that the longer a group's residence and the older its nativity in the United States, the greater was its incidence of intermarriage."[49]

It would be interesting to know specifically how the various ethnic or nationality groups compare with each other in their rate of assimilation through intermarriage. The studies we have referred to by Drachsler, Wessel, and Kennedy do provide such comparative data for a number of ethnic groups within the communities they were studying. Again it would be misleading, I fear, to reproduce these statistics here for the reader's examination. In my opinion it would be better (if we had the space for it) to evaluate the findings of each study separately, taking into consideration the author's definition of intermarriage, the composition of each nationality or ethnic group, and the length of time that each group has been in this country. Other factors that influence the rates of intermarriage for ethnic groups are the relative size of each group in that locality[50] and the sex ratio particularly of the first generation.[51] Rarely have these factors been adequately analyzed or controlled.

Let us summarize now the main points which have been made in this section. Although the term ethnic group can describe people who are conscious of their shared religion or racial origin, we have used it here of those who consciously share a national origin or a language and cultural traditions (in a land foreign to them). We have seen that studies of the intermarriage rates of such ethnic groups depend on a variety of operational definitions which make it inadvisable to compare their findings. We have, however, taken note of Wessel's numerical system for describing marriages according to the number of generations each partner can claim to be rooted in the land of settlement—a system which Bossard applied to marriages in upstate New York. As for out-group marriages, we can say that each ethnic group tends to intermarry at a higher rate in succeeding generations, as the unmixed category becomes smaller and smaller. The principal factors which are thought to contribute to this are the sex ratio in the first generation and the relative size of each group. The other important factors of occupation and religious similarity will be taken up in subsequent pages. However, for the reasons stated here (and in the notes) it is best to avoid broad generalizations that draw on several studies of ethnic intermarriage. Each such study has its own value and should be interpreted in accord with the researcher's operational definitions and the nature of his sample.[52]

Class and Caste: Endogamy and Hypergamy

In this final section of our chapter reviewing the important types of endogamy and intermarriage we take up the variables of class and caste. The principal indices of social class are occupation, education, and income—of which we shall focus mainly on the first. There will also be some overlap here with what we have already said about races and ethnic groups, but the focus will be quite different. Whereas before we were talking only about endogamous rules requiring marriage within one's group or category, now we shall also be talking about rankings within society and about the marriage patterns of people who occupy various ranks. This, in general, is the problem of social stratification as it relates to mate selection.

Kingsley Davis, in the most significant article the present writer has found on this subject, states that stratification is "the master-basis of matrimonial choice."[53] Whether this is completely true or not, the subject certainly cannot be overlooked in a treatment of intermarriage. Stratification is, of course, a major problem area in sociological theory and research. However, to go into matters like the number of social classes and how they are determined, discrete *vs.* continuous classes, status crystallization, vertical mobility in general, class consciousness—all these would take us far afield from our purpose in this chapter. We shall be content with defining the important terms and reviewing the empirical findings which seem most significant.

What is stratification? Barber describes it briefly as: "the structure of differential rankings that seems to occur in all societies."[54] Davis expresses it in a concrete distinction:

Those positions that may be combined in the same legitimate family—viz., positions based on sex, age, and kinship—do not form part of the system of stratification. . . . Those positions that are socially prohibited from being combined in the same legal family—viz., different caste or class positions—constitute what we call stratification.[55]

The two principal modes of stratification which are commonly distinguished are caste and class. The former is simply more rigid than the latter. Caste is inherited from one's parents at birth, and this status is fixed for life. One's class is also inherited at birth, but with adulthood one may achieve a higher (or lower) status.

Most people do marry within their own social class—and they are expected to. Says Davis: "A cardinal principle of every stratified social order is that the majority of those marrying shall marry equals." The functional basis for this principle is this:

> Since marriage is an institutional mechanism for procreating and rearing children, the requirements of status ascription in a caste order practically require the marriage of equals. A wife reared in a social stratum widely different from her husband's is apt to inculcate ideas and behavior incompatible with the position the children will inherit from their father, thus creating a hiatus between their status and their role.[56]

Coupled with the rule of class endogamy is the practice of hypergamy, i.e., of institutionalized intermarriage whereby a woman may marry a man who has a higher status than her own family's. This may occur even between subcastes in a caste system, e.g., in India.[57] If and when it becomes the rule rather than the exception, it will destroy that part of the system of stratification.

The opposite practice, hypogamy, is comparatively rare, whereby a woman marries a man who has a lower status than her family's. An example would be the Japanese practice called *yoshii,* according to which a man with no sons would adopt a lower class son-in-law for one of his daughters. The son-in-law takes the name and title of the father-in-law and inherits his property.[58] In American society we call this "marrying the boss' daughter" (without changing the son-in-law's name).

We have not attempted to review all the studies of social class in this country in which marriage patterns may have been incidentally discussed. As samples, however, we may take note of the following. Hollingshead found class endogamy to be the rule in the community he studied: "If we include immediately adjacent classes, then almost all cases are included."[59] A recent study of 2,706 marriage license applications in Columbus, in which census tracts were ranked economically and social class was determined by the location of addresses in these tracts, concluded that through the years 1933-58 social class endogamy remained in force.[60]

When social class is defined simply by occupation, at least two comparisons can be made. To compare the occupations of husband and wife before marriage, as Thomas Hunt seems to have done, appears to be unrealistic.[61] When sex differences are not controlled, the practice of ranking white-collar higher than blue-collar occupations does not seem to reflect a widespread evaluation of most of these jobs. Perhaps the best that we can do when we are trying to discover whether occupational hypergamy has taken place is to compare the husband's occupation with the occupation of the wife's father, as was done recently by Fitzpatrick in his study of Puerto Ricans in New York. In one way, this puts the husband at a disadvantage, since he is just starting on a career and his father-in-law has probably reached his occupational peak. In another way, the husband will have an advantage because he participates in the general upgrading of occupations in this country in recent decades, i.e., white-collar and semiskilled occupations have increased overall and relative to the skilled and unskilled blue-collar occupations. Given these qualifications (which may cancel each other out), the general finding has been that class endogamy is most common, with hypergamy (generally limited to adjacent levels) being an approved alternative.[62]

So much for occupation as an index of social class. Another index is education, and we have a number of studies concerned with the marriage choices of those who have reached the level of higher education. It is not too surprising to discover that, at least in one university, more college women than men marry someone of a higher or equal educational status.[63] This pattern seems to be functional inasmuch as it corresponds to the male and female roles within marriage and it recognizes the fact that the whole family shares the status of the husband and father. Similarly, a national sample of college students recently showed that, after racial and religious intermarriages, going outside one's educational group was most rejected (compared to nationality or economic intermarriage). In this same survey, students in the three private all-female colleges rejected educational even more than religious intermarriage.[64] As a final example of educational endogamy and hypergamy, there is the fascinating study of the American college sorority by John F. Scott. He shows that the ancient institutions of kinship are not so foreign to modern industrial life as one might think and that the well-supported sorority house maintains familial control away from home in the matter of ethnic and class endogamy for its nubile occupants.[65]

Racial intermarriage has already been discussed in an earlier part of this paper, but let us look at it now as a caste phenomenon. Race relations in this country still have the character of caste relations. Many States outlawed racial intermarriage until the 1967 U.S. Supreme Court decision declared such laws unconstitutional, and the society as a whole forbids it by custom. When it does occur, interracial marriage in this country is more likely to involve a white woman and a Negro man.[66] According to the *caste* system this is hypogamy rather than hypergamy. However, in the *class* system it is hypergamy rather than hypogamy, since the white woman has generally been of a lower class than the husband (who has a relatively high occupation). The woman's caste advantage is traded for the man's class advantage. This is understandable in theoretical terms, since in marriage the man's occupational and economic status belongs to the whole family, whereas the children's caste markings are derived from both parents. A white man marrying a Negro woman would not find this advantage for his children (or this prestige symbol for himself). In fact, we can safely predict that, if the racial caste system ever ceases to exist in our country, this pattern will disappear and we will find the more common practice to be the marriage of Negro (mulatto) women to white men, as is the case in societies without a racial caste. For instance, in Puerto Rico, a woman's attractiveness, regardless of race, will allow her to "marry upwards": "The available evidence indicates that three white men marry mulatto women for every white woman who marries a mulatto man."[67]

So, in summary, class and caste endogamy are the rule. But, because of the levels involved in stratification, we also find an alternative pattern of hypergamy. Actually, this reflects the advantage of the upper-class male, who may select a marriage partner at his own level or reach to a lower level.[68] Rarely does a society approve the opposite pattern; and, when it does, it is usually to give a status-heir to the bride's father. We saw also that a racial caste system does not approve of hypergamy. When intermarriage takes place in spite of caste endogamy, it does so in terms of class hypergamy so far as the bride is concerned, the husband gaining some caste status for himself and his children.

This brings to a close our discussion of several important rules of endogamy: racial, ethnic, caste and class. Intermarriage does occur to some extent in spite of the norms. Endogamy and intermarriage can (and do) coexist, but they are continuously in tension with each other. We shall find the same to be true as we take up now the subject of religious endogamy and intermarriage. Since it is our main topic, we shall discuss its implications at greater length.

IV

Religious Intermarriage:
How Frequent?

To ANSWER THE QUESTION "How common are interfaith marriages?" is much more difficult than would appear at first glance. There are two principal reasons for the confusion, which we will discuss at the beginning of this chapter: one is the fact that our data concerning this question come from such a variety of sources, each with its own limitations; the other reason is that there are quite a few ways of analyzing and reporting these data once they have been gathered. These are important matters to understand for anyone who wants to evaluate realistically the rates of religious intermarriage which have been reported by so many researchers.

After acquiring a sense of caution through the considerations just outlined, we will then turn our attention to the rates of interfaith marriage which have been discovered for each of the three major religious groups in the Western world: Protestant, Catholic, and Jewish. We have no data of this kind outside of Europe and the areas of heavy European colonization. Actually, most of the data available to this writer have originated in the United States. Even in this country for many years little attention was given to religious intermarriages. However, in the last twenty years this type of intermarriage has elicited almost twice as many studies as any other kind. Distinctions might have been made within each of the major religious groups, Protestant, Catholic, and Jewish, since there are many churches and sects among Protestants, several rites among Catholics, and divisions among Jews. However, studies of intermarriage generally ignore these differences, except for a few which are concerned with a specific Protestant denomination. Those people with no religious persuasion rarely appear in the results. Now to the problem of evaluating sources.

Sources and Occasions for Data-Gathering

Data-gathering is always a challenge to the researcher. However, for those who study interfaith marriages in this country, it calls for more than ordinary ingenuity. The basic reasons are that we have no question concerning religious preference or church membership in our national decennial census, and the registration of marriages by state governments generally does not identify the religion of the two people who apply for each marriage license. In many other Western countries such information is readily available. In the United States students of this subject look for substitutes in data-gathering.

In the interest of helping the reader to understand this aspect of our subject, I shall try to outline here the various sources and occasions for gathering information about interfaith marriages—before going on to comment about the advantages and limitations of some of them. One basic distinction to keep in mind is that a relatively few studies are *national* in scope, whereas most are *local.* Beyond this fairly obvious distinction, we can outline the various types of data-gathering as follows:

A. On the occasion of the wedding.
 1. From civil records.
 2. From ecclesiastical records.

B. At a time not relevant to the wedding day.
 1. By access to household addresses.
  a. With complete coverage of an area.
  b. Sampling for partial coverage.
   i. Selection based on a known probability.
   ii. Selection based on the researcher's judgment and/or availability of the respondents.
 2. By contacting individuals directly.

It seems to me that all known studies of interfaith marriages can be located according to their method of data-gathering in one of these categories—or perhaps they use a combination of them. Let us now consider some of the advantages and limitations of these types of data-gathering (with a few examples).

A. Data Taken on the Occasion of the Wedding

Advantages: Presumably this is the most complete information on which to base rates of intermarriage. Marriages which may later be broken by death, divorce, separation, or desertion are here included. The record generally distinguishes first marriages from remarriages. Other useful information will generally be included, such as addresses, ages, type of ceremony. Trends in the frequency of intermarriage can be identified if the records are continuous and standardized.

Limitations: Religious identification is frequently not ascertained, as, for example, in New York City and New Haven. A change in religious identification will not be recorded here. (Hence conversions which occur before the marriage will cause originally mixed marriages to be undercounted.) There will not be an opportunity to ask other important questions about social characteristics or attitudes. In sampling from the records, the researcher may be unaware of biases in his data which are attached to the years or months or days he has selected.

B. Data-gathering on Other Occasions

Advantages: This procedure produces a kind of snapshot portrait of the population being studied. There is an opportunity to ask about religious identifications, past and present, and about other social characteristics and attitudes.

Limitations: A survey of marriages in which the couples are living together will necessarily leave out of consideration those marriages broken by death, divorce, etc. If it inquires only about *present* religious preferences, it will miss the conversions that took place both before *and after the marriage,* thereby underestimating the originally mixed marriages. A trend in rates of intermarriage is not so easily revealed by this procedure, either. Finally, to sample and survey a large population is much more expensive for the researcher than to use available records.

A–1. Civil Records as a Source of Data

Civil records of marriages must include all cases because their function is to verify the existence of legal relationships. Unfortunately, however, in this country only two states include religious identification as one of the questions: Iowa since 1953 and Indiana since 1959. Even so, other civil records do show the name of the officiant and whether it was a civil or a religious ceremony.

A–2. *Usefulness of Ecclesiastical Records*

The most serious disadvantage of ecclesiastical records is that they do not include the marriages of people who identify with a particular church but have not made use of its religious ceremony. The extent to which marriage records of the Roman Catholic Church underestimate the total marriages of Catholics civilly recorded has been studied in the Netherlands,[1] in a city of Canada,[2] and in Iowa.[3] The undernumeration of inter-faith marriages in Protestant and Jewish records will be even greater, since they generally do not require this religious ceremony for their members to remain in good standing, as the Catholic Church does. For instance, Erich Rosenthal reports that, "Between 1953 and 1959, 65.6 per cent of Jewish intermarriages were solemnized in a civil ceremony, as compared with 20.5 per cent of Jewish in-marriages."[4]

On the other hand, data for church-sanctioned Catholic marriages, mixed and unmixed, are published annually for the entire United States in *The Official Catholic Directory*[5] and can be used to study trends in the country or in any Catholic diocese.[6] Both mixed and unmixed Catholic marriages, so registered, will include some "convalidations" by a religious ceremony of marriages that were earlier contracted only in a civil ceremony. Some researchers have gone to the actual records in diocesan chanceries or in parish rectories to analyze the proportion of Catholic marriages that were originally contracted in this religiously invalid manner.[7] However, church records, like civil records, do not register conversions which may have occurred prior to the marriage, thereby underestimating the number of marriages of couples with religiously heterogeneous backgrounds.

B–1–a. *Canvassing All Households of an Area*

Although many countries apparently do include a question about religious affiliation in the decennial census of their population, no study of interfaith marriages known to this writer has tried to make use of such data. The reason is probably that these same countries keep a continuous registration of marriages, including the religious identification of the parties, which provides a better source of data for this subject.

We have, therefore, no studies of interfaith marriages based on national data that cover all households. However, there have been rather intensive studies of small communities[8] or parishes[9] in which mixed marriages were enumerated and analyzed. The chief advantages that this case-study approach has are that more detailed information can be gathered and relationships between variables can be examined in their whole context. For instance, the religious behavior and attitudes of couples in mixed or unmixed marriages can be compared. On the other hand, there is no sound basis for generalizing from such a small locality to the general population of a city or nation. Such research is mainly exploratory.

B—1—b. *Sampling Some Households of an Area*

As social scientists know, when all members of a population are given a known probability of being selected into a large sample, then the laws of probability can make it legitimate to generalize from the sample to the entire population. In the United States the Bureau of the Census has so far used one such national sample to ask about religious affiliations and marriages.[10] Private survey organizations have also sampled the metropolitan areas of Manhattan in New York City,[11] Washington, D.C.,[12] and Detroit,[13] asking questions which could later be related to the study of interfaith marriages. Such samples have the same advantages and limitations as do surveys which canvass all households in an area, besides the added advantage that one can legitimately generalize from the sample to a larger population (recognizing that a known margin of error due to chance has been introduced).

Of course, if the researcher relies on his judgment or on the availability of respondents to select his sample of addresses, there is considerable danger of bias in the results. For example, Stanley Bigman was able to compare his probability sample of Washington households with a "master list" of known Jews compiled from the mailing lists of Jewish organizations. The contrast in the proportion of mixed Jewish families from the two sources is quite significant:

> As might be anticipated, the samples from the Jewish list showed a much lower proportion of mixed families than the sample of blocks. Of the 15,500 Jewish families identified in samples from the list of Jews, 5.2% were mixed, compared to 19.9% of the 11,700 Jewish families identified in the block sample. Or, in other words, 75.6% of the 3,300 mixed families were found in the block sample, 24.4% of them in samples derived from the list.[14]

This should convince the reader that it is important to know the source of the data before one accepts at face value the reported rate of interfaith marriages or compares this rate with any other he may know of.

B–2. *Contacting Individuals Directly*

This procedure is not fundamentally different from selecting households or addresses, except that it underscores the easy accessibility of some respondents. There is even less justification for generalizing to a larger population here than there would be in the instance cited of using membership lists. If the researcher selects such a sample of acquaintances or available people, he must be careful to concern himself only with the internal dynamics of his cases and not generalize beyond them.[15]

Ways of Reporting Rates of Intermarriage

It is time now to move on to a consideration of the other fundamental reason for confusion regarding rates of interfaith marriages, namely, the various ways in which these data are analyzed and reported once they have been gathered in one of the procedures just described. I will try to list these ways of reporting rates of intermarriage in a more-or-less logical order and comment on the reasons for the confusion.

1. *Rates Based on Marriages vs. those Based on Individuals*

One of the most persistent sources of confusion about the reported rates of religious intermarriage has been the failure to pay attention to the distinction between rates based on individuals and rates based on marriages.[16] Until now it has been more common for researchers to report rates of inter-marriage based on marriages, except for those who make use of civil registrations in other countries.[17] The difference between the two rates can be explained by way of a hypo-thetical example: If 30 out of 100 Hindus married across religious lines, we would say that the rate of intermarriage for Hindus is 30 per cent; however, in the same example 46 per cent of the marriages of Hindus would be interfaith marriages. Why the difference? Because it takes twice as many Hindus to constitute an unmixed Hindu marriage as it does to participate in a mixed Hindu marriage. To avoid this type of confusion, Rodman has suggested that researchers distinguish in their reports between "the *mixed marriage* (or intermarriage) *rate for marriages* and the *mixed marriage rate for individuals.*" He has also invented simple formulas for translating one rate into the other without having the raw data to work with.[18] In the future, therefore, we may expect better communications in this respect.

2. *Rates Based on the Whole Population or on One Category*

Most rates of intermarriage, by far, are computed on the base of marriages or married individuals for a particular cat-egory or group in the population: for example, rates of inter-marriage for Protestants, Catholics, or Jews. However, occa-sionally it happens that a single rate of intermarriage is reported for all marriages in a country.[19] If the reader is not alert to this, he may compare such a rate with those he has seen elsewhere for particular groups and be surprised at this low rate of intermarriage. Of course, it is simply due to the larger total number of marriages on which the percentage has been computed and the fact that, when intermarriage rates are computed for separate categories in a population, the mixed marriages will actually be counted twice (once with each mixed category). For instance, the 1957 sample of the United States population by the Bureau of the Census showed that the overall rate of intermarriage for the major religious groups was 6.4 per cent, whereas for each major category alone it was, respectively: Protestants 8.6 per cent, Catholics 21.6 per cent, Jews 7.2 per cent.[20] The rate of intermarriage for the entire population will necessarily be lower than it is for individual categories. (This confusion will occur only when these comparisons are made between mixed marriage rates based on marriages, not when the comparisons are made between mixed marriage rates based on individuals.)

3. *A Ratio which is Adjusted to the Size of the Group*

Whether one is talking about the population of a nation, of a state or province, of a metropolitan area, or of a village, the largest category (by any single criterion) in that area will tend to have the lowest rate of intermarriage. This is simply because members of the largest category will find many more homogeneous marriage partners available to them than will members of the smaller categories. Mere chance distribution of potential marriage partners would produce this effect mathematically. Even though the smallest category may be a group that feels threatened in its very existence by this, the fact that this mathematical tendency is there has nothing to do with a group's solidarity or the strong appreciation that they have for their values.

We have had no dearth of sociologists pointing out that as a group's proportion in the general population goes up, the rate at which its members intermarry goes down. Barron first spelled it out clearly about twenty years ago: "As for numerical size, all other factors being equal, intermarriage incidence varies indirectly and breadth of selection varies directly with the relative size of the group."[21] The same inference has been drawn more recently from the records of Catholic dioceses in this country,[22] from civil records in Canada,[23] and from both state-reported and diocese-reported marriages in Iowa.[24] A group's proportion in the general population is related, of course, to the factor of residential propinquity, which we discussed in Chapter II. Rosenthal has correctly pointed out, however, that this important mathematical factor "becomes significant only in the absence of group cohesion," which we shall consider in a later chapter under the heading of "social control."[25]

Since the factor of relative group size is not, properly speaking, a sociological one, it would seem that sociologists might want to control its influence before trying to explain variations in intermarriage rates as a sociological phenomenon. It is possible to do so by determining how the potential marriage partners would distribute themselves by chance according to the several categories within a given population, but for this one must be able to estimate how many persons there are of marriageable age within each category in the area. The present writer has done this for his data in the Detroit area.[26] In doing so, he simply reconstructed the method that Glick had apparently used for the 1957 national data.[27] Heer has used precisely the same procedure for his Canadian data,[28] and Leonard Broom used a similar one for ethnic intermarriages in Hawaii.[29] These are all not much different from other measures of association that have been in use by statisticians for many years.[30] Although we might wish that such a control for group size were always used in reporting rates of intermarriage, the fact is that in our country one cannot so easily determine the relative size of each religious category in a given locality. Without an enumeration of religious affiliations in our decennial census or in our marriage registrations, we do not have a good basis generally for computing such a ratio of actual to expected rates of religious intermarriage in the United States. So, again, researchers are forced to improvise and to do the best they can with the data available.

4. *Types of Intermarriage, including Conversion Possibilities*

It is my conviction—and one of the principal emphases of this book—that, when the average individual in our country speaks of mixed marriages and the likelihood of their occurrence, he is referring to those matches which involve a person raised in one religious tradition with another person raised in a different religious tradition. The fact that one or the other partner may eventually convert and make it a homogeneous marriage is an important but secondary consideration. In the United States we have, in fact, underestimated the rate of religious intermarriage mainly because of two facts: (a) our data are drawn from surveys which ask only about the present religious preference of the respondents and thereby miss those marriages in which one or other party has converted to make it a religiously homogeneous marriage;[31] (b) our data are frequently drawn from ecclesiastical records which leave uncounted those mixed marriages which are solemnized (at a high rate) in civil ceremonies.[32]

How many married couples with different religious backgrounds are overlooked when one asks only about *present* religious preference or affiliation? So far our evidence is rather piecemeal on this point. Those studies which ask only about religious conversions which have taken place *after* the marriage tell just part of the story.[33] Similarly, a study which asks only about the early religion of the marriage partners (when they were growing up)—and does not ask about subsequent conversions on the part of either one of them—is leaving out an important question from the point of view of social control and does not reveal how many of these marriages are *currently* mixed.[34]

There is growing evidence that conversions between the major religious groups in this country generally are associated with marrying someone of a different religious background. Joseph H. Fichter, S.J., found that "marriage to a Catholic is in some way connected with about 75 per cent of all adult conversions within the limited area of twenty-three urban southern parishes."[35] David M. Eichhorn discovered, through a mailed questionnaire returned by 67.7 per cent of the Conservative and 91.3 per cent of the Reform rabbis actively functioning in the United States, that marriage to a Jewish person was involved in 93.9 per cent of Reform and 96 per cent of Conservative conversions for all these rabbis in their entire careers.[36]

Of course, it does not follow that because people who convert are likely to be involved in intermarriages that therefore those who intermarry will generally convert (one or the other). Murray Leiffer's survey of one community revealed that only 9 per cent of intermarried Catholics changed to Protestant while 7 per cent of intermarried Protestants changed to Catholic.[37] In a survey of Jewish intermarriages in Providence, R.I., it was found that 42 per cent of the non-Jewish partners had converted to Judaism.[38]

In our Detroit data the evidence is stronger that intermarriage is generally accompanied by conversion. In his 1958 sample of that community Gerhard Lenski had found that one-fifth of the marriages which were *unmixed* according to

TABLE 1.—*Types of Interfaith Marriages among Protestants and Catholics in the Detroit Area, 1955, 1958, and 1959*

Types of Interfaith Marriages	Number	Per Cent
Protestant unchanging; spouse changes	87	27
Protestant with Catholic or other	129	40
Protestant changes; spouse unchanging	106	33
Total of Protestant mixed marriages	322	100
Catholic unchanging; spouse changes	104	33
Catholic with Protestant or other	125	39
Catholic changes; spouse unchanging	91	28
Total of Catholic mixed marriages	320	100

present religious preferences were actually contracted by couples raised in different faiths.[39] The situation is presented somewhat more sharply by looking only at the interfaith marriages of Protestants and Catholics in the Detroit area surveys of 1955, 1958, and 1959, as presented in Table 1. Here it can be seen that only *two out of five* marriages of Protestants or Catholics which were originally mixed according to early religious preferences *remained mixed marriages* at the time of the surveys. The remaining marriages involved conversions. one way or the other, with a slight tendency for Protestants to do more changing than Catholics in this combined sample. Furthermore, in a small 1962 sample in Detroit the same proportion of conversions was found among the intermarriages and, in addition, it could be shown that more than three-fourths of the conversions occurred within one year of the date of the wedding.[40]

Later studies may show that Detroit is not typical in these respects. However, the main point that I wish to make here should be clear: If an interfaith marriage means the matching of two people who have different religious backgrounds, then most published rates of intermarriage in this country seriously underestimate the extent to which religious intermarriage has been occurring. They do so because the association of conversions with intermarriage has been ignored.

5. *The "Triple Melting-Pot Hypothesis"*

One of the best known generalizations about intermarriage says that Americans are marrying at increasing rates across

ethnic lines while they continue to marry within each of
the three major religious groups. This is called the "triple
melting-pot hypothesis" from an article published over twenty
years ago by Ruby Jo Reeves Kennedy.[41] It has hardly been
substantiated outside of New Haven, but I do not doubt that
the hypothesis is correct in practically every city in the
country. Nevertheless, I think that the hypothesis should not
have been stated. It is deceptive. Even though the generalization is true enough, it means practically nothing because
it is an artifact of the phenomena described in Numbers 3
and 4 of this section. We saw in No. 3 that the larger the
relative size of a group in a population, the lower will be
its rate of intermarriage—by mathematical necessity. Applying this fact to the "triple melting-pot": If people of Irish, Italian, and Polish origin constitute the Catholic population within
a community, their individual rates of ethnic intermarriage
will be higher than the Catholic rate of religious intermarriage even if marriage partners are distributed at random
(because the ethnic groups are smaller than the religious
group of which they are parts). Furthermore, the unmixed
ethnic groups will shrink in relative size in succeeding generations due to any amount of ethnic intermarriage, becoming
still more subject to this mathematical necessity. On the other
hand, as we saw in No. 4, religious groups need not shrink
in size at all due to intermarriage, since conversions make
many of these marriages homogeneous and the children are
not identified as having a "mixed religion." The hypothesis
will be much less true (even superficially) if you base the
rate of religious intermarriage on early, rather than on present, religious preferences. For these reasons I believe that
the "triple melting-pot hypothesis" should be avoided, since
a comparison of rates of ethnic and religious intermarriage
is deceptive.[42]

6. *Rates Based on First Marriages Only or on All Marriages*

Unless otherwise stated, we can assume that all published
rates of interfaith marriages are based on all marriages in
a specific time and place. However, there is striking evidence that in Iowa, at least, there is a much greater tendency toward religious intermarriage for remarriages than for
the first marriage. Among Jews in Iowa, 1953-59, the rate

of interfaith marriages for first marriages was 36 per cent; for remarriages it was 54 per cent.[43] For Catholics in Iowa, 1953-57, first marriages showed a rate of religious intermarriage of 30 per cent, whereas remarriages had an intermarriage rate of 63 per cent.[44] The reader will want to keep this in mind in interpreting general rates of interfaith marriages which include remarriages as well as first marriages.

7. How Samples Differ by Their Exclusions

I would like to urge on the reader one final caution before presenting published rates of religious intermarriage: In more ways than we can detail here, researchers will elect to exclude certain categories from their samples. These decisions should be known by the reader, if possible, and taken into consideration before comparing rates of intermarriage from different studies. For instance, in the Manhattan study by Heiss and in the Detroit data presented by this writer all nonwhites have been excluded from the computations. My own reason for doing so was the taboo on interracial marriages. The proportion of Catholics among Negroes in Detroit is so small that they could not be expected to marry Negro Protestants at a rate comparable to the white Catholics marrying white Protestants, and there were not enough of them to justify a separate analysis.[45] Ignoring the taboo on racial intermarriage by including nonwhites in the analysis of interfaith marriages will have the effect of enlarging the "expected" rate of religious intermarriage for Catholics and reducing it for Protestants—which is contrary to the real situation. This probably contributes to making the intermarriage rate expected by chance in the 1957 national survey somewhat higher for Catholics and somewhat lower for Protestants than it otherwise would be.[46]

Let me mention one further example of how a category of marriages can be omitted, intentionally or not. If a researcher elects to use civil registrations in computing rates of religious intermarriage, he will automatically be excluding perhaps most of the marriages of the foreign-born, since their marriages will generally be registered in another country.[47]

This section of the chapter has listed and explained some ways of reporting rates of intermarriage. It is hoped that the reader has now acquired the sense of caution which is appropriate for interpreting the published rates of interfaith marriage. Now let us proceed to examine these rates for each major religious group in our country.

Following through on the discussion thus far in this chapter, the tables for rates of intermarriage in the three major religious groups *will not show*

- rates from ecclesiastical records,
- rates from religious membership lists,
- rates from surveys which ask only about present religious preference,

since each of these seriously underestimates the actual rates of interfaith marriage in the population; but they *will show*

- rates from civil records, if religious identification was asked,
- rates based on *all* marriages, including remarriages,
- rates based on *early* religious preferences,
- rates from surveys (complete, or of probability samples), even though these may underestimate intermarriage rates by counting only marriages which have survived.

Rates and Trends: Jewish-Gentile Marriages

Undoubtedly no type of religious intermarriage has been studied so extensively as that between Jews and Gentiles. This is probably because the Jewish community has no shortage of scholars, particularly in the social sciences, and intermarriage has been traditionally a subject of much concern as a threat to group survival.

Before turning to the rates of intermarriage found for Jews on this continent, let us consider briefly the rates reported from civil registrations in Europe from 1875 to 1935. The rates listed by Arthur Ruppin are the most comprehensive. They range from a low of 0.4 (0.2)[48] intermarriages for each 100 marriages of Jews in Lithuania for 1931 to a high of 71.9 (56.1) per cent for the city of Trieste in 1927. In each country or city for which he has data, the rate rises consistently until 1933 and then falls off—the only exception being Hungary where the rate of intermarriage held at the crest through 1934 and 1935. In 1933 the rates of intermarriage per 100 marriages involving Jews were: 20.5 (11.4)

in Czechoslovakia, 24.4 (13.9) in Hungary, 43.8 (28.0) in
Germany, and 43.9 (28.1) in Bohemia. It seems likely that
the decline in intermarriage after this was due in part to
the racist anti-Semitism that accompanied Hitler's rise to power.

Let us turn now to the rates of Jewish intermarriage found
in the United States and Canada. Table 2 shows only those
rates which meet the criteria stated at the end of the pre-

TABLE 2.—*Selected Rates of Intermarriage per 100 Marriages of Jews in the
United States and Canada, 1908-1960*

Area	Years	Per Cent		Reference*
New York City	1908-12	4.3	(2.2)†	Drachsler (1920), p. 121
New Haven	1870	0.0	(0.0)	Kennedy (1944), p. 333
New Haven	1900	1.1	(0.6)	Kennedy (1944), p. 333
New Haven	1930	5.0	(2.6)	Kennedy (1944), p. 333
New Haven	1940	6.3	(3.2)	Kennedy (1944), p. 333
New Haven	1948	5.6	(2.9)	Hollingshead (1950), p. 622
New Haven	1950	3.9	(2.0)	Kennedy (1952), p. 59
Iowa	1953	36.3	(22.2)	Rosenthal (1963), p. 37
Iowa	1954	38.1	(23.5)	Rosenthal (1963), p. 37
Iowa	1955	44.7	(28.8)	Rosenthal (1963), p. 37
Iowa	1956	40.4	(25.3)	Rosenthal (1963), p. 37
Iowa	1957	44.9	(28.9)	Rosenthal (1963), p. 37
Iowa	1958	38.0	(23.5)	Rosenthal (1963), p. 37
Iowa	1959	53.6	(36.6)	Rosenthal (1963), p. 37
Manhattan "Midtown"	1957‡	18.4	(10.1)	Heiss (1960), p. 49
Canada	1926-30	4.9	(2.5)	Rosenberg (1963), p. 62
Canada	1931-35	5.1	(2.6)	Rosenberg (1963), p. 62
Canada	1936-40	6.2	(3.2)	Rosenberg (1963), p. 62
Canada	1941-45	9.6	(5.0)	Rosenberg (1963), p. 62
Canada	1946-50	9.1	(4.8)	Rosenberg (1963), p. 62
Canada	1951-55	11.7	(6.2)	Rosenberg (1963), p. 62
Canada	1956-60	14.1	(7.6)	Rosenberg (1963), p. 62

* References found in this table and not cited earlier in this chapter are:
Julius Drachsler, *Democracy and Assimilation* (New York: Macmillan, 1920);
August B. Hollingshead, "Cultural Factors in the Selection of Marriage
Mates," *American Sociological Review*, 15 (1950), pp. 619-27; Ruby Jo
Reeves Kennedy, "Single or Triple Melting-Pot? Intermarriage in New
Haven, 1870-1950," *American Journal of Sociology*, 58 (1952), pp. 56-59.

† The number in parentheses indicates the rate of intermarriage for *individuals.* Each of these was computed by this writer, using Rodman's formula,
from the rate of intermarriage for *marriages.* For Rosenberg's and Hollingshead's rates the computation was reversed.

‡ This is the year of the survey, not the year when the marriage took
place.

ceding section of this chapter and are therefore thought to be roughly comparable. The rates are all based on the civil registration of marriages, except for the Manhattan rate which comes from a survey that identified *early* religious preferences.[49] Two aspects of these data seem to call for special comment: the exceptionally high rates in Iowa, and the apparent trend toward more intermarriage in Canada and slightly so in New Haven and Iowa. If we could adjust for the relative size of the Jewish community in each of these areas, it is certain that the rates of intermarriage in Iowa would be much closer to the rest, since Jews constitute just .33 per cent of the total population of that state and only 1.5 per cent in Des Moines.[50] As for the trend toward more intermarriage, it seems to be quite consistent in Canada, also in New Haven except for the final decade. In the case of Canada, David Heer has shown that the trend holds true even after one computes a ratio of the actual to the "expected" rates of intermarriage.[51]

The following published rates of intermarriage per 100 Jewish marriages were deliberately omitted from the table for reasons which make them not comparable to the others: 0.0 per cent and 16.7 per cent in Derby, Connecticut;[52] 7.2 per cent for the United States in 1957;[53] 13.1 per cent in Washington, D.C.;[54] 4.5 per cent in Providence, Rhode Island;[55] 7.7 per cent in the largest U.S. metropolitan areas.[56]

Rates and Trends: Catholic Intermarriages

Turning now to Catholic intermarriages, there seems to be little information from European countries available. However, the excellent study from the Netherlands by Van Leeuwen shows that 13 per cent of the nation's Catholics are in mixed marriages, varying from 2 per cent in the most Catholic rural area to over 30 per cent in the urbanized coastal area. He notes the tendency for civil records to show more mixed marriages than church records do. In the large cities of the Holland provinces the increase in interfaith marriages has been quite striking, in Rotterdam rising from 20 per cent in the years 1879-93 to 48 per cent in 1936-38.[57]

Table 3 presents the rates for Catholic interfaith marriages in the United States and Canada. Even though all of these

TABLE 3.—*Selected Rates of Intermarriage per 100 Marriages of Catholics in the United States and Canada, 1926-1961*

Area	Years	Per Cent		Reference*
Derby, Conn.	1929-30	15.6	(8.5)†	Barron (1946), p. 167
Derby, Conn.	1940	8.8	(4.5)	Barron (1946), p. 167
Parish A	1930‡	21.0	(11.7)	Dubius (1930), p. 416
Parish B	1930‡	22.0	(12.4)	Perplexus (1930), p. 313
Parish C	1937‡	50.0	(33.3)	Schnepp (1944), p. 108
New Haven	1948	11.7	(6.2)	Hollingshead (1950), p. 622
Iowa	1953	42.0	(26.6)	Chancellor-Monahan (1955), p. 237
Iowa	1953-57	35.0	(21.2)	Burchinal-Kenkel-Chancellor (1962), p. 26
Manhattan "Midtown"	1957‡	21.4	(12.0)	Heiss (1960), p. 49
Detroit	1955‡	45.0	(29.0)	Besanceney (N=327)
Detroit	1958‡	48.0	(31.6)	Besanceney (N=200)
Detroit	1959‡	35.0	(21.2)	Besanceney (N=262)
Detroit	3 combined‡	42.0	(26.6)	Besanceney (N=789)
Detroit	1961	39.0	(24.2)	Besanceney (N=133)
Canada	1926-30	15.5	(8.4)	Rosenberg (1963), p. 62
Canada	1931-35	17.9	(9.8)	Rosenberg (1963), p. 62
Canada	1936-40	16.2	(8.8)	Rosenberg (1963), p. 62
Canada	1941-45	18.7	(10.3)	Rosenberg (1963), p. 62
Canada	1946-50	19.5	(10.8)	Rosenberg (1963), p. 62
Canada	1951-55	20.3	(11.3)	Rosenberg (1963), p. 62
Canada	1956-60	20.9	(11.7)	Rosenberg (1963), p. 62

* Each of the references in this table has been cited earlier in this chapter. Besanceny's revised rates have not been published before.

† The number in parentheses indicates the rate of intermarriage for *individuals*. Each of these was computed by this writer, using Rodman's formula, from the rate of intermarriage for *marriages*. For Hollingshead's and Rosenberg's rates the computation was reversed.

‡ This is the year of the survey, not the year when the marriage took place.

rates meet the criteria outlined earlier, the first five of them are from case studies of very small areas and therefore we should not be surprised that the rates are so variable, from 8.8 to 50.0. On the other hand, the low rate of 11.7 from New Haven is quite puzzling. In challenging this, Thomas pointed out that even ecclesiastical records for the entire State of Connecticut show an intermarriage rate of 40.2 for Catholic marriages in 1949.[58] It seems to me that much of the difference might be explained through the automatic action of the factor of the relative size of the Catholic population. By taking as his population only those married people having addresses within the city a few months after the wedding, Hollingshead apparently got an unusually large proportion of Catholics (not yet fled to the suburbs). One of his tables shows that, of the wives belonging to a major religious group, 66 per cent were Catholic, 19 per cent were Protestant, and 15 per cent were Jewish. This would automatically bring down the Catholic rate of intermarriage. Furthermore, Italians and those of purely Italian descent constituted about half of the people in this sample, making it less likely that there would be religious intermarriage among Catholics.

The factor of relative size of the group would again explain some of the difference between the rates for Manhattan "Midtown" and for Detroit. In the former restricted area Catholics made up 51 per cent of the married people in the sample, compared with 43 per cent in the Detroit area. For a larger group we expect a somewhat lower rate of intermarriage. However, that would be only a partial explanation. By the same principle, we would expect the rates in Iowa (where Catholics are about 22 per cent of the population) to be notably higher than Detroit's. One influence that would keep Iowa's rates of intermarriage rather low is that civil registrations (which these are) ignore conversions which took place *before* the marriage, thereby undercounting the mixed marriages more than the surveys in Detroit or Manhattan would do. So it should be clear that even these relatively comparable intermarriage rates need careful appraisal.

The rates of Catholic intermarriage in Canada show an increase continuously in the years 1926-60, except for a decline in 1936-40. Heer did his own analysis of rates for every fifth year, 1927-57, and found an increase of 60 per cent, from 7.2 per cent in 1927 to 11.5 per cent in 1957. This trend was true of each province, even when controlling for the relative size of the group.[59]

In the case of the United States, one set of data, which we have not included in the table because it derives from ecclesiastical records, does not show evidence of a trend toward more interfaith marriages for Catholics in the years 1943-62.

Reiss found that church-reported Catholic intermarriages for
the United States in 1943 were 31.7 per cent of the marriages
of Catholics. The rate remained above 30 per cent during
the war years 1944-45, but after that did not go as high
as 29 per cent nor lower than 26.1 per cent.[60] The growth
in the Catholic proportion of the American population in
recent decades would tend to depress the rate of intermarriage, of course. According to the evidence that we have,
therefore, there is no important trend in intermarriage for
Catholics in this country, whatever may be the case in Canada.

Again, many published rates of Catholic intermarriages have
been omitted from Table 2 because they do not satisfy the
criteria stated earlier. All rates based on church-reported data
were omitted because they seriously underestimate the number of intermarriages of those who identify themselves as
Catholics, counting only those whose marriage has been blessed
by the Church. Kennedy's rates for New Haven were not included since her assumption seems to be a dubious one: that
almost all who identify themselves as Italian, Irish, or Polish
will be Catholic, and that the Protestants are those who list their
own or their parents' birthplace as Scandinavian, German, or
British-American (apparently third-generation Americans with
any national background.)[61]

Also omitted from the table was the rate of intermarriage
for individuals of 13 per cent, and for marriages of 23 per
cent, discovered by Charles Westoff *et al.* in their sample
of the largest U. S. metropolitan areas. It was not comparable
to the rates shown in the table because it was based on present religious identifications and was also restricted to couples
who had just two children.[62]

Rates and Trends: Protestant Intermarriages

There are relatively few studies showing the rates of
Protestant mixed marriages. None of those available to this
writer is based on European data. This does not seem to be
due to lack of interest, since many Protestant clergymen have
published warnings concerning the dangers in marriages to
Catholics particularly. It is probably because there is not
the Catholic insistence on a churchman officiating, and consequently no uniform and comprehensive Protestant church

records. However, a number of researchers have published rates for all three major religious groups.

Although each of the studies in Table 4 satisfies the criteria set down before we began to review the rates of religious intermarriage, there are special reasons why the unusually high rates in Derby and in Detroit for 1961 might be questioned. The two rates in Derby together are based on a total of 106 married Protestants in that community, in which they constituted about one-fifth of the population. The 1961 Detroit sample has the fault of underrepresenting the Protestants. White Protestants constitute 40 per cent of this small sample instead of the 49 per cent that earlier surveys indicated they were.[63] Therefore it seems that we can consider these samples atypical and likely to produce high rates of intermarriage for Protestants.

The other rates reported from cities of the United States

TABLE 4.—*Selected Rates of Intermarriage per 100 Marriages of Protestants in the United States and Canada, 1926-1961*

Area	Years	Per Cent		Reference*
Derby, Conn.	1929-30	50.0	(33.0)†	Barron (1946), p. 174
Derby, Conn.	1940	43.8	(28.0)	Barron (1946), p. 174
New Haven	1948	40.8	(25.6)	Hollingshead (1950), p. 622
Manhattan "Midtown"	1957‡	33.9	(20.4)	Heiss (1960), p. 49
Detroit	1955‡	38.0	(23.5)	Besanceney (N=378)
Detroit	1958‡	40.0	(25.0)	Besanceney (N=232)
Detroit	1959‡	31.0	(18.3)	Besanceney (N=287)
Detroit 3 combined‡		36.0	(22.0)	Besanceney (N=897)
Detroit	1961	53.0	(36.1)	Besanceney (N= 97)
Canada	1926-30	10.1	(5.3)	Rosenberg (1963), p. 62
Canada	1931-35	12.2	(6.5)	Rosenberg (1963), p. 62
Canada	1936-40	12.9	(6.9)	Rosenberg (1963), p. 62
Canada	1941-45	15.0	(8.1)	Rosenberg (1963), p. 62
Canada	1946-50	16.3	(8.9)	Rosenberg (1963), p. 62
Canada	1951-55	18.5	(10.2)	Rosenberg (1963), p. 62
Canada	1956-60	20.0	(11.1)	Rosenberg (1963), p. 62

* Each of the references in this table has been cited earlier in this chapter. Besanceney's revised rates have not been published before.

† The number in parentheses indicates the rate of intermarriage for *individuals*. Each of these was computed by this writer, using Rodman's formula, from the rate of intermarriage for *marriages*. For Hollingshead's and Rosenberg's rates the computation was reversed.

‡ This is the year of the survey, not the year when the marriage took place.

center around 35 or 36 per cent. This may be typical of northern cities, where Protestants are sometimes not as numerous as Catholics. Their rate of intermarriage for the country as a whole would certainly not be that high. As we have seen earlier, the 1957 survey by the U. S. Census Bureau underestimated the rate of religious intermarriage for the white population because it included nonwhites and especially because it did not consider early religious identifications. However, the rate that was reported for Protestants then was 8.6 per cent.[64] The correct rate for the country must be somewhere between this and that of the northern cities.

Rosenberg's rates for Protestants in the whole of Canada are somewhere between those extremes. They also show a steady increase in the rates of intermarriage for the years 1926-60. Heer's analysis of the Canadian data for 1926-57 indicates an increase of 132 per cent in the Protestant rates, from 5.0 per cent for individuals in 1927 to 11.6 per cent in 1957.[65] We have no information to show whether there is such a trend in the United States also.

Several rather well-known studies of Protestant intermarriage have been regretfully omitted from this table. Of the published reports on Iowa marriage registrations, only one is concerned with the interfaith marriages of Protestants, and even that one does not indicate the rate of their occurrence as it goes on to discuss related characteristics and behaviors.[66] James H. Bossard and Harold C. Letts base their article concerning Lutheran interfaith marriages on returns from 382 pastors (12 per cent of the questionnaires mailed), relying on their church records. So far as this weak sample shows, there was an increase in intermarriage rates from 46 per cent in 1936-40 to 58 per cent in 1946-50.[67]

Two articles by Murray H. Leiffer describe the findings of a house-to-house religious census in one area of a large city. He gives much information about the 743 interfaith marriages which they discovered there, but he does not tell us how many unmixed marriages there were in the area or give us any rate of intermarriage.[68] Similarly, Alfred J. Prince explores the religious attitudes and behavior of those who have entered into an interfaith marriage—one-fourth of them being across Protestant denominations—but he cannot estimate from his sample the rate of their occurrence. In fact, he depended for his respondents simply on the acquaintance-ship and cooperation of his students.[69]

Two studies which present quite a contrast with each other tell us something more about Protestant interfaith marriages. One is the survey of the seven largest metropolitan areas in this country by Westoff and his associates. Here it was found that 14 per cent of Protestant individuals were in mixed marriages (24.6 per cent of all Protestant marriages.)[70] On the other hand, a very different kind of study would be to look at intermarriage patterns in small communities. In such case studies interfaith marriages are sometimes mentioned but not systematically measured. For instance, Vidich and Bensman reported that in one township of 3,000 people, where there are four Protestant churches in the village, the Episcopalians, Congregationalists, and Methodists intermarry quite freely while the Baptists tend to be endogamous. In these cases it is the practice for the wife to affiliate with the church of her husband.[71]

The question is sometimes asked whether this or that Protestant denomination is more or less likely to marry Catholics. Such information is usually not available. However, for the combined Detroit sample this writer computed the rates at which the largest Protestant denominations (or families of denominations) in the area intermarried with Catholics and other non-Protestants. These are shown in Table 5, the rates of intermarriage for these being arranged in descending order from left to right. The intermarriage rates for the three middle groups are very similar, but the Episcopalians show notably more intermarriage and the Baptists notably less than the others. This corresponds to the general notions as to their

TABLE 5.—*Rates of Intermarriage with non-Protestants per 100 Marriages of the Largest Protestant Groups in the Detroit Area, by Early Religious Preference of Respondents, 1955, 1958, and 1959*

EARLY RELIGION OF RESPONDENT

Type of Marriage	Episcopalian (N=62)	Methodist (N=158)	Presbyterian (N=93)	Lutheran (N=142)	Baptist (N=128)
Unmixed	68	74	76	77	84
Mixed	32	26	24	23	16
Total	100	100	100	100	100

doctrinal and ritual similarities with Roman Catholics. However, because of the relative sizes of these groups in the area, the largest numbers of intermarriages are between Catholics (or other non-Protestants) and Methodists or Lutherans. Unfortunately, we do not have statistics concerning the intermarriages between Protestant denominations.

Cross-religious Mate Choices of Major Religious Groups

The last study mentioned brings us rather easily to the question whether there are any *preferences* evident in the denominational combinations of those who do intermarry between the three major religious groups.

There are five studies that tell us something about the preferences of Jews. In Switzerland they (men and women) select Protestant spouses almost twice as often as they do Catholics. This is consistently true for Swiss Jewish marriages from 1888 to 1960, but it is explained mainly by the fact that Protestants and Jews are concentrated in the same cities of Switzerland.[72] For Canada, Louis Rosenberg enumerates these cross-religious choices in unusual detail, showing in two tables the choices by Jewish brides and grooms of marriage partners in each religious denomination for every five-year period from 1921 till 1960. No other data known to this writer would make it possible to state on a large scale such details as these:

> Among the non-Jews with whom the 5,548 Jews who have intermarried in Canada during the period from 1926 to 1960 have associated themselves are 3,746 Protestants, 1,606 Roman Catholics, 98 Greek Catholics, 60 persons professing no religion, 5 members of Oriental religions; 33 persons have left their religious affiliation unspecified. Of the 3,746 Protestants of various denominations, 1,159 were Anglicans or Episcopalians, 1,029 members of the United Church of Canada, 412 Presbyterians, 250 Lutherans, 184 Baptists and 113 members of the Eastern Orthodox Churches.[73]

Whether this represents a rate of selection proportionate to the distribution of these denominations in the general population of Canada is not clear. Rosenberg does not explain, except to say that the largest Jewish community, that in

Montreal, is attached to the English-speaking sector and that French-speaking Jews are relatively few. This would, of course, reduce the number of marriages of Jews to the Catholic French Canadians.

In the United States the 1957 survey of the Census Bureau found that, besides the 1,258,000 couples (92.8 per cent) who were both Jewish, there were 57,000 Jewish persons with Protestant spouses (4.2 per cent) and 41,000 with Catholic spouses (3.0 per cent).[74] The principal reason that Catholics are overrepresented here is probably that they and Jews are concentrated in many of the same northern cities. On the other hand, Jewish intermarriage in Manhattan "Midtown" seems to favor Protestants over Catholics a little more than one would predict from their distribution in the population.[75] Considering the same factors of group size and the concentration of Jews and Catholics in certain cities of Iowa, Erich Rosenthal concludes that the distribution of Jewish spouses among Protestants and Catholics is to be expected. Even within the Protestant choices, the Jews in 1953-59 intermarried with Lutherans, Methodists, and Presbyterians in that order—the same order in which they rank within the general population of the state.[76]

From the point of view of Protestants, the 1957 national sample showed that, whereas 8.4 per cent of the marriages of Protestants were contracted with Roman Catholics, just 0.2 per cent involved a Jewish partner.[77] In the much smaller sample from Manhattan "Midtown," the percentages were 28.3 and 4.6, respectively.[78] Both sets of numbers indicate somewhat more preference for Catholic partners over Jewish than the relative size of these groups in the population would suggest. Of course, the generally low rate of Jewish intermarriage contributes to this situation.

Finally, the national picture for Catholic data in 1957 shows that 21.2 per cent of their marriages were with Protestant partners, 0.4 per cent with Jewish spouses.[79] In Manhattan "Midtown" Catholics selected Protestants for marriage 17.9 per cent of the time and Jews 2.3 per cent of the cases.[80] The same observations could be made here as in the Protestant choices.

In general, the situation regarding cross-religious mate choices is rather clear. Partly because Jewish marriage partners are less available through their low rate of intermarriage, both Protestants and Catholics marry them less often than one would predict from their relative size in the population. On the basis of what little evidence we have, intermarriage between the major Christian groups is much preferred to Jewish-Gentile matches. Jewish choices themselves follow rather closely the population distribution of Catholics and Protestants.

Pulling the Intermarriage Patterns Together

If we ask which of the major religious groups is most endogamous, there is no doubt about the answer. Examining Tables 2, 3, and 4 shows that Jews have lower intermarriage rates in Canada and the United States. The same was evident in the 1957 Census Bureau findings and in the survey of the largest metropolitan areas. However, the Jewish rates of intermarriage in Iowa demonstrate how overpowering the extreme minority status can be. We might also recall the high rates of intermarriage registered by Jews in central Europe in the 1920's and 1930's.

The best way to compare the endogamous tendencies of different religious groups would be, of course, to control for the influence of the relative size of the group (since this just represents a random probability factor). So far only three researchers seem to have found it possible to do so for religious categories. My analysis of several combined samples in the Detroit area revealed practically an equal tendency toward intermarriage on the part of Protestants and Catholics. The ratios of their actual to "expected" mixed marriages were, respectively, .53 and .56.[81] Although the 1957 national sample may not give a good indication of the actual intermarriage rates, the mixed marriages of all groups should be equally undercounted and therefore comparison between them may be justified. Paul C. Glick computed a ratio of actual to "expected" mixed marriages from these data and found that for Protestants it was .19, for Catholics .26, and for Jews .07.[82] By this reckoning, the Catholics are seen to be the least endogamous (in terms of currently mixed marriages) of all three groups. It is possible (as was the case in the Detroit data) that Catholics are somewhat less inclined to convert in order to bring about a homogeneous marriage and therefore more of their originally mixed marriages would remain in the statistics.

In Canada David M. Heer produced a table showing a similar "Ratio of Actual to 'Expected' Proportion of Brides and Grooms with Interfaith Marriage by Major Religious Group, Each Canadian Province, 1922 to 1957." In the three provinces where he computed a Jewish ratio, it ranged from .020 to .081, being generally twice as high in Ontario as it was in Quebec. The Protestant ratio varied between .068 (Prince Edward Island, 1922) and .576 (British Columbia, 1947). The range for the Catholic ratios was from .068 (Prince Edward Island, 1922) to .546 (British Columbia, 1957). In this country, therefore, the endogamous tendency of the Jews is strong and consistent. There was no consistent difference between Protestants and Catholics, except that the Catholic ratio was notably and regularly higher in Manitoba, Alberta, and British Columbia, while the Protestant ratio was notably higher in Quebec.[83] The fact that these differences in ratios seem to correspond to the actual distribution of these religious groups in Canada makes one wonder whether the factor of group size has truly been controlled here—or whether there is some other factor that operates in a nonrandom fashion concomitantly with this one. Perhaps being a large group is conducive to group solidarity.

One final question before we close our analysis of rates of interfaith marriage in this chapter: Is there an overall trend toward more intermarriage? Outside our own country, where we do not have appropriate data to draw a conclusion, the answer must be "Yes!" If we take a relatively long view of history, we must recall that interfaith marriages were practically outlawed until the time of the French Revolution, when civil marriages began to be recognized. One of the early students of this subject tells us that in Bavaria during the first half of the 19th century and in Prussia during the second half of the same century mixed marriages quadrupled while the number of marriages in general increased about 70 per cent.[84]

Of course, we are now considering all interfaith marriages together, as opposed to unmixed marriages, and this gets around the problem of controlling the relative size of groups in evaluating their respective rates of intermarriage. Jacques David has published this kind of data for Switzerland, by which he demonstrates that the overall rate of interfaith marriages in that country has increased from 3.1 per cent in 1870 to 11.7 per cent in 1941, the greatest increase occurring before 1910.[85] Similarly, Heer shows that in Canada and in each of its provinces the overall rate of religious intermarriage has increased from 1927 to 1957. In the country as a whole it went up from 5.8 to 11.5 per cent. The smallest increase (and smallest rate) was registered in the Province of Quebec, where it has crept up from 2.6 to 3.7 per cent.[86]

J. Milton Yinger has just published an article entitled, "A Research Note on Interfaith Marriage Statistics," which would have been discussed earlier in this chapter under the subheading "Ways of Reporting Rates of Intermarriages" if it had been available when those pages were written. The contributions that he makes in this interesting piece are mainly two: (1) he extends the Glick method (p. 56, above) to apply to rates of individuals who intermarry; (2) he proposes a way of estimating the rates of "pre-conversion" intermarriages when only the intermarriage rates according to present religious preferences are known. A third contribution would be that of his colleague at Oberlin College, John Hewitt, who suggests that a ratio of actual/possible intermarriages is a desirable refinement for Glick's ratio of actual/expected intermarriages. One can hardly evaluate this suggestion, however, since the procedure is not detailed.[87]

This brings to a close our quite lengthy analysis of the rates of religious intermarriage. It is hoped that the reader who has struggled through this chapter will have gained a sense of caution in regard to these rates as well as a sense of confidence that they can reveal much to us concerning the rule of endogamy as an index of group cohesion.

V

Religious Intermarriage: Who?

IN THIS CHAPTER I hope that the reader will discover some of the fascination of exploring an intricate subject. Up till now we have been describing some widely distributed patterns of mate selection. Having looked at the patterns of homogamy, residential propinquity, and heterogamy, we turned our attention to the idea of a rule of endogamy and its violation through intermarriage. Racial and ethnic intermarriage brought us to class and caste hypergamy. Then we focused on the problem of evaluating the many reported rates of religious intermarriage, and we applied our criteria to the rates of intermarriage which have been observed for the three major religious groups. All this has been done mainly in a descriptive way. Now we will try to explain some of these patterns and other data still to be presented.

The next four chapters will discuss the tools of the sociologist as they are applied to this subject. We shall begin by considering how the principles of class endogamy and hypergamy can operate in opposition to religious endogamy, but in doing so we shall also be presenting some of the characteristics of those who marry across religious lines—answering the question "Who?"

In the following chapters we will turn our attention to social control as a way of explaining the extent of adherence to the norm of religious endogamy that we do observe, going on then to consider anomia and some conflicting norms and values that threaten to extinguish the flame of this kind of endogamy.

But now, who are these members of society who select their marriage partners against the rule of religious endogamy? How can we describe their characteristics in such a way that their patterns of behavior in this matter make some sense? The descriptions for the several major religious groups may be quite different, but the explanation so far as their endogamy goes should emerge as a coherent one.

Jewish Intermarriage: Husbands More Than Wives?

"Everywhere Jewish men were found to have intermarried more than Jewish women."[1] This summary statement by Barron is probably 95 per cent correct. However, around the turn of the century in Europe there were some places (such as Prussia, Hungary, Hamburg) where there was no consistent relationship between sex and Jewish intermarriage, and there were other places (such as Alsace-Lorraine, Hesse, Baden, Breslau, Bucharest) where the Jewish women had an edge on the men.[2] Still, as the century grew older (until 1935), Jews increasingly outnumbered Jewesses in the practice of marrying Gentiles, until the ratio became about 2 to 1.[3]

On this continent in more recent years Jewish men have continued to outdo their women in intermarrying, generally by a ratio of at least 2 to 1. This has been true in New Haven (1900-1940),[4] in Washington, D.C. (1956),[5] in Iowa (1953-59),[6] and in Canada (1926-55).[7]

This is one of the most consistent patterns to be found in all mate-selection studies, yet an explanation has hardly been attempted. Someone has suggested that Jewish men have greater freedom and mobility. Do not the men of every religion? John E. Mayer believes that the growth of anti-Semitism is responsible for this sex differential and offers as evidence the data from Prussia beginning with 1876 and continuing in Germany through 1933. He thinks that men and women of a religious group will intermarry equally, except that, "when there is a great deal of anti-Jewish feeling present, more Jewish men than Christian men will be intent upon crossing ethnic lines."[8] Although there may be some tendency for a man who is discriminated against to want to "prove himself," I think that Mayer is misinterpreting the data, particularly from the female standpoint. It seems to me that this pattern is explained adequately by the practice of hypergamy attached to the norm of class endogamy, which we discussed in Chapter III. In other words, Jewish men who are relatively wealthy have simply taken advantage of the prerogative allowed to the unusually "good provider" to select his bride from his own socioeconomic class (and religion) or from a lower socioeconomic level (occupied more dominantly by Gentiles). Jewish men, forced by European land discrimination to develop the skills needed for urban competition, have prospered accordingly as Western nations became more urbanized. Meanwhile, the Gentile girl (and her parents) still cultivates the age-old feminine techniques for "making a good match." From her point of view, we call this hypergamy. Some evidence for this interpretation will be presented when we come a little later to the topic of the economic factor in religious intermarriage.

Catholic Intermarriage: Wives More Than Husbands?

Barron concluded in 1946 that in "most studies" Catholic women intermarried at higher rates than did Catholic men.[9] Some evidence continues to support this generalization. Thomas reported that the ratio was three Catholic women to two Catholic men in mixed marriages in the Bishops' national study, in Whelpton and Kiser's Indianapolis survey, and in Schnepp's study of an eastern parish.[10] The percentage has gone even higher, to 68 per cent in a "Lakeport" parish,[11] and to 73 per cent in "Southern Parish."[12]

However, in other studies of Catholic intermarriage this sex differential gets lower than three to two and in other cases disappears. In Holland, 1935-38, just about 56 per cent of the Catholic intermarriages involved a Catholic bride. The fact that these brides favored Jews and those with no religious affiliation more than did the Catholic grooms suggests the influence of the hypergamy pattern as described above.[13] In one Canadian Catholic diocese, there were an average of three Catholic women to two Catholic men who had intermarried in the urban parishes—but the situation was reversed at five men to four women in the rural Catholic parishes.[14] In a sample drawn from the largest American metropolitan centers in 1957, there was simply no difference between Catholic men and women in the rate of their interfaith marriages with Protestants,[15] as was the case also in a less systematic sample of Midwestern states.[16]

In samples of over 600 marriages of Catholic men and of Catholic women in Detroit (1955-59), the intermarriage rate for the men was 29 per cent, for the women 27 per cent. There is no significant difference here, but it is surprising to find it in the direction contrary to most of the studies reviewed above. If the Detroit rates had been based on present religious preferences, instead of on previous religious preferences, Catholic women would have shown slightly more intermarriage than the men. Furthermore, if you take a closer look at the relatively high intermarriage rates of Catholic women reported above, you will see that almost all of them were based on ecclesiastical records. Why should this influence these rates? Since the pastor of the bride is the proper officiant for a Roman Catholic wedding, since a conversion of the spouse *to* Catholicism before the marriage would cause it to be registered as an all-Catholic marriage, and since those who convert *from* Catholicism or who intermarry without benefit of a Catholic ceremony will not be found in these records, it seems to me that we already have reasons which render it quite doubtful that there is actually any appreciable or widespread tendency for Catholic women to intermarry more than Catholic men do.

To the extent that Catholic women do intermarry more than Catholic men in the church records, it may be explained partially by these considerations: Before a mixed marriage at which a Catholic priest officiates, the Catholic and non-Catholic party must each have agreed that the children of the union will be raised as Catholics. Since the early training of children is necessarily entrusted to the mother and she typically provides the religious influence in the family, such an agreement gives some security to a Catholic woman in a mixed marriage. At the same time, a Catholic husband must rely more on his wife in this matter. If the bride-to-be is not a Catholic, he may become aware of the risk and she may be averse to assuming this alien role, and they may end by calling it off. Or, if his religious convictions are weak, he may abandon his religion and, therefore, will not appear in parish records of marriages. This speculation seems logical but cannot be supported by convincing evidence at this time.

Protestant Intermarriage: Husbands as Often as Wives

We have fewer studies to help us decide whether Protestant men intermarry more than Protestant women, and their evidence is not consistent. In the small town of Derby, Connecticut (1929-30, 1940), the men intermarried somewhat more than the women.[17] In the metropolitan area study by Westoff and in the Midwestern sample of Prince, the rates of intermarriage for Protestant men and women were found to be indistinguishable, just as they had found for Catholics. The only notable study of Protestant intermarriages in this country which relied on church records was the survey by Bossard and Letts which elicited responses from 382 pastors of the United Lutheran Church of America. They reported that 64 per cent of these mixed marriages involved Lutheran women.[18] I would offer the same explanations for this high ratio as was offered above for high intermarriage rates for Catholic women as revealed by church records. In the Detroit surveys of 1955, 1958, and 1959, there was a slight tendency in the same direction: 20 per cent of 718 Protestant husbands intermarried compared to 24 per cent of 758 Protestant wives. Putting all of these statistics together, we do not seem to have any consistent pattern to show that Protestant men intermarry more or less than Protestant women do. More widespread sampling and more thorough analysis is needed. It would be interesting, for instance, to see whether variant sex ratios within religious categories of a given population have any influence on interfaith marriages. Although we know that the Detroit area, similar to practically all cities, has a relatively large population of women in the marriageable ages, we do not know whether one or other religious group is overrepresented among them.[19] This is just one more instance of the handicap involved in not having religious identifications included in our census data.

Religious Intermarriage and Social Class

In our short discussion of which sex tends most to marry outside the group in the several religious categories, we adverted to the socially allowable pattern of hypergamy as a partial explanation of the sex differences in rates of intermarriage. Hypergamy says, of course, that a girl who marries a man somewhat above her own social class has social approval for this—although, in general, most men and women are expected to marry within their social class. Although we do not have sharply defined social classes in this country, except perhaps at the top of the pyramid, there are several characteristics which are commonly taken as indicative of social classes, namely, occupation, income, and education. The question of social mobility as such and its impact on social control regarding interfaith marriages will be taken up in a later chapter. In all of these questions the evidence is spotty and much less extensive than we would like. However, let us see what we can learn when we look at income, occupation, and education in relation to interfaith marriages.

First in terms of income, class endogamy and religious endogamy can be seen either as reinforcing each other or as working against each other. For instance, Barron interpreted the low rate of intermarriage which he found for Jews in Derby, Connecticut, as due partly to the mobility they had in going to neighboring communities for Jewish marriage partners since they were few in number locally. High income was in this case regarded as a facility toward maintaining religious endogamy, and at the same time it would prompt these people to seek others elsewhere in the same social class.[20] On the other hand, my own data for the Detroit area showed that Catholics with high income, in which category they were underrepresented, had higher rates of religious intermarriage than those with medium or low income.[21] (For Protestant intermarriage there was no such relationship with income.) In the case of Detroit Catholics with high income, we have the same facility to look elsewhere for Catholic partners, if desired. However, there would be plenty of Catholic partners of lower social class (by this criterion) locally. Because they are not so numerous in the higher income levels, these Catholics are more likely to be faced with a choice between religious endogamy and class endogamy. The two do not reinforce each other in the local situation. Detroit Catholics of high income do not have a double incentive to go elsewhere, as the Jews of Derby did.

The same line of reasoning could be used to explain any

rates of religious intermarriage in any population in which a particular religious group is underrepresented in one or other social class or income category. I would apply it to the finding of Jerold Heiss in "Midtown" Manhattan that, "Among the Catholics there is a positive relationship between status and intermarriage rates, but the Protestant group shows an inverse relationship."[22] Similarly, it probably explains much of the consistent and positive relationship which John L. Thomas found between graded rental areas and rates of intermarriage for Catholics in thirty parishes of a large urban center.[23] The study by Hollingshead in New Haven indicates that the economic factor, as measured by Maurice R. Davie's ranking of residential areas, operates independently of religion; and he adds: "What is especially significant is that the effects of class position on who marries whom are so strong in each religious group."[24]

If we had more detailed data, we might be able to explain much religious intermarriage not only in terms of the concentration of religious groups in particular income categories (the size of group factor) and of the tendency toward class (or income) endogamy, as above, but we might also incorporate the influence of hypergamy as a subordinate norm. This might not tell us so much about the large Protestant and Catholic groups in our population, since we saw above that it is not too clear yet that for them either sex tends to intermarry more than the other. However, Rosenthal has shown that in Washington, D.C., hypergamy by a Gentile wife helps to describe Jewish intermarriage (predominantly by Jewish men). In his terms, "the family income of intermarried Jewish wives was significantly smaller than that of all Jewish husbands," particularly among the native-born of native parentage.[25]

When we look at occupations as an index of social class, we come upon two studies which report findings that seem to be in conflict with the interpretation just given above for Catholic intermarriage. Monahan and Chancellor show that Catholics were mainly located in blue-collar occupations and in farming according to Iowa marriage records in 1953. They find also that the farmers were overrepresented among unmixed Catholic marriages, whereas blue-collar workers were overrepresented among mixed Catholic marriages.[26] This difference is probably due to two factors: greater social control in the rural setting, and the likelihood that Catholic blue-collar workers constitute a smaller part of a given urban population than Catholic farmers do of a given rural population. (Hence the "interaction-time-cost theory" of Katz and Hill would be applicable here.) The relative weakness of social control by the religious community among poorer people in the urban setting is also suggested by these observations concerning marriages of Catholics outside the Church ("invalid") in a Canadian diocese, 1944-53:

> There was only one white-collar male who married a non-Catholic invalidly in these years. All the other males, both Catholic and non-Catholic, belonged to the unskilled or semiskilled classes. In addition, it was learned that of 55 invalid mixed marriages in one parish, 41 occurred within a space of four city blocks, all of which are populated by industrial workers. Six of the Catholics involved lived in the same boarding house.[27]

Note that these observations concern marriages outside the Church, which are not the same thing as rates of intermarriage. Neither these data nor those from Iowa are actually in conflict with the interpretation given earlier that Catholics will have higher rates of intermarriage at those levels of social class where they are underrepresented. Both sets of data are more a reflection of different outcomes of social control, a factor which we shall begin to discuss in greater detail in the next chapter.

The Detroit area data tell us pretty much the same thing regarding occupations and intermarriage as we have observed for income and intermarriage. The Protestant marriages are somewhat overrepresented in the professional and managerial occupations, whereas the Catholic marriages are more likely than Protestant marriages to be among the semiskilled and unskilled occupations. The criterion used for these samples was the "usual occupation" of the husband's father, since this can more reasonably be treated as a background factor in mate selection than the occupation of the husband himself. As expected, given the distribution of religions among the occupations as just stated, the rate of religious intermarriage for Catholics (50.6 per cent) was higher than it was for Protestants (35.5 per cent) in the professional and managerial occupations; conversely, in the semiskilled and unskilled occupations it was lower for Catholics (35.9 per cent) than for Protestants (41.4 per cent). Class endogamy and hypergamy would both help to account for these differences.[28]

There is one curious difference in the Detroit data regarding occupations which cannot be explained in those terms. The mixed marriage rate for Protestant marriages in which the father was a farmer was only 19.3 per cent; for Catholic marriages in this category it was 30.9 per cent. Why should Protestant rural families have been more endogamous than Catholic rural families? The explanation is probably the following: Of the Protestant respondents, 30 per cent identified themselves as rural migrants, compared to just 15 per cent of the Catholics. It is known that in the Detroit area there has been a large immigration from the Border and Southern states of our country, which are strongly Protestant. These would tend to keep the Protestant intermarriage rate down for rural migrants. Furthermore, to be rural migrants *themselves* places them more under the influence of rural social control, which restrains religious intermarriage, more than being the children of rural migrants—as Detroit Catholics tend to be. Actually, 56 per cent of our Catholic respondents are the children of foreign-born parents, compared to 34 per cent of the Protestants in our sample. Undoubtedly, many of these parents were farmers in the old country. But, being the child of foreign-born parents tends somewhat to weaken social control by the parents, as we shall see in a later chapter. Hence this characteristic of the Catholic population of Detroit would help to explain the high rate of intermarriage for those whose fathers were farmers.

Rosenthal's studies of Jewish intermarriage rates in Washington, D.C., and in Iowa bear out the same relationships with occupation as we saw them to have for income. In Iowa about 83 per cent of the Jewish grooms, 1953-59, were white-collar workers, and about half of these were in professional or kindred occupations. Hence they were three times as numerous among Jewish intermarried couples as were blue-collar workers, in spite of the fact that the latter had a considerably higher rate of intermarriage. From the Jewish point of view, this occupational homogeneity strengthens group solidarity by making religious endogamy consistent with class endogamy, as Rosenthal observes. From the Gentile point of view, the presence of so many professional grooms in intermarriage represents hypergamy for the bride. In his Washington data, by contrast, small numbers of Jewish manual workers were found to intermarry rarely. Professional, clerical, and sales workers had relatively high rates of intermarriage; but managers and officials resisted intermarriage except among the native-born of native parentage. The self-employed in every generation had much lower rates of intermarriage than those employed by others. In Washington, therefore, the pattern of hypergamy still seems to be important, although class endogamy is not here reinforcing religious endogamy.

Finally, we turn to secular education as an index of social class and we find only two studies that have data relevant to our interest in religious intermarriage. Rosenthal's Washington data reveal the rather surprising fact that, although graduate studies encouraged Jewish intermarriage somewhat among the foreign-born, it was a deterrent after that generation, particularly among the native-born of native parentage. On the other hand, among second- and third-generation Jews, intermarriage was about ten times as frequent for Jewish college students or graduates as it was for those who had not gone beyond high school.[30] By the criterion of intermarriage, therefore, it would seem that in Washington the Jewish husbands with the least and the most amounts of education were adhering closest to their traditions, whereas those with an intermediate amount of education were most likely to amalgamate. The other study of interest is that done by Hollingshead in New Haven in 1949. He finds that educational homogamy is present within each religious group, being strongest among Jews and weakest among Catholics. However, his data do not show what relationship this has to rates of religious intermarriage.[31]

Our Detroit surveys showed somewhat different patterns of intermarriage according to educational level for Protestants and Catholics than did Rosenthal's data for Jews in Washington. In the small 1962 sample interfaith marriage was significantly related to being a high school graduate (as distinct from all other educational categories) for Protestant wives; the tendency was in the same direction for Catholic wives, though not statistically significant. In this sample there is a tendency toward the same relationship if one uses the educational level of the fathers as a predictor of the intermarriage rate of the daughters. Similarly, in the case of the Catholic sons, if either they or their fathers attended college, the sons are significantly less likely to intermarry; Protestant sons show only a slight tendency in this direction.

How should we interpret this relationship? It may be that the existence of a norm of religious endogamy is expressed and understood better at the college level of education. In this context it may be regarded as a social norm (what a *religious* man *ought* to do), or it may simply be the perception of a marital risk which is operating (what an *intelligent* man *will* avoid). In any case, we have no evidence here of the sons rejecting the norms of their fathers. In this connection, one is reminded again of John F. Scott's fascinating article on "The Role of the College Sorority in Endogamy."[32] He shows that, to a considerable extent, the sororities provide the families with an opportunity to control the marriage choices of their daughters. Something similar could undoubtedly be said for the church-related colleges and universities, such as exist in Detroit and probably kept the intermarriage rate down for our Detroit collegians referred to above.

Summing up, we have found in our review that class endogamy—by the criteria of income, rental areas, occupation, and education—has its influence in all three major religious groups. In those categories of social class where a particular religious group is underrepresented, class endogamy will work against religious endogamy; otherwise it will reinforce religious endogamy. This generalization explains most of the facts that we have summarized above. The pattern of hypergamy for Gentile wives also helps to explain the intermarriage of Jewish husbands. However, we must leave unexplained some special patterns, such as the various rates of religious intermarriage for the educational categories among Jews in Washington. Let us move on now to consider some other characteristics of the religiously intermarried.

Religious Intermarriage and Nationality Groups

Not much information has been published on the rates of religious intermarriage which are specific to particular nationality groups. Perhaps it is because quite a large sample is needed in a general survey to obtain enough cases to compute religious intermarriage rates *within* nationality groups. The several surveys in which this has been attempted will be reviewed here. Unfortunately, we cannot make use of studies of New Haven done by Kennedy and Hollingshead, even though ethnic origin and religion were both important variables for them. Hollingshead did not have enough cases to get rates of religious intermarriage for specific ethnic groups, and Kennedy did not distinguish between Protestant and Catholic members of the same nationality.[33] This distinction we were able to make in the Detroit area, as is shown in Table 6. Perhaps Kennedy could safely assume in New Haven that all Irish were Catholic and all Germans were Protestants, but certainly we could not do so in Detroit, where these nationalities are well represented in both religious groups. The rates for Protestant and Catholic intermarriage in Manhattan presented in the doctoral thesis by Heiss are directly comparable to ours for Detroit. Of those intermarriage rates which he reports, the following are based on subsamples of more than fifty: Irish Catholics—12.5; German-Austrian Catholics—29.5; German-Austrian Protestants—42.7; Italian Catholics—15.3.[34]

TABLE 6.—*Religious Intermarriage Rate (per 100 Marriages) by Early Religious Preference of Respondents with Selected National Origins on Father's Side, 1955, 1958, and 1959*

National Origin* of Respondent on Father's Side	CATHOLIC RESPONDENTS		PROTESTANT RESPONDENTS	
	Rate	Number	Rate	Number
English			25.4	154
Scotch, Scotch-Irish			19.7	56
Irish	36.8	68	21.7	83
German	31.7	60	19.0	153
Polish	19.4	176		
Italian	22.2	72		

* This table includes only those nationalities which were claimed by more than fifty descendants in one of the major religious groups.

Perhaps the principal factor in determining these rates is the relative size of the ethnic group in the population. Unfortunately, we cannot compute a ratio of actual to expected rates of intermarriage as we did for interfaith marriages as a whole, since we do not have information about the numerical distribution of nationality groups in the Detroit area in a form that would be comparable to these data. As we expected, the Polish Catholics are a large enough group in Detroit to exert an influence toward minimizing the general Catholic rate of interfaith marriages. It is surprising, however, to discover that the German Protestants in Detroit exert the same influence on the intermarriage rates of Protestants. Those Protestants who identify themselves as Scotch or Irish are probably largely migrants from the South, in which case strong ethnic ties would still be expected in them.

Regarding rates of Jewish intermarriage within the several national origins represented, we have some data from New York City and Washington, D.C. The largest national groups among Jews which Heiss found in Manhattan in 1958 were these, with their intermarriage rates: Russia-Poland—13.1 (N= 61), and Germany-Austria—23.9 (N=46).[35]

As far back as 1908-12, Drachsler found much lower rates of intermarriage for Jews in New York City. He reported these rates in ascending order, as follows: Roumania—.45, Russia—.62, Turkey—.80, Austria—.99, Hungary—2.24, England—3.47, Holland—4.00, Germany—5.16, France—6.54.[36] The only surprises in this series of rates are that the rates of intermarriage for Russian and Austrian Jews were so very low and that the rates for German and French Jews were even higher than for Jews from England and Holland. Whatever the reasons, German Jews have intermarried quite a lot, particularly in comparison with those from Russia and Poland.

In Washington, D.C., Erich Rosenthal got similar results in regard to Jews who were second-generation Americans. He had samples of over 12,000 husbands and 11,000 wives, with Jews of Russian origin constituting a large majority. Their rates of intermarriage were: for husbands—Russia—10.1, Poland—1.5, other Eastern Europe—5.8, Central and Western Europe—22.0; for the wives—Russia—7.6, Poland—3.0, other Eastern Europe—0.4, Central and Western Europe—14.5.[37] In each of these sets of statistics, the "older" immigrant groups from Central and Western Europe have higher rates of religious intermarriage—even when we are referring only to second-generation Americans as in Washington. Those Jews of Polish origin apparently resist intermarriage more than do those of Russian origin.

It does not seem to me that we can find a simple way of explaining the national variations in rates of religious intermarriage as reviewed above. Probably some study of the historical relations between religious groups in those countries would be necessary, but that is beyond what we can attempt here. In the next chapter we shall take up the related topic of the influence that Americanization and intergenerational conflict have on religious intermarriage, regardless of national origin.

Religious Intermarriage and Urbanism

A few writers have asked whether there is any relationship between the size of cities (or urbanism) and rates of religious intermarriage. Analyzing the records of 25 parishes in each of four categories of city size, Thomas found that the rate of interfaith marriages rose concurrently with the size of the cities, short of the largest city size. The intermarriage rate was lowest (14.9 per cent) for Catholics in cities of 100,000 people or over.[38] He is inclined to attribute this to the presence of large and cohesive ethnic groups among Catholics in these cities.

Burchinal and Chancellor explored the relationship between Catholic mixed marriages and the proportion of county populations in Iowa which was urban, 1953-57. They also used the variable of the proportion of Catholics in each county and then controlled each of these variables while relating the other to interfaith marriages. In the diocese-reported marriages they found a partial correlation coefficient of $-.62$ for the association between rates of mixed marriage and the proportion of Catholics in the county populations, compared to a partial correlation coefficient of $+.24$ for the association between urbanism and mixed marriage rates. In other words, in Iowa Catholic mixed marriages show a rather strong inverse relationship with the proportion of Catholics in the local population when controlling for the urbanism index. The relationship between urbanism itself and mixed marriages is very slight, even when the influence of the proportion of Catholics in the population has been controlled. These researchers see this as "another instance of declining rural-urban value and norm differences." However, they believe that this may be explained by the large proportions of former urban residents in rural areas. If these city people in the country were not included, the farm-nonfarm differences might be found to exist still, even in the matter of more social control regarding interfaith marriages.[39]

The studies of Erich Rosenthal in Iowa and Washington, D.C., also contain some information on this aspect of Jewish intermarriage. For the years 1953-59 he found the following rates of intermarriage for Jews in Iowa by rural-urban categories: cities of 10,000 and over—34.2 (N=523), towns of 2,500-9,999—64.1 (N=53), rural areas—67.0 (N=100).[40] He questions the usefulness of these data because they indicate places where the marriage occurred, not where the marriage partners were living, and particularly because this threefold classification "precludes the possibility of distinguishing between the relatively large Jewish communities of Des Moines, Sioux City, and Davenport, and the smaller communities in the other cities." Apparently he regards these differences in rates of intermarriage as mainly a function of the relative size of the Jewish community in the various areas. This is a factor that we have discussed at length in the preceding chapter. When the same author tried to relate the intermarriage rates of Jews in Washington with the previous residence of the husband, he found that those from larger Jewish communities had an intermarriage rate of 11.7 per cent, compared to 14.9 per cent for the natives of Washington. However, he did not explain very well the unexpected finding that Jews from "other" previous residences (middle and small towns) had an intermarriage rate of only 10.0 per cent.[41]

In this brief section we have considered what is known about the relationship between urbanism and religious intermarriage. We have seen that it is difficult to separate this variable from that of the relative size of a religious group in a particular population. Even when Burchinal and Chancellor attempted this, they were not satisfied with their

measure for the rural-urban distinction. Perhaps the influence of the farm community in matters of social control is
still there, but we have not found viable ways to measure
this variable.

*   *   *   *   *

This brings us to the end of this chapter on the social
characteristics of those who enter into religious intermarriage.
We have tried to find a partial answer to the question "Who?"
without, however, going into topics which we shall discuss
more fully under the heading of "social control." For each
of the major religious groups we asked which sex was more
likely to intermarry. In the case of Jews, the answer is
clearly that the men have a higher rate of intermarriage.
We are inclined to attribute this largely to their relative
prosperity and the consequent practice of hypergamy on the
part of Gentile women. In the case of intermarriage by
Protestants and Catholics, there is not consistent and convincing
evidence that either men or women participate in this more
frequently, although it is likely that Catholic women intermarry more frequently than Catholic men.

In this chapter we have also examined the influence of
class endogamy on religious intermarriage. In general, if a
religious group is underrepresented at a given socioeconomic
level, these two endogamous norms will work against each
other and we can expect a higher rate of interfaith marriages. Other things being equal (such as strength of religious
convictions), we would expect that a religious group that is
overrepresented in a given social class would have a lower
rate of religious intermarriage within that class (such as
those Jews who have a relatively high income).

In examining the rates of religious intermarriage for speci-
ic nationality groups within each major religious category,
we have not considered the question of the Americanization
process, i.e., the extent to which first, second, and third
generations of an immigrant group behave differently in the
matter of religious intermarriage. We shall look into two
aspects of that question when we consider the ethnic group
as a source of social control and the special relationship
between the members of the first and second generations.
For the present we have simply noted that a larger ethnic

group has a better chance of organizing its marriage market because there are more eligible partners available without crossing religious lines. Other than that, it would be risky to generalize about the rates of religious intermarriage for particular nationality groups from the rather limited information we have.

There may be a relationship between urbanism as such and rates of religious intermarriage. If so, it is fairly well obscured by the factor of the size of the group. Furthermore, there is the fact that even the rural areas of our country are occupied largely by people who work and participate in the city's culture. There is some evidence, however, that among farmers social control is stronger than in other occupations or localities. In stating this much, we are already moving into a discussion of the next important approach to our study of interfaith marriages and how their occurrence can be explained—the normative structure and social control.

VI

Norms, Institutions, Social Control, and Anomia

IN THE EARLY CHAPTERS of this book we tried to place the subject of interfaith marriages in its proper context of mate selection and the various types of marriage norms and intermarriage. Many factors relative to interfaith marriages have already been discussed, and in the last chapter we described some of the social characteristics associated with this kind of intermarriage. Now I feel that it is time to take up more explicitly the approach to this subject which is most distinctive of the sociologist, through a consideration of social norms and the nature of their organization and vitality.

The plan of this chapter is as follows: So that the reader may be clear about the principal focus of the study that I have made of Detroit data, we shall begin by taking notice of some studies, especially that of Heiss, which have used social control as an approach toward understanding interfaith marriages. This will give us an opportunity to state without further delay the hypotheses which have been explored through the Detroit area data. Then we shall turn to a general discussion of the principal concepts which are involved in this typically sociological approach. Social norms, institutions, social control, and anomia are these concepts.

Studies of Social Control and Interfaith Marriages

In Chapter III, we defined endogamy as a social norm and intermarriage as a deviation from that norm. Rates of any type of intermarriage represent degrees of deviation from that particular endogamous norm, or, when they reach a certain undefined point, they may represent the group's abandonment of that norm. For instance, Chancellor and Monahan felt justified in saying, "The role of religious affiliation, in the final analysis, may not be any more important than the other elements in marital selections."[1] So far we have been accepting low intermarriage rates as evidence of a social norm. Later in this chapter other indications of a norm of religious endogamy will be reviewed. In passing, it may also be worth recalling that Katz and Hill, in their "norm-interaction" theory which grew out of their review of studies of residential propinquity, gave as the first assumption of their theory that "marriage is normative."

The research which has best organized data on religious intermarriage from the point of view of social control is found in an article published a few years ago under the unpretentious title, "Pre-marital Characteristics of the Religiously Intermarried in an Urban Area." I have referred to it earlier as the "Midtown" Manhattan study. Actually, it is a notable middle-range theory of intermarriage. To repeat this part from our introductory chapter, the theory assumes that

> the ultimate sources of barriers to interfaith marriages in American Society lie in the family of orientation and formal religious organizations. . . . If, in the case of an intermarried respondent, it can be shown that these sources did not produce effective barriers to intermarriage, we will consider the marriage to be explained.[2]

Heiss sets down six general hypotheses to test this theory, each being particularized by several specific hypotheses. He concludes from his data that the intermarried have:

> (a) non-religious parents, (b) greater dissatisfaction with parents when young, (c) greater early family strife, (d) less early family integration, and (e) greater emancipation from parents at time of marriage.[3]

Taking our lead from this study, but including findings from other studies of interfaith marriages, let us see what can now be said about the following as agents of social control for the norm of endogamy: parents, family, ethnic group. It should also be helpful to consider briefly the social conditions of secularism and *anomie* as they relate to interfaith marriages, before we state the hypotheses for the present study.

First, what are the characteristics of the *parents* of the religiously intermarried? In Heiss' Catholic sample it was reported that "religion was not at all important to both parents."[4] Catholic respondents also reported dissatisfaction with their early relationship with their parents, that they argued with parents over religion, that they often disagreed with their parents, that their parents quarreled often. The Protestant intermarried reported that their parents never attended church. In the Jewish sample, two statements were made concerning parents which are hard to square with each other: The intermarried were significantly different from the intramarried in that fewer of them reported living with both their real parents up until age sixteen, and yet a higher proportion of them said that their parents were *not* divorced, separated, etc. If their parents were living together, yet the respondents were not living with them both, we must assume that the children lived away from home before the age of sixteen in significant numbers. Mysterious? However, for the sample as a whole Heiss found that the parents of the intermarried were more likely themselves to be intermarried. This agrees with the earlier findings of Schnepp and of the present writer.[5] Emancipation from parents by being at least thirty years old at the time of marriage was a characteristic of the intermarried among Catholics and Jews, but among Protestants there was a tendency in the opposite direction.[6]

The failure of the family to exercise social control in the rule of religious endogamy was also indicated in Heiss' study by these results: For the sample as a whole, intermarriage was positively related to having a low Family Integration score, and negatively related to having grandparents living with them. Surprisingly, intermarriage was positively related to being the youngest or only child and negatively to being the oldest child. So far as the present writer is aware, too little is known to make a case for differential social control related to a child's birth-order in the family. However, in our small 1961 Detroit sample, there was a tendency (not statistically significant) for more intermarriage to occur among Catholic husbands and wives who claimed to have just one sibling or none. Heiss found that the Catholic intermarried also had a high Intra-Familial Conflict score, whereas fewer of the intermarried in the Jewish group reported seeing their relatives fairly often.

In an earlier day a person's "people" were thought of as his larger family. Especially when a group is surrounded by a contrasting majority group does their own shared subculture hold them together, their national origin or language or customs. What social control do *ethnic groups* exercise in the matter of religious intermarriage? In the Jewish case, religious and ethnic lines are practically coterminous. However, in the area around Derby, Connecticut, the same could be said about the equally small groups of Greek Orthodox and Greek Catholics (distinguished from Roman Catholics not by church but by rite). Yet, the intermarriage rate of the Jews was much lower than that of the other two groups. Barron was probably correct in identifying one important differential factor as being the Jews' long history of migration and status as a minority group, which conditioned them to develop attitudes and techniques resistant to intermarriage.[7] In the Catholic case, Heiss found that in Manhattan intermarriage was negatively related to being first-generation Americans. Some ethnic groups have remained cohesive much beyond the first generation in America. Thomas attributes to this factor the low rate of Catholic mixed marriages in some large cities.[8] Heer feels that the trend toward increased religious intermarriage in Canada may be due to a lessening of in-group feeling among the French Catholic and British Protestant elements in the population.[9] He also asks whether in the larger society itself there has not been a change of attitude toward intermarriage. It is certainly difficult to assess the impact of ethnic cohesiveness on religious intermarriage; but, to the extent that this exists, it belongs in the category of social control.

We now turn from the agents of social control—parents, family, ethnic group—to the conditions in which it is ineffective to restrain religious intermarriage: secularism and anomie. The first refers to the abandoning of distinctively religious values in some degree. It puts a this-world goal in place of an other-world goal. "Rationality" supplants faith as a guide to action. Worldly "success" is not to be hindered by religious or moral considerations. The radical secularism is religious indifference, which we saw already manifested in the experience of Manhattan's religiously intermarried by the Protestant parents who never attended church and the Catholic parents for whom religion was not at all important.[10] Secularist values may be seen in the positive correlation discovered by Carleton S. Coon between economic prosperity and religious intermarriage for Jews.[11] In the data which Heiss presents, secularism is probably also displayed in both the choice and the experience of those Catholics in mixed marriages who had not attended parochial schools and for whom their interfaith marriage is not their first marriage. The qualification "probably" is made because inaccessibility may explain the first, and widowhood the second type of behavior.

Finally, let us consider briefly the influence of *anomia* on the rates of religious intermarriage. We are talking about the normlessness an individual may experience when the agents which exercised social control over his behavior are no longer present and his own internalization of these norms has been quite superficial. Examples might be found among those who have left the farm to go to the city, or have left home to go to college. We are talking about the normlessness that is likely to be felt in stressful circumstances, such as wartime or oppressive poverty or unemployment or unusual vertical mobility. In the literature on religious intermarriage we find some indications of such a relationship, all of them based on Catholic data. One student in Holland cited urbanization as one of three major factors involved in increased religious intermarriages.[12] In Iowa, as we noted at the close of the preceding chapter, there was a slight positive association of mixed marriages with urbanism, when controlling for the percentage of Catholics in the population.[13] Data from Iowa also showed a negative association between interfaith marriage and having the occupation of farmer.[14] In Manhattan intermarriage was negatively related to being born on a farm (probably in a foreign land).[15]

As illustrations of the normlessness which characterized a people at war, we have data on intermarriage in one parish over twenty-six years, showing the rates to be the highest during World War II.[16] Thomas estimated from records in the Official Catholic Directory that diocesan mixed marriage rates increased by 5 to 10 per cent during both world wars.[17]. That anomia associated with poverty also has its influence is suggested by the fact that the males who married outside the Church in one Canadian city were almost all in unskilled or semiskilled occupations.[18] At the other end of the economic scale, we may see anomia in the positive association of Catholic mixed marriages with those who are upwardly mobile in education.[19]

With this much for background, the reader is now in a better position to perceive the rationale for the hypotheses of this study. It will be noticed that I have followed Heiss in specifying the parents and family as agents of social control. However, Heiss did not include the church or the ethnic group as direct agents of control in his hypotheses. Neither did he make explicit use of the concept of anomia, although some of his data would lend themselves to this kind of conceptualization.

Hypotheses to Be Tested in This Study

The foregoing studies provided the germ for the following system of hypotheses. However, both opportunities and limitations for testing this theory of social control in relation to Protestant-Catholic marriages were dependent on the data at hand. As has been stated in Chapter I, the Detroit Area Study surveys for 1955, 1958, 1959, and 1962 appeared to be suitable for the study of interfaith marriages because they included questions concerning the religious preference of husband and wife. By examining the interview schedules used in these surveys, the writer believed that the following hypotheses could be tested. The phrasing of the subhypotheses, in fact, reflects the wording of these interview schedules.

A. *General hypothesis:*

If the agents of social control do not, or cannot (due to an anomic situation), exercise their influence, the violation of a religiously endogamous rule is more likely to occur.

B. *Specific hypotheses:*

1. If *parents* do not exercise social control, the violation of a religiously endogamous rule is more likely to occur.

    a. Protestant-Catholic marriages will be positively associated with having parents of mixed religions.

    b. Protestant-Catholic marriages will be negatively associated with mother's frequent talking about or participating in religious activities with the family when self was growing up.

    c. Protestant-Catholic marriages will be negatively associated with naming parents as having had "the greatest influence on your religious beliefs."

2. If *family or relatives* do not exercise social control, the violation of a religiously endogamous rule is more likely to occur.

    a. Protestant-Catholic marriages will be negatively related to the statement that friends or relatives would feel "unhappy or disturbed" or "would try to discourage" one from changing to Protestant or to Catholic.

3. If the *church* does not exercise social control, the violation of a religiously endogamous rule is more likely to occur.

    a. Protestant-Catholic marriages will be negatively related to one's education in church schools.

    b. Protestant-Catholic marriages will be negatively related to frequent attendance at religious services the year before marriage.

4. If the *ethnic group* does not exercise social control, the violation of a religiously endogamous rule is more likely to occur.

    a. Protestant-Catholic marriages will be positively related to being an American of the second and subsequent generations.

5. If an *anomic situation* exists, the violation of a religiously endogamous rule is more likely to occur.

    a. Protestant-Catholic marriages will be positively

related to being married during war years—
World War I, World War II, Korean War,
determined from the question on length of marriage.

b. Protestant-Catholic marriages will be positively
related to getting married at a late age, with
consequent emancipation from home.

c. Protestant-Catholic marriages will be positively
related to migration from a farm to Detroit before
age 18.

d. Protestant-Catholic marriages will be positively
related to the husband's extreme upward mobility
in education, compared to his father.

e. Protestant-Catholic marriages will be positively
related to the husband's extreme upward mobility
in occupation, compared to his father.

These are the hypotheses to be tested in the Detroit data.
There were several other subhypotheses which I had hoped
to test, but the data proved inadequate for them. As a
point of clarification, it may also be worth stating here that
the *anomic situation* in the fifth specific hypothesis does not
necessarily infer a state of normlessness in the entire social
system. It refers to a situation which is thought to induce
anomia in the individual personality system, with special
reference to the norm of religious endogamy.

The Assumption of a Normative Order

It has been stated that this book is concerned with a
concrete action—the choice of a marriage partner—insofar
as this conforms with the norm of religious endogamy. My
initial interest in this question was practical, not theoretical.
Nevertheless, the social scientist who reads the hypotheses
which are to be tested here will immediately be aware that
the theoretical ramifications of this research problem are
very extensive. In general, my orientation in the study of
this problem has been that of structural-functional analysis.
Many social theorists have something to contribute to our
understanding of the subject of this study. However, it has

been my experience that the works of Talcott Parsons—because of his broad Theory of Action framework and its articulation on the psychological, social, and cultural levels of analysis—seem to provide more points of contact with our far less abstract theory of interfaith marriages than do the works of any other author. On specific concepts or hypotheses, of course, other social theorists will be better able to further our understanding.

An overview of the hypotheses proposed in the preceding section surely indicates the need for us to rely on the most fundamental of all sociological assumptions, i.e., the assumption of a normative order. If there were no order or regularity in human activities, then behavioral science would be an impossibility. If social norms, i.e., shared standards of behavior, were nonexistent, then sociologists would have to go out of business. Let us consider briefly how this basic concept has arisen and been described.

> In all social phenomena we perceive the working of the physiological laws of the individual; and moreover something which modifies their effects, and which belongs to the influence of individuals over each other—singularly complicated in the case of the human race by the influence of generations on their successors.[20]

In this pregnant sentence we find suggested the interrelationship of psychological, social, and cultural systems. Yet, they are the words not of a contemporary social theorist but of the "grandfather" of them all—Auguste Comte. He has not made explicit, however, the concept of "norms."

In fact, I am not prepared to say who among social scientists first made explicit use of the concept of social or cultural norms. Emile Durkheim certainly was using this notion when he described his "social facts" as "ways of acting, thinking, and feeling, external to the individual, and endowed with a power of coercion, by reason of which they control him."[21] We find the same content with different labels in the folkways and mores of William G. Sumner:

> In fact, the real process in great bodies of men is not one of deduction from any great principle of philosophy or ethics. It is one of minute efforts to live well under existing conditions, which efforts are repeated indefinitely by great num-

bers, getting strength from habit and from the fellowship of united action. The resultant folkways become coercive. All are forced to conform, and the folkways dominate the societal life. Then they seem true and right, and arise into mores as the norm of welfare.[22]

Among anthropologists, Ralph Linton used almost an equivalent concept in his "ideal patterns": "The sum of the ideal patterns which control the reciprocal behavior between individuals and between the individual and society constitute the social system under which the particular society lives."[23] Whoever introduced the precise concept of cultural or social norms, we can see that similar ideas have been around for a long time.

George C. Homans has a clarity of style which will be particularly helpful at this point. A *norm,* he says, "is an idea in the minds of the members of a group, an idea that can be put in the form of a statement specifying what the members or other men should do, ought to do, are expected to do, under given circumstances."[24] His stress on norms as ideas enables him to make a basic distinction: "By our definition, norms are a part, but only a part, of what social anthropologists call the culture of a group."[25] They are statements of what ought to be done, not expressions of actual behavior in a group. The interplay of these two aspects is generally of great interest to a sociologist, as it will be for us in the matter of interfaith marriages.

Underlying all norms are the values of a group. The distinction between these two concepts is rather subtle. We may say that norms, in general, express a group's consensus on what should be done, but that values represent the broader and more fundamental areas of consensus from which other norms are derived. Since individuals belong to various groups, there can easily be conflict between the norms or values of these groups, as we shall find in a later section to be the case with respect to marriage choices. In Parsons' terms, we are concerned not simply with the cognitive or the appreciative modes of value-orientation, but with the synthesis of these two in the moral standards, "that aspect of value-orientation which is of greatest direct importance to the sociologist."[26]

One might think that values express the goals of a group, and norms the means to those goals. However, this is not viewed by most social scientists as an appropriate distinction. As Robin Williams expresses it, cultural norms

> include both cultural *goals* and the approved means for reaching those goals. To be *cultural*, the norms have only to be acquired by learning and to be shared by individuals, but norms shade into one another in many complicated nuances.[27]

He goes on, in the same place, to specify some major dimensions of variation in cultural norms.

1. *Prevalence* within the given collectivity.
2. *Enforcement* and imputed sources of authority.
3. *"Formal characteristics"* of the norm itself, e.g., specificity, rigidity.
4. *Relation to other norms.*

These dimensions will each be examined in our study of interfaith marriages.

These remarks begin to give a theoretical context to our research problem. Before moving on, it may be worth noting that similar ideas are generally found in textbooks on sociological principles and on social psychology.[28] The concept of norms also has been productive of small group research[29] and of cross-cultural studies.[30]

Institutions

There has been considerable disagreement among sociologists about the use of the concept "institution," so much so that Homans chooses to avoid it altogether[31] and Zaniecki asks whether sociology will drop the term and leave it to philosophy.[32] This is unfortunate, since the concept can be a powerful one which lies at the heart of a theory of social organization. The difficulty seems to arise from the uncritical acceptance of usages found in the ordinary English dictionary, where the term receives at least three distinct meanings: (1) an established practice or system of practices; (2) an organization having a social, educational, or religious purpose; (3) the building which houses such an organization.

It seems to me that MacIver and Page have done well to restrict the meaning of institution to "established forms or conditions of procedure characteristic of group activity."[33] They thereby are able to distinguish associations, such as the family or state, from institutions, such as marriage or government. The notions are related, of course: "Every association has, with respect to its particular interest, its characteristic institutions," e.g., a church has its sacraments, etc.[34] In this sense, we can *belong to* an association but not to an institution. We shall try to use the concept consistently in this way. Although Robin Williams restricts the meaning of "institution" in the same way,[35] others who have written extensively on the subject do not (unfortunately, I believe) exclude the notion of association from the concept.[36]

Talcott Parsons, although using the term "collectivity" in place of "association," agrees closely with MacIver and Page, and incidentally specifies our particular interest in this study:

> An institution in this sense should be clearly distinguished from a collectivity. A collectivity is a system of concretely interactive specific roles. An institution on the other hand is a complex of patterned elements in role-expectations which may apply to an indefinite number of collectivities. Conversely, a collectivity may be the focus of a whole series of institutions. Thus the institutions of marriage and of parenthood are both constitutive of a particular family as a collectivity.[37]

Parsons distinguishes three classes of institutions: relational, regulative, and cultural. The first of these, which defines statuses and roles of the parties in interaction, is what will concern us in the problem of mate selection according to a rule of religious endogamy. In discussing the "pattern variables" of role-definition at this point, he notes that "the relative primacies given to choices between them can be treated as constitutive of the patterning of relational institutions."[38] The second (later enumerated as the fifth) of the "pattern variables," which he focuses on the system of relational institutions, is the "Private *vs.* Collective Interest Dilemma" or "Self-Orientation *vs.* Collectivity-Orientation."[39] This expresses aptly the dilemma of a Protestant or Catholic or Jew faced with the alternative of selecting a mate outside his religious group. One might think Parsons had this situation in mind when he wrote:

> There is a moral issue only when the alternatives involve a presumption of relevance to the "integrity" or the "solidarity" of an interaction system when the preservation of that integrity or solidarity is itself a value. . . . The case of self-orientation is the case where, in the choice in question, which alternative is chosen is felt to be or defined as *indifferent* as far as the integrity of a valued social system of action is concerned. That of collectivity-orientation on the other hand is that where such integrity is defined as being involved, so that the actor who chooses one side is violating his *responsibilities*, to the system as a unit and its participant members. It is only when an action system involves solidarity in this sense that its members define certain actions as required in the interest of the integrity of the system itself, and others as incompatible with that integrity—with the result that sanctions are organized about this definition. Such a system will be called a "collectivity." Collectivity-orientation, as it were, involves posing the "Question of confidence"; "are you one of us or not?" Your attitude on this question decides.[40]

It is well to keep this question in the general context of collectivities, since we are interested not only in society-wide norms with respect to mate-selection but also in the viewpoints of the smaller groups which are named in our "agents" of social control, namely the parents, family, church, and ethnic group, insofar as they support a norm of religious endogamy. Therefore, when Hertzler says that, "The control of mating in the interests of society constitutes the essence of the institution of marriage," we can read "religious collectivity" for "society" and "religious endogamy" for "marriage."[41]

Finally, Robin Williams describes the "three main problems" in the study of social institutions in such a way that more than enough work is cut out for us. The third of these will be our principal concern:

> First, one must describe and analyze the normative structure itself: the existing patterns, their causes and interrelations, the sources and mechanisms of institutional integration, and consequences of the norms. Second, one must discover the processes of change in institutional patterns: their

causes, mechanisms, and results. Third, one must study the relation of individual personalities to the normative structure; this is the area of "social psychology" dealing with culture-and-personality problems and facing the complexities of "social control" and of motivations for conforming, innovating, or dissenting.[42]

The Concept of Social Control

Whether we think of the rule of religious endogamy simply as a cultural norm or as an integral part (for the members of a religious group) of the institution of marriage, it clearly is of some concern to the religious group whether the rule is observed or not. To discuss the ways in which its observance is ensured is to enter into what Williams has just told us are the "complexities of 'social control.'" Since it is this concept which gives unity to the hypotheses of our study, we shall hardly be amiss in giving it considerable attention.

First, a few words about the changing popularity of this concept and then an effort to define it satisfactorily. It seems that the first use of the expression "social control" by a sociologist occurs in an early text by Albion W. Small and George E. Vincent.[43] However, it became popular a few years later when it was made the subject of a book by Edward A. Ross.[44] It even provided the theme for the Twelfth Annual Meeting of the American Sociological Society at Philadelphia in 1917, although the papers given there were only loosely related to this concept.[45] Since Ross' work, several authors have contributed books on the subject.[46] Of the several review articles on this concept, the best seems to be that by Georges Gurvitch.[47] In spite of the centrality that is often ascribed to this concept, it is not frequently used in research or theoretical articles. *Sociological Abstracts* sometimes has an entry under this heading appended to the Sociology of Law. *The American Sociological Review* indexes fewer articles on this subject than one finds under such headings as Social Class, Social Participation, or Marital Adjustment. Many well-known theoretical works in the areas of Social Organization and Social Psychology include one or more chapters with "Social Control" in the title.[48] However, only occasionally does a study appear in which this concept is the unifying theme.[49]

What is the meaning of "social control"? Almost a score

of definitions have come to the writer's attention. Most of these stress the relationship of social control to system maintenance or social organization. Social control is defined as one of the "master processes" in the theory of Charles Loomis: "the process by which deviancy is either eliminated or somehow made compatible with the functioning of the social groups."[50] Hollingshead gives us a clue instead of a definition: "The essence of social control is to be sought in the organization of people."[51] Homans is one of those who call attention to what social control means to the individual person. His definition is almost operational: "the process by which, if a man departs from his existing degree of obedience to a norm, his behavior is brought back toward that degree, or would be brought back if he did depart."[52] Rarely, the term "social control" has been used to designate an outgoing process, such as "to control one's environment."[53] For the purposes of our study, the definition given by Loomis is satisfactory. Associated with the rule of religious endogamy, as we shall see, there are regulations by which deviance is "somehow made compatible with the functioning of the social groups."

The means of social control may be conscious, such as rewards or punishment, advertising or propaganda, or even laughter. Or the means may be unconscious, such as the folkways, mores, and societal roles. Law is a conscious as well as a formal means of control by the state. Landis is probably right in his judgment that, "Unconscious forces, imbedded in the culture, are at least as strong as the conscious, formal control devices."[54]

Since the elements of social structure, such as roles and institutions, work for social control by their very existence, it follows that the socialization of the members of society into these roles and institutions is a key process contributing to social control. This has been a special interest of social psychologists and anthropologists.[55] Parsons also stresses its relationship to social control:

> There are such close relations between the processes of socialization and of social control that we may take certain features of the processes of socialization as a point of reference for developing a framework for the analysis of the processes of control.[56]

He sees both processes as involving adjustment to strains through mechanisms of defense and adjustment. This leads him to describe the process of psychotherapy as "a prototype of the mechanisms of social control."[57] The salient mechanisms used by the therapist, in Parsons' view, are those of permissiveness, support, denial of reciprocity, and manipulation of rewards. Later Parsons retains the same terms for the "learning-social control phases" in the socialization of the child.[58] The consistency and scope of Parsons' theorizing are sometimes capable of inducing amazement.

In our study of interfaith marriages, we cannot undertake a thorough and systematic study of socialization as related to social control. However, it is not difficult to see that socialization is involved in our hypotheses relating to the influence of parents and of education in church schools.

It would take us too far afield to go into a detailed discussion of the qualities and functions of social control. Let us note for future reference, however, that the rigidity and effectiveness of a system of social control seem to depend largely on two factors: (1) the homogeny of the group;[59] and (2) the social and physical opportunities for escaping from the group.[60] In an excellent discussion related to this, William R. Catton hypothesizes that conformity of a group's members to its norms will increase with the in-group's ethnocentrism. What consequences this may have for the group as a whole is suggested by this well-phrased observation of his: "If ethnocentrism promotes social control within the group, it may make the group more effective at adaptation *of* environment even when it interferes with the group's adaptation *to* environment."[61]

Approaches to Deviance: Anomia

Deviance and the mechanisms of social control may be defined with reference to the social system involved, or with the focus on the individual actor. We are more concerned about the latter in this book. Hence the definitions given by Parsons are appropriate:

. . . deviance is a motivated tendency for an actor to behave in contravention of one or more institutionalized normative patterns, while the mechanisms of social control are the motivated processes in the behavior of this actor, and of the others with whom he is in interaction, by which these tendencies to deviance tend in turn to be counteracted.[62]

The very complementarity of these definitions suggests the interplay between deviance and social control. It reminds us of Durkheim's well-known passage on the function that crime performs in stimulating a reaffirmation of collective sentiment with respect to the violated norm.[63] As Homans has expressed the same idea more recently: "Crime—not too much of it—is needed; it keeps the controls in good working order. A control is not effective unless it is tested. . . . "[64] In relating these ideas to interfaith marriages, it seems to me that two points should be made at this time: *1.* "Crime" and "criminal" have acquired connotations which make them inappropriate to apply to the violation of a norm like religious endogamy. Even the concept of "nonconformist," which Merton carefully delineates from "criminal," is not always the proper word.[65] We shall generally use the nonrestrictive terms, "deviant" or "deviance." *2.* The point about crime aiding the social system by stimulating sanctions should not be accepted without a distinction. If violation of a norm is a way for a nonconformist to bring about its revision or removal, as Merton observes, it may indeed help the social system toward defining its own boundaries and making new adjustments to the environment. However, the idea that crime, properly speaking, is functional for the system (always "in limited quantities") because it tests the sanctioning machinery is, simply from the point of view of the social system, a point to be studied rather than assumed. Is the social structure stronger or weaker *after* the violated norm has been reaffirmed? If weaker, then how is the criminal act "functional" for the system? If stronger, then why should not each punished crime have the same effect? Why do authors avoid this cumulative notion by adding a phrase such as "not too much of it"?

Enough for the functions of deviance. We are more concerned in this study with predicting its occurrence. This brings us to the question of its relationship to alienation and *anomie*, a subject to which very many have contributed in recent years. It is important for us to be as clear as we can about this, since several of our hypotheses concern "anomic situations."

Historically, the problem stems from Emile Durkheim's use of the term *anomie* both in his study of suicide and in an earlier work.[66] To get to the root of the meaning, this exposition seems to help:

> Thus, social disorganization; discarded and discredited norms; a flat unwillingness to accept in any form a checkrein on pleasures, appetites, production, or prosperity: this constellation of signs Durkheim translated into Greek. To the negative prefix *a*, he added the plural of laws, *nomous*, and turned the "no-laws" of *anomous* into French as *l'Anomie*. That is why Durkheim's first mention of the term occurs as "the state of unbridleness" (to put it awkwardly), or, in French "*L'etat* de dereglement ou *d'anomie*. . . ."[67]

Some have translated Durkheim's term as "normlessness," but it is important to note that for him it originally designated a state of a *society* or a group. Loomis, following Parsons here, defines anomie as "under-institutionalization . . . in which persons are provided with no effective norms to guide them, no meaningful status-roles, no sanctions, and other elements to standardize behavior."[68] One distinction made in the concept as used at this level may be applied to our study. Attributed by Merton to Sebastian De Grazia, it is the distinction between *simple* and *acute* anomie:

> Simple anomie refers to the state of confusion in a group or society which is subject to conflict between value-systems, resulting in some degree of uneasiness and a sense of separation from the group; acute anomie, to the deterioration and, at the extreme, the disintegration of value-systems, which results in marked anxieties.[69]

As we shall see, the principal value-systems which are in conflict in interfaith marriage are the secular and the religious.

Anomie at the societal level has its counterpart in the experience of the individual personality. To avoid confusion in using the term at these two levels, MacIver used the spelling "anomy" to designate the *state of mind* of the individual.[70] A few years later, Leo Srole suggested the spelling "anomia" to distinguish the psychological concept from the sociological concept.[71] His suggestion was taken up by others and is followed in this study also. Apart from spellings, what does this psychological concept actually mean?

It seems to me that clarity of meaning has been lacking until recently in the use of this term and the related concept of alienation. A significant contribution toward eliminating such confusion was made by Melvin Seeman in an article published in 1959.[72] He discussed "five basic ways in which the concept of alienation has been used"—powerlessness, meaninglessness, normlessness, isolation, and self-estrangement. If we assume that these exhaust the meanings which the term has received and if we restrict anomia to its Durkheimian usage of "normlessness," then we can see that anomia as a *psychological* concept (not as a property of a social system) constitutes one *part* of the literature on alienation. One can hope (without any real assurance) that these clear distinctions will be followed by future writers on the subject, but it is necessary to be cautious in interpreting earlier publications. One modification of Seeman's article, proposed by several men at Whittier College, seems to have merit. They reformulate the five meanings somewhat and consider them to represent *stages of a process* of alienation. Seeman, in his reply to them, judges that this view of alienation would be an "over-commitment which leaves too little room for historical circumstances, situational pressure, or personality type in shaping the specific form of sequence that alienation will take."[73] This criticism is probably correct with regard to the *concept* of alienation, but the process idea as the Whittier group proposed it could be regarded as a *hypothesis* to be tested.

Related to the meaning of anomia and alienation is, of course, the problem of measuring these concepts operationally. In 1959, Leo Srole proposed a set of attitudes which he thought would provide a scale of alienation and would "place individuals on a eunomia-anomia continuum representing variations in interpersonal integration with their particular social fields as 'global entities.' "[74] Gwynn Nettler followed with a measure of alienation, which was but slightly correlated with Srole's anomia scale ($+.309$).[75] When one examines the five attitude statements in Srole's scale, it is difficult not to agree with Nettler's judgment that what they measure is largely *despair*. (In view of what was said above about the meanings of alienation in Seeman's article, it is regrettable that this scale has been used by a number of researchers who considered themselves to be measuring *anomia;* the Durkheimian sense of "normlessness" is conceptually not the same as "despair.") In my estimation, the most thoroughgoing approach to the measurement of alienation so far published has been reported by Dwight G. Dean. In selecting items for his three subscales of Powerlessness, Normlessness, and Social Isolation, he enlisted the aid of seven sociologists as judges of 139 attitude items, finally retaining 24 items.[76]

Conclusions resulting from the use of these scales will be cited (in a later chapter) if they relate to the "anomic situations" of our study. Here we may mention two characteristics which have been thought to be associated with anomia: socioeconomic class and religion. Interest in the question as to whether anomia is related to religion stems from the finding by Durkheim that anomic suicide was more characteristic of Protestant than of Catholic populations (divorce rates being his index of anomy).[77] Using Srole's anomia scale in San Francisco, Meier and Bell report that, when socioeconomic status and age are controlled, "the Protestants generally show lower anomic scores than the other religious groups," though "the relationship is more obscure."[78] Dean and Reeves used the "normlessness" subscale developed by the former and found that women at a midwest Protestant college had significantly higher normlessness scores than women at a midwest Catholic college.[79] Since *divorce rates* and *normlessness* seem more relevant to interfaith marriages than does *despair* (these being the criteria for anomia used in these three studies), we may have some slight reason here to expect our hypotheses concerning "anomic situations" to be better predictors for Protestant mixed marriages than for Catholic.

Interest in the relationship of socioeconomic status to anomia was stimulated by Robert Merton's study of the subject. He shows that in a society such as ours, in which the achievement of "success" is held out as the goal for all and in which those in the lowest socioeconomic strata find the means to this goal relatively unavailable to them, people in these strata will experience a "strain toward anomie," "the breakdown of the regulatory structure."[80] (This is not quite the same as our hypothesis that vertical *mobility* is related to anomia.) By contrast, Durkheim had found anomic suicide to be most characteristic of those with independent means, among those in professional, industrial, and commercial occupations.[81] Although Merton takes account of "white collar crime" in one deviant adaptation (Innovation) to this conflict between the "success" goal and limited accessibility of culturally approved means toward the goal, his analysis suggests, in general, that "the greatest pressures toward deviation are exerted upon the lower strata."[82] Nevertheless, the association between social class and anomia is still in doubt, as Ephraim H. Mizruchi observes:

> Is the association an inverse one, as Srole and Bell report, or is it "negligible," as Roberts and Rokeach suggest? Different indices of class were used in these three studies, which probably accounts for some of the discrepancy between the findings. No standard index of social class has as yet been applied systematically in the various attempts to evaluate its role in relation to anomia.[83]

His own data from a small city in upstate New York did show a significant inverse relationship between scores on Srole's anomia scale and Hollingshead's two-factor Index of Social Position as well as the respondents' subjective class identifications. However, if we wish to apply this generalization to the interpretation of interfaith marriage rates, we must remember the large element of "despair" in the Srole scale which was used for each of these studies. This may not be related to the "normlessness" which we look for in our hypotheses concerning anomic situations.

In Merton's study of social structure and anomie, he goes to considerable trouble to develop and describe a typology of modes of individual adaptation to cultural values, based on their acceptance or rejection of the goals and institutionalized means.[84] Parsons modified the paradigm by adding the dimension of activity vs. passivity.[85] Robert Dubin greatly expanded the typology and ended with fourteen categories of deviant behavior.[86] At this point in our study it does not seem worthwhile to go into detail concerning these typologies. Our hypotheses are not intended to validate them, and our data are only partly suitable for this.

Finally, having considered at length sources of deviant behavior and its typologies, let us bring this section to a close by mentioning the study of some *reactions* to deviance. We have already called attention to the point that crime and nonconformity are thought to stimulate the reinforcing of the social structure. Small group studies have shown that deviates do not fare well in sociometric choices, that they also experience pressures to change in the form of increased communication received.[87] On a more theoretical level, Howard Becker's Presidential address to the American Sociological Association in 1960 dealt with reactions not only to deviates but to the condition of normlessness itself.[88]

Before closing this discussion of the basic sociological concepts which underlie our study of interfaith marriages and the hypotheses which are to be tested with Detroit area data, I would like to call attention to two very recent contributions to our understanding of them. Clark and Gibbs have given this helpful definition of *social control:* "social reactions to behavior defined as deviant, including over-conformity to, as well as violations of norms."[89] Since they allow for the inclusion of "deliberate anticipatory reactions" and wish to encompass not only formal sanctions but also informal and nonlegal reactions to deviations from a norm, it seems to me that my use of the term in this book is in full agreement with theirs.

In another very recent and noteworthy article by Gibbs, his typology of norms is a very logical one, which he recognizes cannot be applied without extensive research. Perhaps at the end of this book it will be appropriate to apply this typology to the norm of religious endogamy. Meanwhile, it should help to keep our thinking clear at this point in our discussion if we accept his definition of a norm as involving: "(1) a collective evaluation of behavior in terms of what it *ought* to be; (2) a collective expectation as to what behavior *will* be; and/or (3) particular *reactions* to behavior, including attempts to apply sanctions or otherwise induce a particular kind of conduct." Gibbs also recognizes that "the degree of conformity to norms is a contingent but not a definitional attribute."[90] In the chapters which reviewed the rates of intermarriage we were, in fact, addressing ourselves to the problem of determining the degree of conformity to endogamous norms.

Now that we have considered rather thoroughly the theoretical context of our problem, it seems to me that we can move logically to examine some expressions of the norm of religious endogamy which we have continuously referred to. We shall see that a norm such as this does not exist in a vacuum; it is woven into the fabric of human life and feeling. Neither does one norm have an existence cut off from all other norms. Such a norm as religious endogamy has a number of rivals for the individual's adherence because, in a given situation such as selecting a marriage partner, not all relevant norms can be easily followed or are felt to be equally important. So let us proceed to considerations such as those just stated.

VII

The Norm of Religious Endogamy– and Contrary Trends

THE FOREGOING THEORETICAL FRAMEWORK for this study of Protestant-Catholic marriages is important, but the reader may have some misgivings at this point. After all, we have not even shown so far that a norm of religious endogamy exists in our society. Well, that is precisely what we are going to do now—as well as examine the current trends which work against it. We have already interpreted low rates of interfaith marriage as some evidence of an endogamous norm, of course, but it is time now to look at some explicit expressions of the norm. We shall first take a historical view, then draw on many statements of this norm, official and unofficial, and show that it is widely shared and expressed in the general population. Then we shall consider some of the trends and values which are contrary to this norm, namely, urbanization, industrialization, secularism, and individualism reflected in romanticism.

A Norm That Persists

As a starting point in the history of religious endogamy, the command given by God through Moses to the Israelites as they were about to enter the promised land is clear enough. Regarding the other peoples they would find living there, God said: "Neither shall you take their daughters as wives for your sons; otherwise, when their daughters render their wanton worship to their gods, they will make your sons do the same."[1] Jewish opposition to marriage with Gentiles through later centuries is well known. However, our concern in this study is with norms of Catholics and Protestants regarding intermarriage.

115

In the Christian era, the first known prohibition was stated by the Council of Elvira, Spain (306 A.D.), which "forbade Christian girls to marry pagans, Jews, heretics, or pagan priests." Girls are singled out since "under the civil law of the time (i.e., in the Greek-Roman empire) the man had the right to dictate the religious profession of his wife and children." In 339 A.D., the Emperor Constantius "forbade the marriage between Christians and Jews under the penalty of death."[2] One council at Constantinople in 692 declared that, if marriage is attempted by a Catholic with a heretic, it is null and void. However, the Scholastic teaching in the 13th century was that such marriages were forbidden but not invalid.

No provisions were made during the Middle Ages for ecclesiastical dispensations for such marriages.[3] This practice arose (for the newly discovered lands, especially in the Far East) in the late 16th century. For Europe the dispensation had to be obtained from the Holy See, although "a custom developed in Germany, England, Poland, and the Netherlands to marry freely mixed couples without a papal dispensation and without the abjuration of heresy."[4] The tenor of these times is also represented by the Presbyterian Confession of Faith, Chapter XXIV, Section III, which reads:

> It is lawful for all sorts of people to marry who are able with judgment to give their consent; yet it is the duty of Christians to marry in the Lord, and, therefore, such as profess the true reformed religion should not marry with infidels, Papists, or other idolaters. . . .[5]

How did the much-discussed promises required of partners to a mixed marriage in the Roman Catholic Church arise? When Pope Pius VI (1775-99) was reigning, Belgian civil law required that Catholic pastors witness mixed marriages. The Belgian bishops asked the Holy See what they were to do if the Catholic party could not be dissuaded and the Protestant party did not want to become Catholic. The answer:

> . . . the pastor could be present as a mere material witness to the declaration of the marriage consent, and only under the following conditions (called the *cautelae*): (1) that the marriage be not celebrated in a sacred place, that the

pastor wear no sacred vestments, recite no ecclesiastical prayers over the parties, and shall not bless them; (2) that the pastor demand and receive from the heretical party a written declaration under oath and in the presence of two witnesses, who together with the party shall sign the declaration by which the Protestant binds himself to permit the Catholic party the full and free exercise of his religion and that all the children without distinction of sex will be raised in the Catholic Faith; (3) that the Catholic party give a written declaration under oath in the presence of two witnesses and subscribed by him and the witnesses that he will never apostatize from the Catholic Faith, that he will educate all the children to be born in the Catholic religion, and endeavor to induce the non-Catholic partner to join the Catholic Church; (4) as to the proclamation of the banns of mixed marriage which the imperial decree has ordered, the Holy Father does not approve of such proclamation and directs the bishops to petition the emperor that he exempt them from making such announcements, at least that they may not be in church. [July 13, 1782][6]

The Code of Canon Law of the Roman Catholic Church, promulgated on May 19, 1918, and still in effect, reads as follows in the pertinent sections:

The Church most strictly and everywhere forbids marriages between a Catholic and a person enrolled in an heretical or schismatical sect. If there is a danger of perversion [i.e., "danger of loss of faith or of Christian life," p. 634] for the Catholic party and the offspring, such marriage is forbidden also by the divine law. [Canon 1060]

The Church does not dispense from the impediment of mixed religion except under the following conditions: (1) there must be good and weighty reasons; (2) the non-Catholic party must promise to avert all danger of perversion from the Catholic party, and both parties must promise to have all the children baptized and raised in the Catholic Faith; (3) there must be moral certainty that the promises will be kept. The promises are, as a rule, to be made in writing. [Canon 1061]

The Catholic party has the obligation to work prudently for the conversion of the non-Catholic. [Canon 1062]

Though the Church has granted the dispensation from the impediment of mixed religion, the parties are forbidden either before or after the Catholic wedding to approach

either in person or by proxy a non-Catholic minister as a
minister of religion to give or renew the matrimonial consent.
If the pastor knows for certain that the parties will violate
or have already violated this law, he shall not assist at their
marriage except for very serious reasons until he shall have
consulted the Ordinary and all danger of scandal has been
removed. If the civil law demands it, the Church does not
censure parties for appearing before a non-Catholic minister
who is acting merely as an official of the Government, provided that their purpose is solely to comply with the civil
law and to get civil recognition of their marriage. [Canon
1063][7]

These canons do not exhaust the regulations of the Catholic
Church regarding interfaith marriages, but they express the
main principles.

Needless to say, churchmen of other faiths have been disturbed by the requirement of these promises. In fact, a new
awareness of these regulations seems to have prompted the
most recent declarations of Protestant bodies against marriages
with Catholics. One of the first on record was the 1948
General Convention of the Protestant Episcopal Church, which
unanimously adopted a resolution patterned after that adopted
by the last Lambeth Conference:

> Resolved, that this convention earnestly warns members
> of our Church against contracting marriages with Roman
> Catholics under conditions imposed by modern Roman Catholic
> canon law, especially as these conditions involve a promise
> to have their children brought up under a religious system
> which they cannot themselves accept; and further, because
> the religious education and spiritual training of their children
> by word and example is a paramount duty of parents and
> should never be neglected nor left entirely to others, we
> assert that in no circumstances shall a member of this Church
> give any understanding as a condition of marriage, that the
> children should be brought up in the practice of another
> communion.[8]

It should be clear already that the rule of religious endogamy
gets much of its strength from concern about the religious
education of the children of a mixed marriage and the fulfilling
of that obligation by parents who are not agreed on the
direction this education should take. Except for this problem,

the churches might very well leave the mixed couple to their own devices. As it is, the following church assemblies echoed (each with its own specific motivations) the resolution just cited:

1950 — General Assembly, Presbyterian Church of the United States.
— American Baptist Convention (Northern).
— International Convention of Disciples of Christ.
1951 — Southern Baptist Convention.
1953 — Convention of the Lutheran Church—Missouri Synod.[9]

The sanction imposed by the Catholic Church until recently in these matters was excommunication reserved to the Ordinary (i.e., the bishop of the diocese), applied to Catholics who contract marriage before a non-Catholic minister contrary to Canon 1063, or who marry with the explicit or implicit agreement to educate some or all of their offspring outside the Catholic Church (Canon 2319). In addition, *for members* of the Catholic Church, only those marriages are valid which are contracted before the parish priest or the local Ordinary or a priest delegated by either of them and before two witnesses (Canon 1094).

The two canons just cited have been withdrawn, at least in part, within the past few years. A decree on the Sacrament of Matrimony, authorized by Pope Paul VI and effective on March 28, 1966, abrogated (even retroactively) the sanction of excommunication for those Catholics who marry before a non-Catholic minister. Such a marriage is still viewed as invalid and illicit, however. The same decree allows a mixed marriage in a Catholic church to take place with the same Mass and blessing which are ordinarily prescribed for an all-Catholic wedding.[10] Another decree, effective March 25, 1967, recognized as valid the marriages entered into in Orthodox ceremonies between Latin Rite Catholics and Orthodox Christians. If the Catholic bishop's permission has first been obtained, such a marriage would be licit as well as valid.[11] This provision goes beyond the Decree on Eastern Catholic Churches by the Second Vatican Council.[12]

The larger Protestant denominations have not specified any

consequences which follow for members who do not observe the resolutions cited above. However, "several small Protestant sects excommunicate members who marry outside of their particular churches."[13]

The reader may be convinced by now that a norm of religious endogamy exists in the official statements of the churches of the United States. How is this norm kept before the eyes of their members? There are occasional high-level conferences, such as that held for two days by the Herzl Institute of New York on "Intermarriage and Jewish Life," February, 1960. There are teaching aids such as the 27-minute film, "One Love—Conflicting Faith," produced by the Department of the Christian Family, the General Board of Education, and the Television, Radio and Film Commission of the Methodist Church. We can assume, no doubt, occasional warnings against mixed marriages in sermons, Sunday school classes, and family counseling sessions of individual congregations. However, there are two means of dissemination which are rather easy to identify: textbooks for high school and college courses and "guide" books for young people and families.

Sister M. Evodine McGrath, O.S.F., made a study of twenty-eight Catholic colleges for women and five for men in the Midwest, to determine their offerings relative to marriage and the family. One of her findings was that mixed marriages were discussed in a variety of courses (usually a religion or family course)—a total of 47 courses for the 55 colleges.[14] Father Edgar Schmiedeler, O.S.B., has written one text for high school students and another for college use, each warning against mixed marriages.[15] Even nonsectarian marriage and family textbooks discourage such unions.[16]

Protestant authors are more prominent in the production of "guide" books for young people and families. Besides the three cited earlier by Black, Bossard and Boll, and Pike, we should mention that John C. Wynn has written a good one.[17] In a slightly different class is the scholarly comparison of Roman Catholic and Protestant views on marriage, with special reference to mixed marriage, written by Mario Colacci.[18] Apparently an Evangelical Protestant, the author does not fully understand some Catholic teachings, but he uses official Catholic sources (often with the most "conservative" commentators) and tries to be accurate and fair. Among

Catholic authors of marriage "guide" books, perhaps the best known is Father George A. Kelly of New York.[19] All of these warn against interfaith marriages.

Granted that the churches try by various means to maintain the norm of religious endogamy, is the general population aware of it? It would be possible to cite a dozen references from nonreligious sources which show an awareness of this norm in our country—which is the only point I want to make just now. To show the variety of contexts in which this may occur, we mention Alfred M. Lee's discussion of socialization, J. O. Hertzler's book on social institutions, and George Simpson and Milton Yinger's master work on minority groups.[20] One curious indication of awareness of the norm of religious endogamy is found in the complaint by Glenn M. Vernon that social scientists show their own bias against interfaith marriages by consistently reporting the increased percentage of divorces which follow such marriages instead of comparing the percentages of unbroken marriages, in which the contrast is not so great.[21]

Although one cannot base a statistical generalization on a small set of case reports, it is of interest that a number of people who have entered interfaith marriages and stuck it out have written about them afterwards to dissuade others from arriving at the same choice.[22] So far no similar report has come to my attention in which a couple in a mixed marriage urged others to do the same. However, a different viewpoint will be considered in our final chapter.

Another indication of the acceptance of the norm of religious endogamy can be found in studies of attitudes toward interfaith marriages. Among the many which might be summarized here, we will select just a few of the better studies which are closest to our subject matter.

As an indication that the official norms are not without some influence, Alfred Prince found that Catholic college students were more willing to intermarry than Protestants, but also twice as likely to specify the condition that the children be raised in their religion.[23]

Father Harry E. Hoover made a study of the attitudes of Catholic high school students toward mixed marriages, drawing on nine Master's theses written earlier at Catholic University on the same subject. His analysis was based on 4,000 questionnaires returned from eleven Catholic high schools in eight dioceses. His conclusions: Girls are more opposed to mixed marriages than the boys are; senior boys are more opposed than the other three classes.[24] When he matched the seniors on seven variables and correlated their attitude scores (regarding mixed marriages) with an eighth factor, "the following significant results" were obtained: Those were most opposed to mixed marriages (a) whose homes were most Catholic (an index based on ten behavioral items), (b) who had above average I.Q.'s, (c) who were high achievers in school.[25]

Another indication of the wide acceptance of the norm of religious endogamy comes from one of the Detroit area surveys being used for the present study. Lenski asked his sample of Detroiters whether they thought it wiser for members of their group to marry within the group. "The overwhelming majority of white respondents said that it *was* wiser. This was true of 92 per cent of the Jews, 81 per cent of the Catholics, and 75 per cent of the Protestants."[26]

Finally, Rabbi Albert I. Gordon has surveyed 5,407 students in forty colleges and universities of many types on the subject of intermarriage. Some of his findings are the following: Only 29 per cent of the students dated outside of their religion "frequently" or "almost always." In the total sample which included 47 per cent Protestants, 31 per cent Catholics, and 12 per cent Jews, 74 per cent said they would be willing to marry Protestants, 56 per cent would marry Catholics, and 37 per cent would marry Jews. In the eight Catholic colleges the percentages were 45, 85, and 17, respectively. When asked what kind of intermarriage would be hardest for them to accept, the total sample indicated that marrying outside their color group would be hardest; however, marrying outside their religion group would be next hardest, followed by their educational, national, and economic groups.[27]

This brings to a close our evidence for the existence of a norm of religious endogamy in the United States. The historical development of the norm is continuous with its current status, although there has been a mollifying of the sanctions involved. Recent statements of the norm by the churches and religious advisers have been clear and frequent. The endogamous norm is also reflected and shared, at least to some extent, by the general population. It has not been our intention here to try to show just how strong or universal the norm is, but rather that it is a viable element of the current American scene.

Multiple Group Memberships in the Modern Scene

Now let us consider what conflicts may be involved in choosing a marriage partner. Here we find the stuff of which great dramas and novels are made: the impulsive individual struggling with his own ideal self-image and with the many-voiced social structures *around* him and *in* him. Any treatment of this subject will seem too brief because it will always be outdone by the complexity of human motivation and especially of modern society. MacIver and Page, whose treatment of this subject is excellent, state that there are two main types of conflict between the individual and the code:

(1) that in which personal interest or personal valuation is opposed to a prevailing code, and (2) that in which the individual is pulled opposite ways by the prescriptions of different codes when two or more are applicable within the same situation.[28]

Most of what is said in this section of the chapter will be related to the second conflict, always understanding that the choice made in terms of this conflict may be a kind of rationalization to resolve the first conflict. At the end we shall consider explicitly some aspects of the self-collectivity dilemma.

Two concepts have been developed in social psychology which are relevant to the momentous choice we are considering: reference group and marginal man. George Mead's "generalized other" and Charles Cooley's "social self" are usually given credit as forerunners to the reference group concept. However, Georg Simmel's "web of group-affiliations" was at least as perceptive in this matter.[29] The actual term "reference group" was coined by Herbert Hyman in 1942, stimulated by Roper's opinion polls. After this, interest in the concept received new impetus from Newcomb's well-known Bennington study, which contrasted the relative influence of campus *vs.* home environment in shaping political ideology.

What is meant by "reference group"? One dictionary defines

it as: "any group with which a person *identifies* and/or compares himself to such an extent that he tends to adopt its standards, attitudes, and behaviors as his own."[30] The term has been used loosely, and will be so used here, to include membership and nonmembership groups, collectivities, social categories, and individuals. In the modern world the average person looks for approval to many different groups and individuals beyond his own family of origin. Hence we must not overlook the concept's potential for interpreting interfaith marriages.

The "marginal man" is, in Merton's paradigm, just one category of persons in reference group theory—those who aspire to membership in a group but are regarded as ineligible by the group itself.[31] The concept of marginal man, however, antedates that of reference group. Robert E. Park invented the term, and Everett V. Stonequist ensured its fame by writing a book about it. The latter's definition of it is:

> The individual who through migration, education, marriage, or some other influence leaves one social group or culture without making a satisfactory adjustment to another finds himself on the margin of each but a member of neither. He is a "marginal man."[32]

The concept has often been applied to the offspring of intermarriages of every type, but it is mentioned here because the writer believes that it sometimes characterizes the participants in religious intermarriage. For instance, the interfaith marriage choice of an upwardly mobile individual or of a second-generation American may be influenced by this sociopsychological condition. In any case, its relationship to conflicting values and reference groups and its similarity to anomia should be evident.

The social changes which have taken place in recent centuries easily breed "marginal men" and give rise to value conflicts which would not have to be faced in a simpler, more homogeneous society. Urbanization, which began about five thousand years ago and has become dominant in our country only in the last couple of generations, has brought with it much heterogeneity in a dense population and a large degree of anonymity at least in the central city. Industrialization adds its impetus to reference group conflicts by the spatial and occupational mobility which it fosters. These may be considered the chief historical forces which have established the conditions for more frequent intrapersonal conflicts, whether in the choice of a marriage partner or in any other important decision.

Trends toward Secularism and Individualism

If urbanization and industrialization sum up the chief *conditions* fostering intrapersonal conflicts in modern societies, then the chief *value orientations* which sum up the opposition to religious endogamy would seem to be secularism and individualism. Let us consider each of them in turn.

Lenski shows some concern with secularism, but his meaning is somewhat different from that which I will give to the term. He says:

> In short, norms of *tolerance* and *secularism* inevitably arise in urban centers. Norms peculiar to one religious group or another are de-emphasized, leaving a common core of moral norms which are shared by all the various faiths represented in the community.

Then he adds in a footnote: "Secularism is used here in the sense of religious neutralism."[33] This use of the concept "secularism" seems to make it a characteristic of *society,* a kind of moral "common denominator" in which religious differences in the population are submerged.

A good illustration of this phenomenon would be the influence of the "social gospel" in bringing about dialogue and cooperation between members of different religious bodies as they try to meet the challenge of modern social problems. It has been said that the cause of better race relations has done more to bring together Protestants, Catholics, and Jews than any earlier influence. This is an attractive aspect of secularism which, nevertheless, provides more occasions for the violation of the norm of religious endogamy.

In the present study the term "secularism" will be used mainly to describe a value orientation for the *individual member* of a society, in which this-world considerations take precedence over the requirements of a faith in an other-world goal.[34] Mine is therefore closer to the meaning which Landis gives to the term, although I will not follow him in the rest of his analysis:

> In the long view of history, two prevailing conceptions of authority are seen: (1) the sacred, and (2) the secular. The trend away from the mystical interpretation of life toward the rational interpretation of it is known as secularization.[35]

Will Herberg has discussed at length and with remarkable insight the problem of secularism in American religion itself. "Under the influence of the American environment," he says, "the historic Jewish and Christian faiths have tended to become secularized in the sense of becoming integrated as parts within a larger whole defined by the American Way of Life." Citing Robin Williams' observation that religion in the United States tends not to be regarded as an ultimate value but as a good because it is useful in furthering other major values, reversing the former ends-means relationship, Herberg goes on:

> Insofar as any reference is made to the God in whom all Americans "believe" and of whom the "official" religions speak it is primarily as sanction and underpinning for the supreme values of the faith embodied in the American Way of Life. Secularization of religion could hardly go further.[36]

Later he contrasts European with American secularism. The former is militant, generates anti-religious sentiments; the latter is covert, makes anti-religion almost impossible because it would have to be expressed by religious people. Herberg concludes:

> The witness to authentic Jewish-Christian faith may well prove much more difficult under these conditions than when faith has to contend with overt and avowed unbelief.
>
> The spirit of secularism has always been pervasive and powerful and has always had its effect on religious institutions. The unique feature of the present religious situation in America is that this secularism is being generated out of the very same conditions that are, in part at least, making for the contemporary religious revival. The sociological factors that underlie the new urge to religious identification and affiliation are also factors that enhance the secularization of the religiousness they engender. It is not secularism as such

that is characteristic of the present religious situation in this country but secularism within a religious framework, the secularism of a religious people.[37]

A number of writers have noted also the secularization of marriage and family life, a tendency which makes the norm of religious endogamy less meaningful. Elliott and Merrill approach the matter from the viewpoint of social disorganization. After stating that the "secularism of the modern world has fostered a corresponding secular attitude toward marriage," they observe that the Catholic Church "mobilizes every element in its powerful institutional machinery toward the continuance of the religious conception of marriage." However, the sacramental nature of marriage was not tenable to the Protestant reformers, even though they "generally maintained the essential sanctity of the monogamic relationship."[38]

Bossard and Boll studied data concerning rituals in more than four hundred families, data from various sources and covering a span of eighty years. The first trend which they say "may be clearly identified" for these years is the trend "from predominance of the religious to predominance of the secular."[39] The same authors, in their book on interfaith marriages, state the following as the third type (out of four) of lay reaction to church opposition to these marriages:

> that religion and the church are no longer important—at least, not important enough to be considered in so personal and serious a matter as choice of a lifelong mate. This is a secular age, an age of change, dominated by science, we are told.[40]

Is secularism, as we are using the term, now more characteristic of one religious group than another? Only two studies attempting to answer this question have come to the attention of this writer. Samenfink's study was based on a sample at a state college in Louisiana. After matching the subjects on five variables, he concluded:

> When contrasted with the equivalent findings for a matched group of Protestants, however, the Roman Catholic respondents were less accepting of the secular position, with one exception. In the matter of equalitarianism in family living, the Roman Catholic position was more secular than was that of the Protestant respondents.[41]

Another study compared the attitudes of 156 college students belonging to the three major religious groups. In answer to the question "To whom do you owe your greatest loyalty?" 74 per cent of Catholics said "God" and 24 per cent said "Family"; for Protestants, the percentages were 50 and 39; for Jews, 11 and 74, respectively—these two responses being the most frequent for each group. When asked "What is most important in life?" the first and second choices of Catholics were these: "Live in accord with religious beliefs," and "Make world a better place." For both Protestants and Jews, the first and second choices were, respectively: "Make world a better place" and "Own happiness."[42] Behavior may be far different from expressed beliefs, of course.

If these differences hold up in other studies, they will be consistent with the finding that Catholics in this country are somewhat less successful in the competitive struggle for this world's goods than are the other two religious groups, since these differences imply that they may not be so highly motivated to succeed in this matter. Lenski, for instance, cites Neil J. Weller's doctoral dissertation to this effect and from his own data concerning attitudes toward work, after controlling for class position, states this conclusion (in italics):

> To sum up, it appears that Protestantism is conducive to more positive attitudes toward those positions in society which are more demanding (and also more rewarding), while Catholicism is conducive to more positive attitudes toward the less demanding (and hence less rewarding) positions.[43]

In a similar vein, he observes that Catholic-Protestant differences in fertility rates (Detroit, 1952-59) have been greater in the middle class than in the working class, which he suggests "could well be a factor contributing to our earlier finding that differences in rates of mobility are greater in the middle class than in the working class."[44] Large families do not make for upward mobility in an urban society.

Albert J. Mayer and Harry Sharp, using data from the Detroit Area Study from 1954 through 1959, apply a "handicapping" system (based on rural, foreign, and specific Detroit background) to the members of religious denominations and conclude that Catholics rank lowest in achievement of worldly success of all denominations in both white and Negro populations.[45] In Iowa the tendency seems to be in the same direction, though not so pronounced except in professional occupations, when comparing "church-Protestants" with Catholics. Other Protestants (i.e., those who do not specify a denomination) and those of no religion had lower occupational status levels than Catholics.[46]

It seems to me that the surprising results reported after a thematic apperceptive measure of achievement motivation was administered to a national sample of 1,620 adults also have relevance for our discussion of secularism as a value orientation. The authors of this study, contrary to expectation, found that Catholic n Achievement scores were higher than those of Protestants in middle age, even with several controls.[47] They then looked more closely at the middle-age group and found that Catholics with larger families have higher n Achievement scores than those with smaller families, true at each income level. Income was independently and *negatively* related to these scores for Catholics. For Protestants there was a slight *positive* relationship between income and n Achievement scores, but no association with the number of children.

The authors of this article seem to arrive at more precise statements than are warranted by the size of their Catholic sample, but our purpose now is not to review their long analysis. Rather, let us note that these findings fit our analysis of secularism as related to religious identification. Catholics do not seem to be particularly motivated toward success in this world as such. Their other-world orientation generally requires them to look for a *reason* for more-than-average striving for this world's goods, such as family duties or special economic stress.

If these differences represent variant degrees of secularism as a value-orientation on the part of Protestants and Catholics, we need not see this simply as a choice between this world and the future world. It may be, instead, a perceived difference in relationship between success in the two worlds, as Mayer and Sharp remind us:

> The powerfully reinforced and traditional Roman Catholic Church tends to orient its members toward the hereafter; successful performance in the market place and the acquisition of the symbols of economic achievement are of relatively little

importance as an indication of the Catholic's status after death. On the other hand, adherents of Protestantism are assumed to be highly concerned with worldly success and the attainment of material possession, status and the prestige that is associated with upward social mobility. These things often are viewed as indications that salvation is assured, or at least is more probable.[48]

What does all of this have to do with religious endogamy? Our discussion has been long enough to obscure the point. To the extent that secularism represents an orientation toward this world in opposition to orientation toward a future life, it is a value orientation which will often conflict with adhering to the norm of religious endogamy. If Protestants and Jews, in this country at least, are more influenced by the values of secularism than are Catholics, as some studies just cited seem to suggest, then we should expect that Protestants and Jews are less likely than Catholics to adhere to the norm of religious endogamy—other things being equal.

Now let us turn to the other major value orientation which is in conflict with religious endogamy—individualism. Paul Landis has stated the problem in its broadest terms:

> To what extent the personality of the individual shall be submerged into the social unit is a key problem of all social orders, and of every social institution. The question involves not only the degree of uniformity and variation in behavior, but also that of the extent to which the individual will seek out his own interests or that of the group.[49]

The rapid rate of social change, as expressed in the forces of urbanization and industrialization, has certainly contributed to the importance of the individual vs. the group in recent generations. That this growing individualism will manifest itself in the choice of a marriage partner is to be expected. Hertzler is one of many who have taken note of this change:

> Marriage is more and more a matter of individual choice of mate. It is usually regarded as an arrangement between the two individuals immediately concerned rather than between the two families or even kinship groups as was to a considerable extent the case a century ago. Whom a person marries is considered to be a matter of personal concern. . . . Marriage,

instead of serving group ends, is aimed at immediate personal satisfactions, sexual gratification, affection, and companionship.[50]

As every American moviegoer knows, romantic love is the only reason for marrying. This emphasis on personal attraction was probably an inevitable development to fill the vacuum left by the decline of the earlier system of arranged marriages, which itself could not persist in the absence of a land-based stable community with a clear-cut status system and kinship ties. Now young people are still emotionally dependent on their parental family when they are urged to undertake the responsibilities of an independent household, yet have no clearly defined mate-selection process to make the transition smoother for them. Hence we should not be surprised that, as Robin Williams observed, "An almost compulsive emphasis upon romantic love emerges in part from this situation."[51]

When it comes to interfaith marriages, the story is the same, as Bishop Pike states it: "But no amount of reasoning, no number of case histories necessarily downs the aphorism so typical of American culture: 'Love will find a way.' "[52]

To the extent that romantic love is stressed, there is probably little chance for a young couple to discuss the practical aspects of marriage. However, many sociologists and others have taken the position that American courtships are not quite as quick and thoughtless as Hollywood would have us think.[53] Companionship in marriage seems to be the norm most often expressed. This may take any number of forms in actual married life, as Robert Blood's study of married couples in the Detroit area showed. One of the bases for companionship is, of course, religious homogamy. That study found that the greater the difference in religious backgrounds, the less was the wife's marital satisfaction.[54] In one sense, therefore, the strain toward companionship in marriage should contribute toward observance of the norm of religious endogamy, rather than be a force in conflict with it as is romantic love. However, in another sense, it may manifest the secularism of religion that Herberg was writing about. This is suggested, perhaps, by Lenski's finding that "one fifth of the homogeneous marriages had been contracted by persons raised in different faiths." Moreover, conversion of one partner or the other was more frequently found among third-generation than among first- and second-generation respondents.[55] Americanization seems to promote religious homogenization. Herberg's point is validated in Lenski's finding only to the extent that these conversions were motivated by the desire to have religion serve as a means toward marital companionship rather than as an end in itself.

This brings to an end our discussion of conflicting norms and values in selecting the marriage partner. We have seen that the two concepts, reference group and marginal man, have some potential for explaining the internal conflicts that individuals experience in choosing their marriage partner. Urbanization and industrialization have been given credit for providing the conditions which foster multiple group memberships and consequent personal conflicts in American society. The value orientations which are in conflict with the norm of religious endogamy were summed up in the forces of secularism and individualism, the latter being manifested here in romantic love. The recent stress on companionship in marriage can contribute either to religious endogamy or to a secularist view of conversions.

In the next chapter we shall consider how the agents of social control play their role in reinforcing the norm of religious endogamy.

VIII

Some Agents of Social Control

It is time again to pull together some of the pieces of our discussion in this book. We began by observing that the selection of a mate for marriage is a subject that social scientists can and have generalized about. The sociologist in particular views this choice as being guided by social norms. One such norm is the rule of endogamy, and religious endogamy is one of its varieties. This norm, like any other, is subject to a certain amount of deviance, which we here call intermarriage. Whatever the norm, the sociologist is interested in the extent of deviance and in the characteristics of those who are deviant. These questions we have summarized in the "Who" of our title and have discussed them in Chapters IV and V. Beginning with Chapter VI we have been dealing with the "Why" of our title, first giving the background for some hypotheses to be tested, then explaining the meaning of important concepts which are at least implied in our theoretical viewpoint here. In Chapter VII we established the existence and vitality of the norm of religious endogamy as well as some trends which operate against it. Now, in the next two chapters, we resume our consideration of agents of social control and some conditions of anomia which we introduced in the first half of Chapter VI. In doing this, the topics will be supplied by the hypotheses tested in the data of the Detroit Area Study which will also be supported or rejected, when appropriate, by relevant data cited from other sources.

Social Control of Interfaith Marriages by Parents

As the reader will recall from Chapter VI, we stated as our general hypothesis to be tested with Detroit data that: If the agents of social control do not, or cannot (due to an anomic situation), exercise their influence, the violation of a religiously endogamous rule is more likely to occur. Our first subhypothesis relating to one of these agents of social control was the following:

    1a. Protestant-Catholic marriages will be positively associated with having parents of mixed religion.

The reasoning behind this statement was that parents who were themselves in a religiously mixed marriage would not be in a good position to support a norm of endogamy, even if they wanted to. Table 7 shows that the predicted relationship is statistically significant at better than the .05 level of probability for Catholics, not so for Protestants (although tending in that direction). Actually, the number of parents who are in mixed marriages according to this table is smaller than one might expect. The fact is that in these marriages of parents we could identify their religious preferences only at one point in time, when their children were growing up. We have seen that in the younger generation three out of five marriages involving couples from religiously different backgrounds actu-

TABLE 7.—*Rates of Intermarriage (per 100 Marriages) for Protestants and Catholics in the Detroit Area, Related to Interfaith Marriages of Their Parents, 1958 and 1959*

Religious Type of Parents' Marriage	Rates of Intermarriage among Their Children	
	Protestant	Catholic
Parents not mixed	26.3 (395)*	25.2 (345)*
Parents mixed	34.0 (50)	55.6 (27)
Totals	27.2 (445)	27.2 (372)
χ^2 (1 d.f.)	1.32	8.45
p	.40†	.002†
V	.045‡	.152‡

  * Numbers in parentheses indicate the number of cases in each category

  † This level of probability is based on a one-tailed test of significance, since the direction of the relationship had been predicted. Cf. Hubert M. Blalock, Jr., *Social Statistics* (New York: McGraw-Hill, 1960), p. 218.

  ‡ V, like the more conventional *phi*, gives us a measure of strength of relationship which standardizes for the number of cases contributing to each *chi square*. Its upper limit is 1.0. Unlike *phi*, its upper limit will still be unity if we come upon a table with more than two columns or rows. *Ibid.*, p. 230.

ally became religiously homogeneous marriages. Hence, if there was a similar situation in the older generation, these three out of five would appear in our table among the "Parents not mixed," even though such parents would be no more likely to give effective support to religious endogamy than our "Parents mixed." This is not a very satisfactory way to test our hypothesis. It is therefore all the more notable that we still find a statistically significant relationship in the Catholic sample.

In Chapter VI we cited studies by Heiss and Schnepp which supported the hypothesis represented in Table 7. To those we can add the evidence for the same which has been published by Bigman[1] and by Prince.[2] It is therefore rather well substantiated that interfaith marriages in one generation lead to interfaith marriages among the children of those families.

We proposed to test two other hypotheses with respect to parents as agents of social control for religious endogamy. They were as follows:

1b. Protestant-Catholic marriages will be negatively associated with the mother's frequent talking about or participating in religious activities with the family when self was growing up.

1c. Protestant-Catholic marriages will be negatively associated with naming parents as having had "the greatest influence on your religious beliefs."

We tested the first for a sample taken in 1962 and the second for a 1958 sample of the Detroit area. In each case the results were in the direction predicted but were not statistically significant, partly due to the small size of these samples.

However, there is no doubt that parents frequently have acted to discourage their children from entering into interfaith marriages. The delicate situation that parents are confronted with here has been well expressed by Harry M. Johnson:

During the child's early dating experiences, the parents' prohibitions and expressions of approval and disapproval may be regarded as part of socialization. Later, when the "child" is old enough to marry, the parents' influence may be regarded as *sanctioning* the norms they have been teaching implicitly for years. When the parents disapprove now, however subtly, they are exercising *social control*, in the technical sense of checking incipient deviation from norms. This control, however, must very often be subtle or even covert, because the institutionalized right to individual freedom of choice on the basis of romantic love makes it legitimate for the "child" to rebel. The point at which socialization passes over into social control is somewhat arbitrary in our society, and the ill-defined boundary is one of the causes of conflict between parents and children. Conflict is sometimes intensified, of course, by the fact that parent or child, or both, being unconsciously dependent, make "unreasonable" demands.[3]

One reason for intergenerational conflict regarding prospective marriage partners is that parents sometimes apply a different set of priorities here.[4] They seem more inclined than their children to give to "same religion" a high rating as a criterion for mate selection.[5]

As we have seen before, the Jewish community has traditionally been strongly opposed to intermarriage. Frequently, the influence that Jewish parents have in this matter is underscored.[6] The day seems to have passed, at least in this country, when "a father would say *Kaddish* (a prayer for the dead) over the child who was intermarried, as if he had died."[7] However, John E. Mayer has shown that Jewish parents and their Christian counterparts will take vigorous action when faced with the prospect of a mixed marriage, treating it as a serious moral transgression and applying some harsh sanctions.[8] He concluded that the parental opposition failed to prevent these Jewish-Gentile marriages for the following reasons:

> The parents' image of the affair failed to keep abreast of its actual course. To this degree, the couple was exposed to less pressure than would have been the case otherwise. In addition, a number of conditions reduced the effectiveness of whatever pressure parents did bring to bear: Our respondents tried not to expose themselves to the objections of their parents; they viewed certain objections as unimportant or exaggerated; they regarded others as illegitimate; and finally, they felt their parents would "come around" in the end.[9]

Of course, if we look beyond the question of religious endogamy for a moment, the activity of parents with respect to their children's choice of marriage partner seems to be quite general, particularly on the part of the mothers. Alan Bates found that among a sample of college students 79 per cent of males and 97 per cent of females said that their mothers attempted to influence them during their courtships.[10] Marvin Sussman showed how such influence among well-to-do Protestant families included consciously living in the "right" neighborhood, planning social activities for children on summer weekends, and threatening to withdraw support when their children were courting disapproved persons.[11]

Social Control by Family or Relatives

Looking outward from the point of view of *ego*, we frequently speak of a person's widening circle of influence. Conversely, there would seem to be a widening circle of social control agents who have their influence on *ego*. Beyond one's parents, the next rings of social control should probably be designated as one's siblings and then the extended family of close relatives. As in the case of parents, however, these are not likely to be agents of social control for religious endogamy if they are themselves participants in interfaith marriages. As an illustration of this, Stanley Bigman found that 29.2 per cent of Jews in mixed marriages had a brother or sister who had also intermarried, compared to 16.4 per cent of Jews who were in an all-Jewish marriage.[12]

The same line of reasoning would lead one to expect that intermarriage is more likely to occur when one has among his relatives a large proportion of people who are of a different religion. When such a question was asked of people in the Detroit area who were already married, this expectation was significantly verified—but the appropriate causal nexus is missing unless one can get such information *before* the marriage. This is not easy to do.

Under these circumstances, a somewhat better index of social control on the part of relatives is the expression of pressure which is felt by the respondent to maintain religious ties. Hence we hypothesized:

2a. Protestant-Catholic marriages will be negatively related
to the statement that friends or relatives would feel
"unhappy or disturbed" or "would try to discourage"
one from changing to Protestant or to Catholic.

From studies such as the one by Mayer, we have reason to
believe that friends as a category do not exercise social control for religious endogamy.[13] Therefore relatives were probably the ones intended by those who answered affirmatively
to this question. The hypothesis, as stated, is supported by the
data of Table 8 with statistical significance for both Catholics
and Protestants. The respondents who answered that their
relatives would try to discourage them from changing religions
were more likely *not* to have contracted an interfaith marriage. (Those who have already changed religious preference
are not included among the respondents found in this table,
even though in terms of background they are in an interfaith marriage. This gives more meaning to the relationship
in the table.)

We cannot be sure how much the experience of marriage
has influenced the respondents' perceptions of their relatives'
attitudes toward maintaining religious ties. Nevertheless, when
I compared the detailed categories of marriage type (cf. Table
4) with the answers to this question, it appeared that those
who are in marriages which are still mixed are more likely
(than are those who have married a convert) to respond that
their relatives "would *not* try to discourage" them from changing

TABLE 8.—*Rates of Intermarriage (per 100 Marriages) for Protestants
and Catholics in the Detroit Area, Related to Perception that Relatives
Would Try to Discourage Respondent from Changing His Religion, 1958*

Perception of Relatives' Attitudes toward Change in Religion	Rates of Intermarriage*			
	Protestant		Catholic	
Would try to discourage change	20.8	(96)	20.4	(103)
Unsure or would not try	41.7	(48)	40.0	(15)
Totals	27.8	(144)	22.9	(118)
χ^2 (1 d.f.)	7.69		4.24	
p	.01		.05	
V	.231		.187	

* The same notes apply here as in Table 7.

religions. In other words, in terms of social control, those in a marriage that is still mixed seem more likely to think of themselves as being close to leaving their religious group. To the writer this seems quite significant. Even though none of these respondents has changed his (her) religious preference, those who are in currently mixed marriages were inclined to say that relatives would not try to discourage them from changing religions. This suggests that interfaith marriage can be thought of as a step toward leaving one's religious group. Hence inmarriage–intermarriage–change of church membership seem to constitute a continuum. (Note that tolerance for a "change in religion" probably indicates a blurring of lines between Christian denominations, not a loss of religious interest.)

The reader who has been exposed to the many treatises written on the disappearance of the extended family as a consequence of modern urbanization may be skeptical about attributing much influence to relatives in such a matter as religious endogamy. However, a number of studies demonstrated not long ago that a modified extended family has considerable cohesiveness even in our urban society.[14] Therefore it seems reasonable to think of it as an agent of social control.

It may be well to note in passing that these studies and the relationship shown in Table 8 are contrary to an observation made by Lenski regarding the Protestant families in the Detroit area. He believes that Protestant churches weaken kinship ties, at least with the extended family. Marginal Protestants were more likely to be involved in the kin group, he found, but less likely to participate in voluntary associations than were the churchgoing Protestants. In fact, Lenski sees the Protestant church, in its characteristic American form, as a training ground for participation in voluntary associations, with consequent strains on family ties.[15]

Social Control by the Churches

Most of Chapter VII was, in a sense, concerned with the churches as agents of social control for religious endogamy. We reviewed many expressions of this norm and showed by attitude studies that it is widely accepted. Furthermore, the fact that rates of interfaith marriages are considerably lower than one would expect by chance is evidence that the three major religious groups have some success in promoting this norm.

However, we would still like to test the relationship between some specific religious experiences and the incidence of intermarriage. To do so, the Detroit area surveys allowed us to set up the following hypothesis:

3a. Protestant-Catholic marriages will be negatively related to one's education in church schools.

The results for samples of Catholics taken in 1958 and 1962 have already been published by this writer. They showed the relationship was not a statistically significant one, even though it was in the predicted direction. This was observed to be consistent with Lenski's finding in the Detroit area that there was little difference between Catholics who attended Catholic schools and those who did not in their attitude toward interfaith marriages. Eighty-four per cent of the former opposed intermarriage, compared with 79 per cent of the latter.[16]

Nevertheless, a somewhat different relationship appeared when we analyzed the 1958 sample further. When we used our distinction between the different types of interfaith marriages, it became evident that Catholic women who had four years or more of their education in Catholic schools were less likely to change their religious affiliation when they intermarried than those who had not ($p<.001$); this relationship was not statistically significant for Catholic men. Hence the norm that was communicated to these women was not so much "Marry only a Catholic," but "If you marry one who is not a Catholic, retain your own identification with your religion."[17] This, of course, is also social control.

Hypothesis 3a finds some support in other studies as well. Brother Gerald J. Schnepp, S.M., found the relationship to be quite pronounced in one parish of an eastern city.[18] Computations based on Father George A. Kelly's survey of Florida Catholics showed that parochial schools accounted for a difference of only 3 or 4 per cent in intermarriage rates.[19] A recent national study, like ours in Detroit, failed to show a statistically significant relationship between Catholic schooling and intermarriage rates, but there was a significant relationship with being married by a priest and with considering endogamy very important.[20]

The data of the 1962 Detroit area survey included a question which allowed for the testing of another hypothesis concerning the influence of the church on religious endogamy:

3b. Protestant-Catholic marriages will be negatively related to frequent attendance at religious services the year before marriage.

The wives answered this question for themselves only, not for their husbands.

Unfortunately, there was no basis for establishing the predicted relationship among the Catholic wives, since only *eight* out of 101 reported attending services less than once a week during this time. There was no consistent relationship either for the wives who were originally Protestant. It was somewhat surprising here to discover that 16 out of the 55 who reported at least weekly attendance were wives who had changed *to* Catholic. Apparently they had already adopted the Catholic practice of weekly Mass during most of the year before their marriage.

If we had a large enough sample and appropriate measurements, this hypothesis would probably be verified. We can say this because high school and college samples in Iowa have indicated an inverse relationship between frequency of church attendance and attitudes toward cross-religious dating.[21] Also, at the University of Idaho students who attended church less frequently were more willing to enter interfaith marriages.[22]

Social Control through Close Ties to Ethnic Groups

When a nationality group is transplanted into an alien society, their own shared subculture will tend to hold them together. However, we may expect that the longer an immigrant group resides in a host country, the more its in-group feeling will be weakened—other things being equal. Therefore we hypothesized as follows for the Detroit data:

4a. Protestant-Catholic marriages will be positively related to being an American of the second and subsequent generations.

When we ask what social control ethnic groups exercise in the matter of religious intermarriage, we are assuming both that an ethnic group can function as an agent of social control and that it would be concerned about enforcing a rule of religious endogamy.[23]

Is the ethnic group an effective agent of social control, in general? This seems to depend on the speed with which it Americanizes and merges its differences with the general population. The greater the cultural differences—such as in race, language, religion, peasantry among urban dwellers—the more slowly these differences will dissolve and cease to be a rallying point for in-group sentiments. The largeness and residential segregation of a group will also slow this rate of change. At least for the first generation, ethnic groups in this country have been an effective agency for social control. However, by the time their children become adolescents, their control has sometimes been challenged sharply especially in the matter of courtship and matchmaking.[24] The third generation, being the native-born children of native-born parents, will generally be quite assimilated unless they live in a large segregated subcommunity.

Now our second major question: Would an ethnic group be concerned about enforcing a rule of religious endogamy? There is little doubt about the feelings of the first generation in this matter. Many students of the subject have called attention to this in one way or another:

> The more thorough the separation from the other aspects of the old life, the greater was the hold of the religion that alone survived the transfer. . . . the immigrants directed into their faith the whole weight of their longing to be connected with the past.[25]

> The church structure to an ethnic group threatened with the loss of identity serves more than any other structure to organize the group as a community system.[26]

> Intermarriage is a serious matter in the eyes of many parents, particularly when religious lines are crossed.[27]

Is the second generation interested in maintaining a rule of religious endogamy? The picture here is not clear. Will Herberg tells us that those who rejected their ethnic identification rejected their religion also, but that in most cases "the ties with the old religion were never completely broken."[28] So far as religious activity is concerned, Lenski's Detroit data show that this falls off in the second generation only in the case of Jews; otherwise there is a steady rise from generation to generation.[29] Father Joseph P. Fitzpatrick, on the other hand, found that the percentage of Catholic marriage ceremonies (compared to civil and Protestant) was decreasing in Puerto Rico at the same time that this percentage was increasing among Puerto Ricans in New York City. Furthermore, there was a reversal from a high percentage of Protestant marriage ceremonies ("performed by Spanish-speaking ministers of Pentecostal and Evangelical sects") in the first generation in New York back to a higher percentage of Catholic ceremonies in the second generation.[30] These apparently inconsistent findings having to do with the attitude of the second generation toward religion all underscore the fact that we are dealing with a multi-factor phenomenon here. Language, social class, intergenerational conflict, and the strain toward assimilation all play their part in religious intermarriage and other forms of behavior that reflect religious affiliation.

How about the third generation? Will they accept a norm of religious endogamy for themselves, and will they pass it on to their children? Herberg believes that since they are no longer anxious about their American-ness, they seek to confirm the tie that binds them to their ancestors in the only important way that remains to them. He quotes Marcus Hansen to this effect: "What the son wishes to forget, the grandson wishes to remember."[31] He also believes that the kind of religion that they return to is more secularized, one which functions to identify its members as one of three religious sub-communities—all equally parts of the "American Way of Life." His analysis may fit the Jewish subcommunity best, but we have no reason to doubt that it applies in some degree also to other third-generation Americans. They want a religious identification, but the secularism, pluralism, and individualism of American culture probably make it relatively easy for them to accept an identification different from their ancestral one—if this will contribute to a companionate marriage and homogeneous family.

With that much for general rationale, let us return to Hypothesis 4a. We noted in Chapter VI that Heiss found Catholic intermarriages in Manhattan to be negatively related to being first-generation Americans, that Heer attributed the trend toward increased religious intermarriage in Canada to a lessening of in-group feeling among the French Catholics and British Protestants of that country, and that Thomas believed the low rate of Catholic intermarriages in some large cities to be due to the presence there of large and cohesive ethnic groups.

We can add to those studies two others which give direct verification to this hypothesis. Stanley Bigman showed that among Jews in Washington intermarriage was rare for the foreign-born (0.8 per cent), but rose in the second and third generation to 6.6 per cent and 7.4 per cent, respectively.[32] Using the same Washington data, Erich Rosenthal found that this relationship between nativity and intermarriage was pronounced and consistent for Jewish men, but that the rate of intermarriage for Jewish women rose in the second generation and then fell again in the third and later generations, instead of rising. He then makes this observation: "It can be assumed that there was indeed a rise, but that those women either were converted to Christianity or otherwise abandoned their identification with the Jewish group entirely.[33] Although Rosenthal's data on Iowa do not permit him to test this relationship, he does cite a historian of the Jews in that state who supports the truth of this relationship between nativity and religious intermarriage.[34]

TABLE 9.—*Interfaith Marriages Related to Number of Generations in the United States for Protestants and Catholics in the Detroit Area, 1958 and 1959*

Marriages of Protestants	GENERATIONS IN THE UNITED STATES				
	1st	2nd	3rd	4th	Totals
Inmarriages	21	101	61	138	321
Intermarriages	8	49	33	32	122
Totals	29	150	94	170	443
Marriages of Catholics					
Inmarriages	45	153	50	21	269
Intermarriages	12	54	28	8	103
Totals	57	207	78	29	372

Protestants: χ^2 (3 d.f.) = 11.37; p<.01
Catholics: χ^2 (3 d.f.) = 4.08; p<.30

It is rather surprising, therefore, that when we tested this hypothesis for Protestants and Catholics in the Detroit area, the relationship was not a consistent one. For both groups there is a tendency for intermarriage rates to increase from the first through the third generation, for in the fourth and later generations the tendency is reversed—particularly for the Protestants. Although the chi-square value for that part of the table has a probability of less than .01, the relationship represented is not unilinear but curvilinear.

It is not easy to interpret these results, but a glance back at Table 6 will show that the largest ethnic groups in Detroit tend to have the lowest rates of interfaith marriages—Polish Catholics (19.4) and German Protestants (19.0)—with the exception that the English Protestants have a rather high rate, 25.4. Since the last named would be mostly in the fourth or later generations, I must assume that the unexpectedly low rate of intermarriage for the fourth-generation Protestants in general must be due to the presence in the Detroit area of large numbers of immigrants from the states in the South. Although they are "old Americans," the areas they come from are overwhelmingly Protestant and rural, with relatively little intermarriage.

This concludes our investigation of the agents of social control which would seem to be concerned about interfaith marriages. Except for parents who are themselves in mixed marriages, the evidence favors the view that parents seek to dissuade their children from marrying outside their religious group (and sometimes succeed). Family and relatives also play their role in this, particularly in preventing some defections from their religion. The ethnic group has a similar function, which apparently diminishes with each generation. The churches themselves have forcefully expressed the norm of religious endogamy, as we saw in Chapter VII. However, at least for members of the Catholic Church, it is subsumed from a stronger, more general norm: If you choose to intermarry, do not abandon your religion. The findings of this chapter support the notion that we are dealing with a continuum of the effectiveness of religion's social control: inmarriage, intermarriage, intermarriage with defection.

IX

Anomia: The Weakening of Social Control

SINCE OUR APPROACH to understanding the various rates of interfaith marriages is through the concept of social control, it seems important to consider not only the norms about which social control is exercised and the agents which try to exert such control but also the circumstances in which social control will be abnormally difficult. In Chapter VI we called such circumstances "anomic situations" and explained at some length the derivation and meaning of this term. Now it is time to examine such situations concretely and to see what evidence we have for their association with higher rates of interfaith marriages.

Wartime Marriages

That wartime brings about disorganization, and possible normlessness, in the lives of a nation's citizens hardly needs demonstration. It should be sufficient to summarize the situation in the words of Ernest R. Mowrer:

> The war as a crisis period is characterized in part by: enhanced social consciousness and identification with the goal of the group (the nation), instability and mobility of both soldiers and civilians, economic well-being particularly of those engaged in war production, high tempo of life, and grief and depression for those involved directly and indirectly in the casualties of war.[1]

Our hypothesis (5a) that Protestant-Catholic marriages will increase in wartime is based on the assumption that norms which are not directly related to the common war effort will be weakened (if not discarded) at this time. Hasty marriages between departing servicemen and their sweethearts, with the fearful thought that he may not come back anyway, have been a common observation. In World War II, at least, it was also not uncommon for these marriages to eventuate in divorce even before a battlefront death could dissolve them.

Our data for testing this hypothesis come from the 1955 and 1959 Detroit area surveys. Only the respondents in their first marriage were included. Most of these wartime marriages took place during World War II, with about two-thirds as many in the Korean War, and just nineteen in World War I (454 marriages of Protestants, 431 marriages of Catholics). The results of this analysis show no relationship between interfaith marriages and being married in wartime. Before dismissing the hypothesis as of no value, however, we should recall that studies by Coakley and Thomas were cited in Chapter VI showing that the rate of Catholic intermarriage increased in both world wars. The same conclusion would be drawn for World War II (but not for the Korean War) from the statistics published by Paul J. Reiss.[2] My conclusion would be that this anomic situation is not felt enough to influence interfaith marriages except when the nation undergoes total mobilization. Furthermore, the high rate of divorce for wartime marriages makes it likely that many of these hasty marriages were broken up before 1955 or 1959 and therefore were not included in our interviews.

Late Marriages

I have classified late marriages with anomic situations in this study because it would seem not only that the offspring's advancing age would give the parents less influence, but also that those who are not married and are still eligible for marriage have thinned out by the late twenties, especially for women. Under such circumstances, it seems that the strain to overlook the rule of religious endogamy would increase. Hence I have proposed this hypothesis:

5b. Protestant-Catholic marriages will be positively related to getting married at a late age, with consequent emancipation from home.

This hypothesis could be tested only for the 1962 Detroit survey. Because the sample was small it seemed best to use only a gross distinction for age at marriage. In the case of men, those aged 25 years and over were considered "late marriages"; for women, it was those who were 23 years old or over who were so defined. There were not enough older brides and grooms in this sample to do otherwise. My hypothesis was not supported by this sample. In fact, for Catholic women and for both Protestant and Catholic men, there was a slight tendency in the opposite direction, i.e., for intermarriage to be associated with the younger age category. Even when setting up this hypothesis I had recognized that very early marriages can also manifest an anomic situation, if they represent a rejection of parental influence. In any case, the size of this sample did not permit us to compare the oldest and the youngest with those in the middle.

There is some evidence that both early and late marriages are likely to be out-group marriages. In Chapter VI it was noted that Catholic and Jewish intermarriages were more common among those who were at least 30 years old at the time of marriage, according to the Manhattan study by Jerold Heiss. An analysis of marriage records in Iowa, 1953-57, showed higher rates of intermarriage of Protestants and Catholics both for 18-or-under brides and for the 30-and-over brides.[3] For the grooms the relationship was clear only at the lower age level. John H. Burma found the same two age categories to have higher rates of interethnic marriage in Los Angeles.[4]

The facts presented here for Iowa and Detroit concerned only *first* marriages. For the Manhattan and Los Angeles studies *all* marriages were aparently included. This is worth noting because there is evidence that second or later marriages are more likely to be mixed than are first marriages.[5] We would like to know, of course, whether the relationship between interfaith marriages and older brides (or grooms) will hold up even for first marriages.

Rural-Urban Migration as an Anomic Situation

Earlier students of urban sociology have led us to expect manifestations of anomia on the part of those who migrate from the farm to the city. Just thirty years ago Niles Carpenter was able to write:

> This *shock-effect* of migration into the city is discussed at length elsewhere. Here it may merely be pointed out that, in the author's opinion, many of the disorganizing effects of the city upon the individual . . . are to be interpreted not so much as effects of city life as such, but rather as the effects of the *sudden impact of the characteristically urban set of conditioning influences upon a personality that has been accommodated to a characteristically non-urban set of influences.* In short, certain individuals break down as a consequence of their failure to become adequately reconditioned to the city.[6]

This is precisely the kind of situation we had in mind in predicting that those who move from a rural environment to a city before they marry are likely to depart from the norm of religious endogamy (Hypothesis 5c). The same might be said for those who originate in a small town, and for the same reasons. However, the last three decades have seen an increasing urbanization of our entire society, even the rural areas. This can be credited to the electrification of rural areas, the prosperity of many of those who remain on the farm, innovations and expansion in mass communication, and growth of the means and routes of transportation. For these reasons, the experience of anomia on the part of farm-to-city migrants has probably become less and less pronounced. If we had examined just the older marriages among the farm-to-city migrants in Detroit, we might have found the kind of anomia that Carpenter was writing about—but this we have not done.

As it is, the hypothesis under consideration is not supported by the data in Table 10:

5c. Protestant-Catholic marriages will be positively related to migration from a farm before age 18.

This specific age was chosen partly because the coders of the Detroit Area Study had already made use of it, and partly because it seemed an appropriate age at which to try to separate those who migrated before their marriage from those who migrated afterwards. The underlying rationale was as above. Those who had married while still living on a farm

TABLE 10.—*Rates of Intermarriage (per 100 Marriages) for Native-born Protestants and Catholics in the Detroit Area, Related to the Respondent's Experience of Migration to Detroit, 1955, 1958, and 1959*

| Types of Migration to Detroit | Rates of Intermarriages | | | |
	Protestant		Catholic	
Detroit area native	39.5	(223)	28.5	(284)
Urban migrant	18.6	(86)	19.7	(61)
Small town migrant	25.5	(161)	31.6	(79)
Rural migrant, before age 18	16.1	(155)	37.3	(61)
Rural migrant, after age 18	16.7	(51)	41.7	(12)
Totals	26.3	(676)	29.4	(497)
χ^2 (4 d.f.)	20.28		7.45	
p	.001		.20*	

* These probabilities represent a two-tailed test of significance since the direction of relationship was not predicted for a table having all of the categories that are presented here.

would probably have the low intermarriage rates which are associated with homogeneous, stable communities; those who left the farm and then found their marriage mate in the city might be expected to feel emancipated from the norms of their place of origin and to tend to contract interfaith marriages.

Although it does not support our hypothesis, Table 10 does show us some interesting aspects of migration and intermarriage rates among the American-born current residents of the Detroit area. Let us look at the distribution of cases across the types of migration. Small town and rural migrants constitute the majority of all Protestants in the Detroit area, whereas native Detroiters (probably the children of the foreign-born) make up a majority of all Catholics in Detroit. In neither group are city-to-city migrants a very large category, nor do these migrants show much intermarriage. This latter finding is rather puzzling in view of the fact that the Detroit area natives, the only other urban people in our sample, show high rates of intermarriage—most striking in the Protestant sub-sample. In fact, it is the remarkably high rate of intermarriage among the Protestant Detroit area natives, the largest single category of Protestants, which mainly accounts for the statistically significant distribution of marriages in the Protestant sample. Here again the relative size of the group seems to be an important factor. Among native Detroiters, the people in our sample who grew up to marriageable age in the same locality, Protestants are a smaller group than the Catholics. Hence we should expect the former to have a somewhat higher rate of intermarriage than the latter.[7]

In general, the Catholic subsample comes closer to fulfilling our prediction than does the Protestant sample. For them, migration to a more urbanized center seems to be associated with higher rates of intermarriage, whatever the age of migration. The intermarriage rates for these categories among Protestants, however, are much lower. If these categories of Protestants and Catholics (so different in actual size) could be properly standardized to remove some of the arithmetic influence of the size of group, we might find that Protestant and Catholic migrants from rural and small town areas are not so different from each other.

Educational Mobility and Interfaith Marriages

It is a commonplace observation that parents are likely to lose some of their influence over their children if the latter acquire a college education which the former did not have. With this in mind, we called this an anomic situation and predicted:

5d. Protestant-Catholic marriages will be positively related to the husband's extreme upward mobility in education, compared to his father.

In none of the Detroit survey samples did we discover enough cases of this kind of upward mobility to be able to test this relationship; actually, the basic information needed was available in only two small samples. As was pointed out in Chapter VI, Heiss found a significant relationship between educational mobility and intermarriage for Catholics in Manhattan, but that seems to be the only study in which this hypothesis has been previously tested.

Quite apart from educational mobility, one might ask whether interfaith marriages for a particular denomination are associated with one or other level of education. The reader is reminded that a discussion of this question was included at the end of Chapter V under the heading of "Religious Intermarriage and Social Class."

Intermarriage and Vertical Mobility in Occupation

The condition of society which for Durkheim was almost the ideal type of *anomie* will here be adapted to the situation of an individual. In Durkheim's view, man's appetites are unlimited unless he is restrained by the social conscience. In times of social crisis or abrupt transition, when the public conscience is reclassifying men and things, society is unable to supply this restraint; it is in a state of deregulation or *anomie*. "The less limited one feels," he says, "the more intolerable all limitation appears."[8] The position implied in Hypothesis 5e is that extreme upward mobility in occupation places the individual in such a situation so far as his personal life is concerned. He must reclassify everything that is associated with his unaccustomed economic status; hence religious endogamy is likely to be discarded with other rules of restraint. Therefore we have predicted as follows:

5e. Protestant-Catholic marriages will be positively related to the husband's extreme upward mobility in occupation, compared to his father.

We have expanded the hypothesis just stated to include the downward mobile with the upward mobile partly because of Lenski's finding that in the Detroit area: "Those who were highly involved in their socio-religious sub-communities were likely *either* to have risen *or* to have fallen in the class system than were those who were more marginal to the group."[9]

To define our terms before we go on, by occupational mobility we are referring to *vertical*, not horizontal, mobility, i.e., the movement of an individual from one level to another in occupational ranks. We make only the gross distinction between blue-collar and white-collar occupations, the latter being ranked higher for males than the former, so that we can use the terms "upward" and "downward" with reference to these ranks.[10] Our hypothesis will be tested only for *intergenerational* mobility, i.e., comparing a man's occupation with that of his father, rather than with his own earlier occupation, which would be intragenerational mobility. Lipset and Bendix tell us that in the United States from 31 to 35 per cent of the sons achieve upward mobility in this sense. A smaller minority is generally found to be downwardly mobile. However, when comparisons are restricted to urban occupations for both fathers and sons, those reported upwardly mobile have ranged from 17 to 21 per cent of the total and the downwardly mobile from 8 to 13 per cent.[11]

A look at the numbers in parentheses in Table 11 shows that Detroit men have experienced somewhat more than their share of upward and downward mobility compared to the national rates, especially in the case of the Protestants. Furthermore, the rates of interfaith marriage are higher for the occupationally mobile than for the nonmobile, as was predicted. This relationship is statistically significant for the Catholic sample at the conventional level, not quite so for the Protestant sample. The distinction between blue-collar and white-collar occupations provides only a crude measure of occupational mobility, but I am not aware that this particular relationship with interfaith marriages has ever been tested before.

However, there have been other studies of relationships approximating this one, which may be worth reviewing briefly at this point. Some researchers have asked the question: Is occupational mobility associated with religion? At least in the United States, Jews "have markedly higher rates of upward mobility than non-Jews, according to a number of studies."[12] Regarding Protestant *vs.* Catholic occupational mobility the evidence is not conclusive. Some data for the United States from the Survey Research Center of the University of Michigan show almost no difference in manual-nonmanual mobility

TABLE 11.—*Rates of Intermarriage (per 100 Marriages) for Protestants and Catholics in the Detroit Area, Related to Husband's Intergenerational Occupational Mobility, Upward or Downward, 1955, 1958, and 1959*

Intergenerational Occupational Mobility	Rates of Intermarriage			
	Protestant Husbands		Catholic Husbands	
No occupational mobility	19.7	(314)	24.5	(286)
Upward or downward mobility	25.0	(180)	31.2	(141)
Totals	21.7	(494)	26.7	(427)
χ^2 (1 d.f.)	1.87		2.67	
p	.10		c. .05*	

* These probabilities represent a one-tailed test of significance since the direction of relationship was predicted.

between Protestants and Catholics of the second generation, but somewhat more upward mobility for Protestants than for Catholics in the third and later generations. A further analysis of the samples shown in Table 11 reveals that Protestants have just slightly more mobility, upward and downward, than do Catholics. Furthermore, investigations in four countries indicated "no significant differences between mobility rates of Catholics and Protestants."[13] However, Lenski finds fault with the analysis of mobility in the United States by Lipset and Bendix, just cited, as well as with a study by Mack, Murphy, and Yellin, which also reported no differences in upward mobility for Catholics and Protestants.[14] The existence and qualifications of a relationship between occupational mobility and Protestant-Catholic religions are still in doubt and need further investigation.

Are there consequences of occupational mobility which would seem to be relevant to religious endogamy? The trouble with discussing "consequences" is that this assumes that we can establish the order of causality, whereas this is generally impossible. Take, for example, the confusion about consequences that can arise from comparing these two authors: Merton writes of "anticipatory socialization," adopting the values of a group to which one aspires but does not belong. This would make mobility a consequence of having acquired the characteristics of a higher occupational level.[15] Richard F. Curtis, on the other hand, finds in the mobile male a "gradual assumption of the culture of his stratum of destination," which seems to make these characteristics the consequents or concomitants of his mobility.[16]

Whether consequences or not, some variables have been found to be associated with occupational mobility for males. Curtis and Morris Janowitz suggested a few years ago that social mobility "is likely to have disruptive consequences on primary group structures, such as family, clique, and friendships."[17] However, the investigations of Eugene Litwak indicate that extended family cohesion is not weakened by occupational mobility itself but by geographical mobility, the criterion for family cohesion being family visits.[18] To the extent that his conclusions are valid, they would argue somewhat against my hypothesis that violations of religious endogamy are associated with occupational mobility, due to anomia. My position is closer to that of Curtis and Janowitz.

The research of Richard L. Simpson and H. Max Miller might be cited as contrary to the association between occupational mobility (at least downward) and anomia.[19] Their work is admirable and worth noting, but it must be pointed out that they made use of Srole's anomia scale, which is mainly a measure of despair (cf. Chapter VI, above). The dimension of alienation which we think is related to interfaith marriages is not powerlessness or despair (as Srole's scale measures it), but normlessness. Such normlessness we have attributed both to the upwardly mobile and to the downwardly mobile. A measure for this normlessness was not developed for the testing of this hypothesis (since we are using available data), but Hypothesis 5e, expanded to include the downwardly mobile, is borne out to some degree by our data and fits into our general theoretical approach. Therefore the reader will probably concede that it has some validity, until contrary evidence based on better measurements is forthcoming.

✿ ✿ ✿ ✿ ✿

To review briefly the conclusions of this chapter: We have examined five situations in which the norm of religious endogamy (among other norms) has been hypothesized to be weakened. They are wartime, late marriages, rural-urban migration, extreme upward mobility in education, and upward or downward mobility in occupation. Does the evidence we have brought together warrant such an approach to this subject matter? First, even though our Detroit data show us no relationship between intermarriage and wartime, other studies of Catholic data substantiate such a relationship at least in the two world wars, when the country was fully mobilized. Secondly, studies made in Manhattan and in Iowa show more interfaith marriages at the extreme ages, 18-or-under and 30-or-over; no adequate test of this relationship could be made for the small Detroit sample. Thirdly, rural-urban migration *as an anomic situation* is probably a thing of the past; our Detroit data do not support the hypothesis that it is related to interfaith marriages. Fourthly, an association between intermarriage and upward educational mobility has been demonstrated only for Catholics in Manhattan so far; the data were not adequate for testing this hypothesis in Detroit. Fifthly, a relationship between interfaith marriages and occupational mobility (upward and downward) was substantiated with respect to the Detroit data; again, anomia is viewed in this context as normlessness, not as Srole's despair or powerlessness.

In sum, there is good (though not extensive) evidence for three of our five hypotheses having to do with anomic situations: those of wartime, extreme ages at marriage, and vertical occupational mobility. A fourth hypothesis regarding educational mobility has some evidence to support it, but this relationship is particularly difficult to test. Hence it would seem reasonable to continue to use this approach to study the factors in interfaith marriages. Other anomic situations may well be more relevant than those that have been examined here.

X

Conclusions and Recent Developments

THIS HAS BEEN a thorough review of the research and insights of social scientists on the subject of the choice of marriage partners across major religious lines. It has been my purpose to put interfaith marriages into a broad empirical and theoretical context. In this final chapter I would like to do two things: (1) I would like to enumerate what seem to me to be the principal conclusions and insights relating to our subject matter which are found in these pages; (2) I intend to review some recent developments, particularly in the ecumenical movement, which seem to me to suggest that new patterns of interfaith marriages will become prominent in the future. That done, it will be left to the reader to decide what this hopefully objective presentation means to him in terms of his own values.

Principal Conclusions and Insights

It is important in the treatment of any subject matter to try to balance caution with incisiveness. Caution has been the principal emphasis in this book until now, since both empirical and theoretical statements have been put forward tentatively and with various qualifications. Now it is time to let incisiveness play its part. Therefore it is my intention to begin with Chapter II and to list successively those generalizations and conceptualizations which seem to me to have greater importance, either because of the empirical evidence that supports them or because of the explanatory value which they seem to have at least potentially. Many of them will not be new, of course, to readers who are familiar with the literature of this subject matter. The order in which they are listed is the same as the order of the chapters from which they are drawn, in turn. If you find some of the statements to be unacceptable as they stand, you are invited to turn back to the corresponding place in the text and footnotes to see what evidence is presented there and what qualifications or sources are indicated.

1. Less than 10 per cent of the men and women in our country reach old age without having married.

2. During the first half of this century there was a steady decline in the median age at first marriage for both men and women in almost all countries where data were available.

3. The most recent available statistics show that men (not women) in this country marry at an earlier age than anywhere else except India (granting that this says nothing about the many countries where such statistics have not been kept).

4. Additional years of education and urban residence still tend to lower marriage rates and to raise the age at marriage, at least in this country.

5. Homogamy, a pattern of "like marries like," has been substantiated for most biological, psychological, and social characteristics studied.

6. Heterogamy, a pattern of "opposites attract" in the form of complementarity of needs, probably has some influence in the last stage of the mate selection process.

7. Residential propinquity of bride and groom just before marriage is an index to the time and cost factors which influence marriage choices particularly in the middle and lower socioeconomic classes.

8. Intermarriage, in general, is best conceptualized as a deviation from a rule of endogamy whereby one is expected to marry a mate who is of one's own kind or group.

9. Such endogamous norms define the "field of eligibles" for the selection of a marriage partner, and segregated residential patterns are one way that parents have of reinforcing these norms.

10. Adherence to endogamy is seen by many as a test of group solidarity.

11. For well-known historical reasons, Negro-Caucasian intermarriage in this country has occurred at very low rates, rarely more than .5 per cent of Caucasian marriages or 5 per cent of Negro marriages. Other kinds of interracial marriage have occurred at somewhat higher rates, and data from

Los Angeles indicate a slight trend toward more interracial marriage in the decade before 1959, the last year for which such data are available.

12. In Hawaii (pre-union) and in Latin America interracial marriages have been quite common, more accepted than interclass marriages.

13. The commonly high ratio of males to females in immigrant groups is an important factor in promoting interracial marriages.

14. Each ethnic group, in the restricted sense of a nationality or cultural group, tends to intermarry at a higher rate in succeeding generations, as the unmixed category becomes smaller and smaller; the principal factors influencing this rate seem to be the high sex ratio in the first generation and the relative smallness of any particular group.

15. Endogamy according to class (indexed by income, occupation, or education) is the practiced rule in our system of social stratification.

16. An approved alternative to class endogamy is the practice whereby a woman marries a man above her social class, known as hypergamy. The opposite pattern, hypogamy, is much less acceptable.

17. The caste (race) system and the class system in our country can be observed to meet in the dominant pattern of interracial marriages whereby a Caucasian woman marries a Negro man (who generally has a relatively high occupation). The woman's caste advantage is traded for the man's class advantage. In the *class* system it is hypergamy, whereas in the *caste* system it is hypogamy.

18. Due to the absence of questions about religious identification in our census-taking and in our public registrations, researchers studying interfaith marriages must use substitutes. Each source and occasion for such data-gathering must be examined closely for its advantages and limitations.

19. Similarly, ways of reporting rates of interfaith marriages need to be understood and watched carefully when interpreting data. In particular, one should be alert to the effect that controlling for the size of the group (done in some studies) would have on the rates.

20. If we define interfaith marriage as the matching of two people who have different religious backgrounds, then

most published rates of intermarriage in this country seriously underestimate the extent to which religious intermarriage has been occurring. The reason is that they ask only about present religious preferences and not about conversions that have occurred. Table 1 shows that in the Detroit area studies only *two out of five* marriages which were originally mixed were still mixed at the time of the interviews.[1] The other three out of five involved conversions one way or the other.

21. Due to the mathematical influence of the relative size of groups and due to frequent religious conversions associated with intermarriage, I believe that the "triple melting-pot hypothesis" is deceptive and should be avoided as a way of comparing ethnic and religious intermarriage.

22. Jewish-Gentile marriages have been the most widely studied interfaith marriages; and the rate of these intermarriages is almost universally lower than those of Catholic or Protestant intermarriages, even when it has not been possible to adjust the rates for the relative size of the groups—which would further accentuate this difference.

23. When rates can be adjusted for the relative size of groups, there is little difference between Protestant and Catholic rates of intermarriage; if anything, the Catholics are the least endogamous.

24. Studies of marriages between members of different Protestant denominations are generally lacking, but the Detroit surveys showed that some differences appear in their rates of marrying Catholics. The Episcopalians had the highest rate of intermarriage with Catholics (32 per cent) and the Baptists the lowest (16 per cent), with the Methodists, Presbyterians, and Lutherans in between.

25. European and Canadian statistics indicate a long-range trend toward higher rates of intermarriage for all three major religious groups. If there is such a national trend in this country, we cannot substantiate it; official Catholic records for the nation show no consistent trend.

26. The consistently reported tendency for Jewish men to intermarry more than Jewish women can be largely explained by the accepted pattern of class hypergamy by Gentile women.

27. The reported tendency for Catholic women to intermarry more than Catholic men is probably exaggerated, due to the nature of the ecclesiastical records on which it is based.

Lutheran women have also shown this tendency according to their pastors' records.

28. Differential rates of religious intermarriage at different class levels (by the criteria of income, rental areas, occupation, and education) can usually be explained for all three major religious groups as follows: In those categories of social class where a particular religious group is underrepresented, class endogamy will work against religious endogamy; otherwise it will reinforce religious endogamy.

29. A larger ethnic group has a better chance of organizing its marriage market because there are more eligible partners available without crossing religious or ethnic lines.

30. The norm of religious endogamy has been shown to exist in the official statements of the churches of the United States; it is disseminated by various educational methods; and it is widely held among the general membership, including college students.

31. Because the average person in the modern world looks for approval to many different groups and individuals beyond his own family of origin, the concept of "reference group" has potential for interpreting some interfaith marriages.

32. To the extent that secularism represents an orientation toward this world in opposition to orientation toward a future life, it is a value orientation which will often conflict with adhering to the norm of religious endogamy. Some studies show that Jews and Protestants are more subject to this orientation than are Catholics.

33. Romantic love, an expression of individualism and personalism, exerts a strong pressure in opposition to the social forces which support religious endogamy.

34. It is rather well substantiated that interfaith marriages in one generation lead to interfaith marriages among the children of those families.

35. Parents often try to influence the selection of marriage partners by their children, not always successfully, in favor of religious and other kinds of endogamy.

36. From the Detroit survey of 1958 it appears not only that relatives are an agent of social control for religious endogamy, but also that interfaith marriage belongs on a continuum between inmarriage and loss of church membership.

37. There is some evidence that the churches effectively

influence their active members toward religious endogamy; but the norm communicated through the Catholic schools may be not so much "Marry only a Catholic" as it is "If you marry one who is not a Catholic, retain your own identification with your religion."

38. The influence of ethnic groups on religious endogamy is shown by the rising rates of intermarriage through the first, second and third generations of residence in America; in the fourth and later generations the trend may be reversed, for reasons that are not clear.

39. Catholic data indicate that World War I and II (anomic situations) weakened the adherence to religious endogamy in this country.

40. There is some evidence that both early and late marriages are likely to be out-group marriages.

41. Rural-urban migration seems no longer to constitute an anomic situation in our country; at least it does not demonstrably weaken religious endogamy.

42. Intergenerational occupational mobility, whether upward or downward, is probably associated (as an anomic situation) with interfaith marriages.

The above list of generalizations and conceptualizations does not pretend to be exhaustive of all that might be said about interfaith marriages, but it does represent a summary of what has seemed most significant to me as a result of this study.

Recent Developments

Times do change.

The truth of this statement can be verified in almost any segment of human life, but I would like to take some time now to verify it in the expressions relating to the norm of religious endogamy. I am convinced that this could be done equally well from Jewish, Protestant, or Catholic sources. I am going to do so from Catholic sources, by way of illustration, because I have a larger number of them at hand.

The ancient sanctions of the Emperor Constantius (339) and the Council of Constantinople (692) were cited in Chapter VII, as well as the Canons of 1918 still in force. Ten years later a canon lawyer–priest wrote an article for a leading journal for Catholic clergy in which he answered "Yes" to the question posed in the title of his article: "Should Dispensations for Mixed Marriages Be Absolutely Abolished?"[2] He argued that the law for dispensations was useless because they were given freely for no adequate reason, in spite of the Church "strictly and everywhere" forbidding such marriages, that "mixed marriages are a great public evil and cause the loss of many souls," and abolishing all dispensations would do more good than harm, etc. He also wrote that one diocese in England and three in the Netherlands had instituted such a policy. The responses of 23 readers were published in subsequent issues of this journal. One reader made a compromise proposal, *nineteen favored* such a ban, and *three opposed* the author's suggestion. (Most, if not all, responses came from priests.)

A decade later the hope for more drastic legislation on mixed marriages was still being expressed, as in this paragraph:

> To date a prudent delicacy and patience have marked the attitude of the Church in our country toward this difficult question. Dispensations have been granted in numbers which have led many to the practical conclusion that the impediment does not exist, or that it is of no great importance, and that mixed marriages can easily be "arranged.". . . If the salvation of souls is at stake, however, the Church knows neither reticence nor false delicacy. Excessive caution and fear of hurting feelings have exacted their toll. Kindly warnings, counsel, pleadings have proved of no avail. And the Church, ever prudent Mother, is considering more severe measures. May they benefit souls![3]

In the late 1940's one no longer finds such expressions of the desire to shut the door altogether on Catholic interfaith marriages. Now the warnings stress the seriousness of the promises required if a mixed marriage is to be performed under Catholic auspices. John C. Heenan's treatment of the subject is straightforward and sympathetic in his book. He says: "The Catholic Church is frankly opposed to marriages between Catholics and non-Catholics. She forbids them and makes exceptions only with reluctance. The reason is that they prove more often than not to be unhappy."[4] (This was an impression shared by many pastors, though not scientifically verified.)

A decade ago several guidebooks were published to help Catholics in their marriages. Here again the stress is on avoiding mixed marriages as much as possible, as in this chapter heading: "How to Avoid a Mixed Marriage in Your Family."[5] If the mixed marriage does occur, then the Catholic must take great care to keep his promises made before the marriage.[6] The best solution is seen to lie in the conversion of the other partner to the Catholic faith.[7]

Then the Catholic Church entered officially into the ecumenical movement during Vatican Council II, publishing its "Decree on Ecumenism," its "Declaration on the Relationship of the Church to Non-Christian Religions," and its "Declaration on Religious Freedom."[8] From this point on Catholic authors and clergymen made serious efforts to understand the viewpoint of the partner in a Catholic mixed marriage who is *not* a Catholic. Even while these documents were being formulated, Cardinal Cushing of Boston was proposing that some changes be made in the regulations regarding mixed marriages:

> As it is now, the requirement that a non-Catholic partner make the famous promises before marriage is an irritant to many, and some, it is clear from what happens subsequently, make the promises in bad faith. If we no longer required the promises, we would not be revoking any divine law; we would not be changing any dogma of the Church. There are good reasons for considering such a move. Remember when mixed marriages could not be performed in church, but had to take place in the rectory? We changed that and permitted the use of the church. Instead of separating that ceremony from a holy environment, we now start these marriages off in a context of church, which opens up the possibility of many actual graces being given instead of the generating of feelings of frustration, hostility.[9]

The reactions of *America*'s readers to these statements were immediate. The editors thought it necessary to interpret the Cardinal's mind for him:

> They thought the Cardinal meant the Church should allow mixed marriage couples to bring up their children in different faiths. He intended no such thing. . . .
> Would dropping the law mean denying the obligation of bringing children up in the true faith? Not at all. The obligation would remain, squarely confronting the individual Cath-

olic conscience. If Cardinal Cushing discerned that Catholics did not want to be left without the force of a Church law backing up a basic moral requirement, he would no doubt withdraw the question he raised. However, that would mean limiting a development he has encouraged for some years: increasing the range of responsible action by the laity. . . . His question about the premarital promises was intended to suggest a practical way for the laity to exercise their co-responsibility in the Church.[10]

In Chapter VII reference was made to the change in Catholic regulations which did away with the sanction of excommunication incurred by any Catholic who married before a non-Catholic minister and which provided that a mixed marriage under Catholic auspices would take place in circumstances very much like any Catholic wedding, with the option that the non-Catholic's clergyman might participate in certain formal ways. At the same time, these provisions were made regarding the promises:

> The non-Catholic party, with due delicacy . . . must also be informed of the Catholic party's grave obligations to safeguard, preserve and profess his faith and to have the offspring which will be born, baptized and educated in the Faith.
> And so that this obligation may be guaranteed, the non-Catholic spouse should also be invited to promise openly and sincerely that he will not create any obstacle in the fulfillment of that duty. If then the non-Catholic party thinks he may not formulate this promise without violating his conscience, the ordinary must refer the case with all its particulars to the Holy See.[11]

It is left up to the local bishop to decide whether the promises, which are to be asked of the non-Catholic, must also be in writing.

In pleading for the removal of most canons regarding mixed marriages and leaving the decisions and responsibilities to the conscience of the Catholic party, Ladislas M. Orsy, S.J., makes this observation on Christian history:

> This approach does not deny the duty of the Catholic parent, but it stresses the moral obligation above the legal one. It requires a greater alertness on the part of the clergy, and stronger faith in our laity. We should also not forget that the

Church was never so dynamic and never expanded so rapidly as in the early centuries, when hardly any legal provisions existed about marriages, and certainly not about the education of the children. All was done by the living faith of the Christian party to the marriage—and with how great success![12]

It is still impossible to say what, if any, further changes will be made in Roman Catholic regulations on interfaith marriages. However, it is certainly interesting to see what new attempts are being made to minister to the needs of the persons who have entered into an interfaith marriage. Books that show a pastoral concern are being published.[13] Joint Protestant-Catholic ministries have been attempted for couples in interfaith marriages in Bavaria and in Pennsylvania.[14] The Protestant and Roman Catholic ecumenical commissions of one eastern city have jointly drawn up a document (as yet unpublished) entitled: "Living the Faith You Share: Ten Ecumenical Guidelines for Couples in Roman Catholic-Protestant Marriages." It opens in this way:

> This pamphlet is to help couples in mixed marriages—to acquaint you with the recently changed attitudes of the Churches; to help you live a life of Christian love and unity despite the dividedness of your churches. In brief, it is to help you make your mixed marriage ecumenical.

Finally, contrary to the observation I made in Chapter VII that all couples who so far had written about their interfaith marriages were trying to dissuade others from arriving at the same choice, expressions of the good points in an interfaith marriage are now beginning to be written by those who speak from experience.[15] It is not their wish to minimize the problems, but they see these in the context of adjustments that any married couple must make. Their emphasis is on the deep religious involvement of each partner in his (her) own church, respect and love for each other, and highlighting the moral-religious beliefs and practices that unite them.

When one puts this all together, it does not prove that we are going to have a rising rate of interfaith marriages as a result of the ecumenical movement (and dialogue with non-Christians), but it does suggest that the attitude of many toward such marriages is changing. The social norm of religious endogamy will persist because no one wants to add problems to the adjustments which all married couples must make to each other. However, I think we will see somewhat less tendency for conversions to occur in order to make the marriages homogeneous—less than we have discovered to be the case in the Detroit area study, even though this is still going to be perhaps the majority experience in mixed marriages. Now I think the advice will not so often be given that, "If you want your mixed marriage to succeed, you are better off if one partner has no strong religious convictions." Henceforth this will more frequently come out: "If you want your mixed marriage to succeed, you are better off if both partners have strong religious convictions, provided they are also tolerant and respectful of each other's position."

Times do change.

Appendix A

NOTES ON THE SETTING AND METHODOLOGY

Since the data presented in this book are scattered through-out the discussion of earlier research, we had better take time to describe briefly the setting from which they were drawn—Detroit. Then we shall take a closer look at the Detroit Area Study and its procedures and particularly the restrictions placed on the samples used for reanalysis in this book. After-wards we shall take some care to define operationally our dependent variable: interfaith marriages. As a consequence of these steps, the reader should be in a better position to under-stand and to evaluate the Detroit findings interspersed through the rest of the book.

Population, Autos, and Religion in the Detroit Area

Detroit was founded by Antoine Cadillac and his French Canadian settlers in 1701 as a fortress protecting their fur trading.[1] Although it reached a population of about 2,000 under the French and later the British flag, the town was all but abandoned by its settlers when the American flag, with its fifteen stars, was hoisted in 1796. It looked like the end when a fire completely leveled the town in 1805. However, laid out anew by Governor William Hull and Judge Augustus B. Woodward, Detroit showed even then its power to recover from hard times.

The opening of the Erie Canal in 1825 and the early devel-opment of railroads in Michigan, particularly to the East through Canada, brought Irish workers and settlers to Detroit in large numbers. A little later the Germans came in such numbers that they totaled nearly 35,000 by 1874, or about one-third of the population.[2] By 1930 it was the Polish who constituted the largest single national group, with about 300,-000.[3] Canada, Great Britain, Italy, Russia, and Hungary were consistently among the largest contributors to Detroit's popu-lation during this and the following decades. Two other ethnic groups, not foreign, must be mentioned. Negroes and whites from the Border states migrated to Detroit especially during and after World War II. On the whole, Detroit's growth has been phenomenal. Perhaps the most striking indication of it is the following. Of the fourteen Standard Metropolitan Areas with a population of over one million in 1950, the highest *rates* of growth, 1900-1950, were:

Los Angeles	2,199.0%
Detroit	606.6%
San Francisco	312.7%
Cleveland	218.0%
Chicago	163.6%[4]

No city can touch Los Angeles in breakneck expansion, but neither does Detroit have a close rival for second place.

As everyone knows, Detroit is the home of the mass-produced automobile. The Oldsmobile of 1901 started the parade of popular cars coming from this city, but Henry Ford introduced new excitement into this development when in 1913 he announced the fantastically high wage scale of $5 a day. In 1925, the Ford Motor Co. employed 51,533 persons in Highland Park and 70,682 in the River Rouge and Dearborn area.[5] In 1940, the automobile industry directly provided one-third of all employment in the area; directly and indirectly it was then the source of 80 per cent of all employment in the area.[6] As a consequence of this concentration, Detroit has experienced severe growing pains in the peak years of auto sales and in wartime, followed by extreme unemployment in the Great Depression and in the transitions from wartime to peacetime production. In addition, the annual retooling for the production of new models has created much seasonal unemployment, a condition which has been largely corrected in recent years.

The data of the Detroit Area Study over the years of its existence give us the best information concerning the religious preferences of people in this tri-county area. Among 7,738 white adults interviewed in the six surveys, 1954-59, 49.0 per cent gave some Protestant group as their preference, whereas 42.7 per cent indicated Roman Catholic. Jews, Eastern Orthodox, and those of no preference—in nearly equal numbers—

together constituted the remaining 8.3 per cent. The largest denominations among white Protestants were the Lutherans (dominantly Missouri-synod), Methodists, Baptists, and Calvinists. Of the Negroes, the Baptists made up about two-thirds; Methodists were next with slightly more than one-fifth, other denominations being much smaller.[7]

The few paragraphs above are admittedly a very incomplete picture of Detroit and its growth. However, the facts selected do have some special relevance to our subject matter.

Methods of the Detroit Area Study

In 1951, the Department of Sociology at the University of Michigan established the Detroit Area Study to aid the research efforts of faculty members in the social sciences and to provide training for graduate students in a cooperative survey research project. The faculty member whose research proposal is accepted by the executive committee in a given year takes responsibility for seeing the project through to its final analysis, aided by the director and staff of the DAS.[8]

The selection of the annual sample for the Detroit Area Study is carried out in consultation with the Sampling Section of the Survey Research Center at the University of Michigan. With the exception of the 1962 sample, which will be described a little later, the other surveys used in our study were based on the following sampling procedures: The population to be sampled in each case consisted of all adults living in private dwelling units within the areas of Macomb, Oakland, and Wayne counties, tracted in 1950. The area included, on February 1, 1958, approximately 87 per cent of the total population of the Detroit Standard Metropolitan Area, with boundaries determined according to the 1950 Census of the United States. In general, the sampling method was a combination of a stratified systematic selection from city directories and a chunk and segment method (a form of area-probability sampling) for parts of the population not included in city directories.[9]

Because the entire population was not interviewed we must, of course, take account of "sampling errors." The size of the sampling error will depend on how large a sample was selected and how large the variation is found to be for any given characteristic. The sampling error for reported percentages can be found in published reports for the 1955 and 1958 surveys.[10] In the survey of 1959 it was equal to that of 1958, since the sampling method for these two surveys was practically identical.[11] The sampling error for 1955 is sometimes 1 per cent larger than these later surveys for a given sample size and sample percentages. Similar statements could be made regarding the statistical significance (with 95 per cent probability) of differences in percentages in each sample.

Nonsampling errors are of two types: "reporting errors" and "nonresponse errors." The size of such errors cannot be determined mathematically. The directors of the Detroit Area Study have regularly tried to keep reporting errors at a minimum by careful training of the interviewers, with the aim of motivating the respondent to answer questions to the best of his ability. Interview responses are also checked for inconsistencies. The response rate in these surveys has been about 87 per cent. It is over 90 per cent for subgroups, such as those in the age group 21-34, and those who are married and have children present. Those found to have the lowest response rate (60 years of age or older, the widowed, and the never married) are the least likely to appear in this particular study of unbroken marriages. An average of 2.9 calls were made to obtain a single interview. Some demographic information was obtained concerning almost all possible respondents, and a comparison between respondents and nonrespondents on such items showed relatively small differences.[12]

In the next step in the process of handling the interview data, which is that of coding the interview responses, there is also the possibility of error. However, in the present study almost all of the questions used were pretested and precoded, the major exception being the husband's occupation. Hence the interviewer usually needed only to check one of a set of possible responses to a question, leaving relatively little room for error.

Several times in the course of this study the IBM data cards were revised in some way. The writer used the code books of the surveys of the DAS to select those items which he could use in this analysis. The Data Processing staff of the Survey Research Center at the University of Michigan filled this request by preparing new decks of data cards for the writer's use at Michigan State University. To make use of the Chi-Square Program on the MISTIC computer at Michigan State, a revision of the code was needed which would remove 11- and 12-punch codes and reduce all double column fields to single columns. This was done according to the writer's directions by the Data Processing staff of Michigan State University. Later checking uncovered only two small errors in this process. The writer's own combination of responses to interview questions into various indices was also carefully watched for mechanical errors.

There are still two features of the original interviews which need to be pointed out here. One is that although the adult to be interviewed in a specific dwelling unit was designated by using a random selection table in 1958 and 1959, the respondent was always the wife in the studies of 1955 and 1962. Therefore, when the three large samples of 1955, 1958, and 1959 are combined in one table, only about 27 per cent of the respondents are male. The writer has examined the implications of this in each case and does not see that the data reported here are thereby being distorted appreciably. (When the samples of 1958 and 1959 are used separately or in combination, there are about as many males as females.)

The other special feature refers only to the study of 1962. In this sample only newlyweds are included. As part of a larger study of "family growth" and its motivation, a number of women were interviewed from six to eight months after their marriage. At first just 101 interviews were sought and obtained with those who had been married in July, 1961. Later it was decided to double the size of this subsample in the larger study. Hence we have 90 interviews with wives who had been married in October, 1961. All of these were selected from the marriage records of the State of Michigan from among those married at ceremonies within the boundaries of the Detroit Area Study. No marriages of nonwhites or second and later marriages were included, and age limits of 15-34 years were set. Within these restrictions, the sample was drawn on a random basis. The response rate in the 1962 study as a whole was 92 per cent, which is very high.[13]

Restrictions Here Imposed on These Samples

The very title of our study indicates that we do not intend to generalize from our data to the entire population of the Detroit area. When the writer arranged for the data cards to be made up in Ann Arbor, he specified that only married people were to be included in the sample, since this is a study of marriage choices. The broken marriages of the divorced or separated or widowed could not be analyzed because questions were generally not asked about the former spouse in such cases. This is unfortunate for our purposes. It would be better if our respondents could have been interviewed at the time of their marriage, when couples later to be separated would not have been removed from our sample. However, we have no choice (except in the 1962 sample) but to catch our respondents at some point in their life experience after the honeymoon is over.

As was stated in Chapter I, several categories were eliminated from our sample of married people in each of the four surveys: nonwhites, Jews, Eastern Orthodox, and those with no religious preference. However, a few who are neither Protestant nor Catholic will appear in our sample if they have married a Protestant or a Catholic. In this case, they will be designated here simply as "other."

Originally, it had been intended to analyze only the *first* marriages among our unbroken marriages. In the surveys of 1955, 1958, and 1959 the *respondents* were asked whether this was *their* first marriage. However, only in 1958 was the respondent asked whether this was the first marriage for his (her) *spouse* also. Therefore only for this sample have we been able to put together a couple of tables which are restricted to first marriages. Otherwise, all marriages (first and later) are included because we have inadequate information to restrict the samples of 1955 and 1959. How much difference will this make in our results? In the three surveys combined for our analysis, this was *not* the first marriage for 17 per cent of the respondents (whatever it was for their spouses). Among these remarried respondents, the first marriage ended by death for 31 per cent and by civil divorce for 69 per cent.

Although most studies of interfaith marriages do not try to separate the first from later marriages, there would be an advantage in doing so. It seems that remarriages involving Catholics are much more likely to be mixed marriages than are first marriages.[14] Therefore we can expect our sample to have a somewhat higher rate of mixed marriages than it would if it were restricted to first marriages.

Operational Definitions: The Dependent Variable

Our dependent variable, the characteristic whose occurrence in the population we are trying to predict, is the religious type of marriage entered into by those who are either Protestant or Catholic. Since every respondent in each of the surveys included in this study was asked "What is your religious preference?" and was asked the same question about his (her) spouse, it is a simple matter to discover which Protestants are now married to non-Protestants and which Catholics are now married to non-Catholics. However, as is generally recognized, many couples share the same religion after marriage because one of them has changed his (her) preference. For instance, Gerhard Lenski reports that in the DAS survey of 1958:

> One of our important findings was that it is most unwise to assume that spouses who are *currently* of the same faith were *always* of the same faith. Although 85 per cent of the white Protestants and Catholics in our sample reported that they and their spouse were of the same major faith (i.e., Protestantism or Catholicism), a check of their religious background revealed that only 68 per cent had been reared in the same faith. In other words, one fifth of the new homogeneous marriages had been contracted by persons raised in different faiths.[15]

To classify married couples simply by their *present* religious preference would put us in the position of having many in the *unmixed* category who were socialized in *different* religious traditions. Furthermore, our group of mixed marriages would be greatly reduced.

Fortunately, all of our respondents (except in 1955) were asked whether they or their spouses had changed religious preference. Hence it seems to the writer that we can get a better picture of the situation at the time of the marriage, regarding the religious tradition in which each partner to the marriage was socialized, if we use this information about previous religious preference to classify our marriages in this study. To do so, we shall have to assume that the change in preference occurred near the time of marriage.

Is it a valid assumption that a change in religious preference by a married person probably occurred about the time of marriage? Not always, of course. However, informal observation would give us some confidence in making this assumption if the change means crossing the line either way between Protestant and Catholic affiliations. Moreover, in our small 1962 sample of couples who were all married in 1961, there were thirty individuals among the 185 couples included in this study who changed either to Protestant or to Catholic. One changed after the wedding; twenty-two changed in 1961 or 1960; only seven changed before 1960. So it appears that, for *more than three-fourths* of these cases, changing religious preference was associated with meeting one's marriage choice.

Another nearly parallel indication of the tendency which we are assuming here is found in some data regarding converts received by Jewish rabbis. A mail questionnaire returned by 68 per cent of the Conservative and 91 per cent of the Reform rabbis actively functioning in the United States in 1953 showed that between 1,500 and 1,750 conversions to Judaism occurred every year. Of these, marriage to a Jewish person was involved in 93.9 per cent of Reform and 96 per cent of Conservative conversions for all rabbis in their entire careers.[16]

With the above evidence to support us, we shall therefore assume in this study that married persons who have changed their religious preference did so about the time of their marriage. For the surveys of 1958 and 1959 we have direct evidence to identify the original religious group, since respondents were asked (about themselves and their spouses) whether their religious preference had always been what it is now—and, if not, what it was previously. Changes between Protestant denominations will not enter into our analysis, only those between Protestant and non-Protestant or between Catholic and non-Catholic.

In the survey of 1955, we have only indirect evidence about previous religious preference. The respondents were asked (about themselves and their husbands) not what their previous religious preference had been but what their mothers' religious preference was when they were growing up. To test whether we might assume that these two questions are equivalent, the writer analyzed the data of 1958 and 1959 to see how many cases would have to be reclassified as to marriage type if he were to classify these on the basis of *mother's* religious preference instead of on the *respondent's (and spouse's) previous* religious preference. As is clear from Table 12, we would make few errors (3 per cent for Catholics, 1 per cent for Protestants) if we assumed that the two questions yield equivalent answers in the samples of 1958 and 1959. Therefore to make this assumption for the 1955 data, as we do, should not produce many errors.[17]

Now, if we compare the *present* with the *previous* religious preference of all respondents and their spouses, we shall discover several religious types of marriage. Not only are there the two types which are *currently* mixed or unmixed religiously, but there are also the two types in which married persons who were previously either Protestant or Catholic have changed their religious preference. With these types of marriages in mind, the writer sorted out for inclusion in this study all the marriages in the surveys of 1955, 1958, and 1959 which involved *at least one* partner whose *previous* religious preference was either Protestant or Catholic. The detailed distribution of marriages is shown in Appendix B.

The types of marriages which can be defined in these terms are too numerous to be used efficiently for cross-tabulations. Combinations of categories must be used. The reader may recall that we are trying to make a double comparison: marriages involving Protestants which are not mixed compared

TABLE 12.—*Previous Religious Preference of Respondent and Spouse, Reclassified by Mother's Religious Preference in the Former's Childhood Days, Detroit Area Study, 1958 and 1959*

Previous Religious Preference of Respondent or Spouse	MOTHER'S RELIGIOUS PREFERENCE			
	Catholic	Other	Protestant	All
Catholic	375	0	5	380
Other	0	9	0	9
Protestant	10	6	410	426
Total	385	15	415	815

with those that are mixed, and marriages involving Catholics which are not mixed compared with those that are mixed. Therefore the writer constructed an index of marriages for each religious group, assigning all marriages in the sample to one category in each index, as follows:

Marriages of Protestants	*Marriages of Catholics*
1. Both Protestant at marriage	1. Both Catholic at marriage
2. Protestant and changing partner	2. Catholic and changing partner
4. Mixed marriage still	4. Mixed marriage still
5. Protestant partner changes	5. Catholic partner changes
9. Neither partner was Protestant	9. Neither partner was Catholic

These distinctions will be useful for some of our comparisons. However, it should also be clear that Numbers 2, 4, and 5 of each index can be combined into a single category which contains all marriages which can be defined as mixed according to the previous religious preference of the partners. This simplified comparison between mixed *vs.* non-mixed marriages will also be used in our analysis.

With this our operational definition of the dependent variable is complete. One final note must be added, however, regarding the use of an index such as the above. We must not forget that we are trying to predict from background characteristics of *individuals* to the religious type of *marriage*. Hence the index of marriages above represents only half of the equation. It is not enough to know, for instance, that we are analyzing in a given instance only marriages involving Protestants, whether mixed or unmixed. It is also necessary to know whether the person answering a given question was raised as a Protestant; in a mixed marriage we might be talking to the non-Protestant partner. Therefore it was necessary to construct an index for the religion (former) of the respondent, and a second index for the religion (former) of the spouse, so that these could be used as controls before attempting a cross-tabulation of the religious type of marriage with any other variables. Each of these indices is simple and looks like this:

Religion (former) of the Respondent	*Religion (former) of the Respondent's Spouse*
1. Catholic	1. Catholic
2. Other	2. Other
3. Protestant	3. Protestant

Where the religion of the *respondent* was given as "other," this marriage would not get into the analysis at all—except for those few variables in which a background characteristic of the *spouse* is involved. Incidentally, after using this control, no mixed marriage will be counted twice (as would have been the case when using only the two indices for marriages of Protestants and Catholics), since each *respondent* will appear only once. This naturally gives us about half as many mixed marriages in any relationship as we would have had before using this control.

So much for the special handling which is called for in the analysis of data of this type. One who has read these pages carefully is now in a better position to evaluate what social scientists have discovered about mate selection in general and interfaith marriages in particular—incorporating our new data from the Detroit area.

Appendix B

Year of Detroit Area Survey

1955	1958	1959	All Years	Religion of Partners
				Husband always Catholic
178	104	168	450	Wife always Catholic
18	17	22	57	Wife formerly Protestant, now Catholic
30	17	11	58	Wife always Protestant
		1	1	Wife formerly Catholic, now Protestant
				Wife formerly Catholic, now other than Catholic or Protestant
				Wife formerly Protestant, now other than Catholic or Protestant
	1		1	Wife formerly other, now Catholic
				Wife formerly other, now Protestant
3	1		4	Wife always other
(229)	(140)	(202)	(571)	Subtotal
				Husband formerly Protestant, now Catholic
17	5	11	33	Wife always Catholic
2	1		3	Wife formerly Protestant, now Catholic
				Wife always Protestant
				Wife formerly Catholic, now Protestant

* This table categorizes the marriage choices only of those in the population who have been Protestants or Catholics. Hence each marriage will include at least one who was a member of either of these groups. The "other" on which these choices sometimes fall may include Jew, Orthodox Christians, or a person with no religious preference.

Year of Detroit Area Survey				Religion of Partners
1955	1958	1959	All Years	
				Wife formerly Catholic, now other than Catholic or Protestant
				Wife formerly Protestant, now other than Catholic or Protestant
				Wife formerly other, now Catholic
				Wife formerly other, now Protestant
				Wife always other
(19)	(6)	(11)	(36)	Subtotal
				Husband always Protestant
17	20	21	58	Wife always Catholic
3			3	Wife formerly Protestant, now Catholic
229	137	195	561	Wife always Protestant
18	10	9	37	Wife formerly Catholic, now Protestant
2			2	Wife formerly Catholic, now other than Catholic or Protestant
				Wife formerly Protestant, now other than Catholic or Protestant
1			1	Wife formerly other, now Catholic
2			2	Wife formerly other, now Protestant
2	2		4	Wife always other
(274)	(169)	(225)	(668)	Subtotal
				Husband formerly Catholic, now Protestant
				Wife always Catholic
				Wife formerly Protestant, now Catholic
12	12	8	32	Wife always Protestant
6	5	2	13	Wife formerly Catholic, now Protestant
				Wife formerly Catholic, now other than Catholic or Protestant

1955	1958	1959	All Years	Religion of Partners
				Wife formerly Protestant, now other than Catholic or Protestant
				Wife formerly other, now Catholic
1			1	Wife formerly other, now Protestant
	1		1	Wife always other
(19)	(18)	(10)	(47)	Subtotal
				Husband formerly Catholic, now other than Catholic or Protestant
3	1	1	5	Wife always Catholic
1			1	Wife formerly Protestant, now Catholic
5	4	2	11	Wife always Protestant
		1	1	Wife formerly Catholic, now Protestant
1			1	Wife formerly Catholic, now other than Catholic or Protestant
				Wife formerly Protestant, now other than Catholic or Protestant
				Wife formerly other, now Catholic
				Wife formerly other, now Protestant
2				Wife always other
(12)	(5)	(4)	(21)	Subtotal
				Husband formerly Protestant, now other than Catholic or Protestant
3		3	6	Wife always Catholic
				Wife formerly Protestant, now Catholic
2	2	2	6	Wife always Protestant
				Wife formerly Catholic, now Protestant
				Wife formerly Catholic, now other than Catholic or Protestant

Year of Detroit Area Survey

Year of Detroit Area Survey				Religion of Partners
1955	1958	1959	All Years	
2			2	Wife formerly Protestant, now other than Catholic or Protestant
				Wife formerly other, now Catholic
		1	1	Wife formerly other, now Protestant
1			1	Wife always other
(8)	(2)	(6)	(16)	Subtotal
				Husband formerly other than Catholic or Protestant, now Catholic
3	3		6	Wife always Catholic
				Wife formerly Protestant, now Catholic
1			1	Wife always Protestant
				Wife formerly Catholic, now Protestant
				Wife formerly Catholic, now other than Catholic or Protestant
				Wife formerly Protestant, now other than Catholic or Protestant
(4)	(3)		(7)	Subtotal
				Husband formerly other than Catholic or Protestant, now Protestant
				Wife always Catholic
				Wife formerly Protestant, now Catholic
3	1	1	5	Wife always Protestant
				Wife formerly Catholic, now Protestant
				Wife formerly Catholic, now other than Catholic or Protestant
				Wife formerly Protestant, now other than Catholic or Protestant
(3)	(1)	(1)	(5)	Subtotal
				Husband always other than Catholic or Protestant
3	3		6	Wife always Catholic

Year of Detroit Area Survey				Religion of Partners
1955	1958	1959	All Years	
	1		1	Wife formerly Protestant, now Catholic
3	4	2	9	Wife always Protestant
				Wife formerly Catholic, now Protestant
3		2	5	Wife formerly Catholic, now other than Catholic or Protestant
3			3	Wife formerly Protestant, now other than Catholic or Protestant
(12)	(8)	(4)	(24)	Subtotal
580	347	463	1390	*Grand totals*

Notes and References

Chapter I

1. The principal findings of this first stage were published under the title "Unbroken Protestant-Catholic Marriages Among Whites in the Detroit Area," *American Catholic Sociological Review*, 23 (1962), pp. 3-20. The hypotheses were divided into two temporal categories, "before" and "after," to include both background factors and familial-religious behavior of the couples after marriage.

2. *Ibid.*, p. 11. More than one well-known sociologist has misread reports of mixed marriage rates.

3. Some findings from these data were published in two articles: "Interfaith Marriages of Catholics in the Detroit Area," *Sociological Analysis*, 26 (1965), pp. 38-44; and "On Reporting Rates of Intermarriage," *American Journal of Sociology*, 70 (1965), pp. 717-21.

4. Jerold S. Heiss, "Premarital Characteristics of the Religiously Intermarried in an Urban Area," *American Sociological Review*, 25 (1960), pp. 47-55.

Chapter II

1. For example: Karl Pearson, "Assortative Mating in Man," *Biometrika*, 2 (1903), pp. 481-98; Roswell H. Johnson, "Mate Selection," *Proceedings, Second International Congress of Eugenics*, 1 (1921), pp. 416-25.

2. Robert Cook (ed.), "Spotlight on Marriage," *Population Bulletin*, 17 (1961), pp. 61-79.

3. William Ogburn, "Recent Changes in Marriage," *American Journal of Sociology*, 41 (1933), p. 298.

4. Paul Popenoe, "Recent Trends in American Marriages," *Eugenical News*, 32 (1947), p. 10.

5. Cook, *op. cit.*, p. 62. Thomas P. Monahan is highly critical of nearly all data on age at marriage prior to 1950 in his *The Pattern of Age at Marriage in the United States* (2 vols.; Philadelphia: Stephenson, 1951), p. iii.

6. *Ibid.*, p. 67.

7. *Ibid.*, p. 64.

8. Howard H. Punke, "Marriage Rate among Women Teachers," *American Sociological Review*, 5 (1940), p. 511. In 1910, the age of women at marriage was found to increase with high social status, according to Frank W. Notestein, "Differential Age at Marriage

according to Social Class," *American Journal of Sociology,* 37 (1931), p. 22.

9. G. W. Hill and James D. Tarver, "Marriage and Divorce Trends in Wisconsin, 1915-45," *Milbank Memorial Fund Quarterly,* 30 (1952), p. 16.

10. Paul H. Landis, "Rural-Urban Migration and the Marriage Rate," *American Sociological Review,* 11 (1946), p. 158.

11. Paul Glick, *American Families* (New York: Wiley, 1957), p. 116.

12. Cook, *op. cit.,* p. 71. Also, see John Hajnal, "Differential Changes in Marriage Patterns," *American Sociological Review,* 19 (1954), p. 153.

13. Walter C. McKain, Jr., and C. Arnold Anderson, "Assortative Mating in Prosperity and Depression," *Sociology and Social Research,* 21 (1937), p. 412.

14. Joseph Greenberg, "Sex Distribution and Marital Status," *Sociology and Social Research,* 33 (1949), p. 371.

15. In an early unsigned article, attributed primarily to Karl Pearson, two definitions were given which came to be commonly accepted and are, therefore, probably worth repeating here:

Preferential mating is that "in which male or female classes with certain values of a character find it less easy to mate than other classes with different values."

Assortative mating is that "in which, while all classes of males and females find mates, certain classes of males appear to be attracted to certain classes of females."

Homogamy is therefore one type of assortative mating. Cf. "Assortative Mating in Man," *Biometrika,* 2 (1903), p. 481.

16. Ernest W. Burgess and Paul Wallin, "Homogamy in Personality Characteristics," *Journal of Abnormal and Social Psychology,* 39 (1944), pp. 480-81.

17. Ernest W. Burgess and Paul Wallin, "Homogamy in Social Characteristics," *American Journal of Sociology,* 49 (1943), p. 110.

18. Paul C. Glick and Emanuel Landau, "Age as a Factor in Marriage," *American Sociological Review,* 15 (1950), p. 523.

19. August B. Hollingshead, "Cultural Factors in the Selection of Marriage Mates," *American Sociological Review,* 15 (1950), p. 626.

20. Karl M. Wallace, "An Experiment in Scientific Matchmaking," *Marriage and Family Living,* 21 (1959), pp. 342-48.

21. Reuben Hill, "A Critique of Contemporary Marriage and Family Research," *Social Forces,* 33 (1955), p. 268.

22. C. Arnold Anderson, "Our Present Knowledge of Assortative Mating," *Rural Sociology,* 3 (1938), p. 299.

23. Anselm Strauss, "The Influence of Parent-Images Upon Marital Choice," *American Sociological Review,* 11 (1946), p. 557.

24. Anselm Strauss *et al.*, "Personality Needs and Marital Choice," *Social Forces*, 25 (1947), p. 332.

25. *American Sociological Review*, 19 (1954), pp. 241-49.

26. Thomas Ktsanes, "Mate Selection on the Basis of Personality Type: A Study Utilizing an Empirical Typology of Personality," *American Sociological Review*, 20 (1955), pp. 547-51. Robert F. Winch, "The Theory of Complementary Needs in Mate-Selection: A Test of One Kind of Complementariness," *American Sociological Review*, 20 (1955), pp. 52-56. Robert F. Winch, "The Theory of Complementary Needs in Mate-Selection: Final Results on the Test of the General Hypothesis," *American Sociological Review*, 20 (1955), pp. 552-55. Robert F. Winch, Thomas and Virginia Ktsanes, "Empirical Elaboration of the Theory of Complementary Needs in Mate Selection," *Journal of Abnormal and Social Psychology*, 51 (1955), pp. 508-13.

27. Robert F. Winch, *Mate Selection: A Study of Complementary Needs* (New York: Harper & Bros., 1958).

28. *Ibid.*, p. 10.

29. *Ibid.*, p. 92.

30. *Ibid.*, pp. 95-96.

31. Charles Bowerman and Barbara Day, "A Test of the Theory of Complementary Needs as Applied to Couples during Courtship," *American Sociological Review*, 21 (1956), pp. 602-5.

32. James Schellenberg and Lawrence Bee, "A Re-Examination of the Theory of Complementary Needs in Mate Selection," *Marriage and Family Living*, 22 (1960), p. 231.

33. Alan Kerckhoff and Keith Davis, "Value Consensus and Need Complementarity in Mate Selection," *American Sociological Review*, 27 (1962), pp. 295-303. Their instruments included Bernard Farber's index of value consensus and William Schutz's FIRO-B scales, the latter being modified before the analysis so as to conform to the concept of complementarity.

34. *Ibid.*, p. 303.

35. James Bossard, "Residential Propinquity as a Factor in Marriage Selection," *American Journal of Sociology*, 38 (1932), p. 219.

36. A recent study in Minnesota concluded that "propinquity generally operates to a lesser extent and with less force in mate selection than previously. Propinquity, in the sense of nearness of potential marriage mates, has been spatially expanded." Cf. Ronald G. Klietsch, "Propinquity: Distance and Direction in Mate Selection," *University of Minnesota Miscellaneous Bulletin #1079*, May 2, 1961, p. 10.

37. Elina Haavio-Mannila found that in Finland, "the proportion of geographically homogamous marriages is declining at a rate of approximately one per cent per year. Intermarriages between com-

munes are constantly increasing." Cf. his "Local Homogamy in Finland," *Acta Sociologica*, 8 (1964), p. 156.

38. William R. Catton and R. J. Smircich enter some strong pleading for the importance of residential propinquity as opposed to endogamous norms for explaining marriage choices, and they propose a modification of Zipf's P_1P_2/D formula in preference to the Stouffer "intervening opportunities" model for analyzing their Seattle marriage data. See their "A Comparison of Mathematical Models for the Effect of Residential Propinquity on Mate Selection," *American Sociological Review*, 29 (1964), pp. 522-28.

39. Alvin M. Katz and Reuben Hill, "Residential Propinquity and Marital Selection: A Review of Theory, Method, and Fact," *Marriage and Family Living*, 20 (1958), p. 33. (In the original text the quoted material appears in italics.)

It is quite possible that analysis of additional data will show that Catton and Smircich were correct in wishing to substitute Zipf's "intervening distance" for Stouffer's "intervening opportunities," as we have just noted. In this case, the third assumption in the Katz-Hill theory can be modified accordingly. However, two of the studies reviewed by Katz and Hill showed that data interpreted by distance only could be misleading unless one took population density into account.

40. *Ibid.*, p. 31. (In the original text the quoted material appears in italics.) The decision-making theories in economics and psychology are reflected here, and one can recognize here also an application of the cost theory elaborated by George Homans in his *Social Behavior: Its Elementary Forms* (New York: Harcourt, Brace and World, 1961).

41. Daniel Harris, "Age and Occupational Factors in the Residential Propinquity of Marriage Partners," *Journal of Social Psychology*, 6 (1935), p. 260.

42. Marvin R. Koller, "Residential Propinquity of White Mates at Marriage in Relation to Age and Occupation of Males, Columbus, Ohio," *American Sociological Review*, 13 (1948), p. 615.

43. A. Philip Sundal and Thomas C. McCormick, "Age at Marriage and Mate Selection: Madison, Wis., 1937-1943," *American Sociological Review*, 16 (1951), p. 57.

Chapter III

1. One other exception would seem to be developing in the Israeli pattern of marrying outside one's own communal peer group. Cf. the excellent and recent article by Yonina Talmon, "Mate Selection in Collective Settlements," *American Sociological Review*, 29 (1964), pp. 491-508.

2. Kingsley Davis, "Intermarriage in Caste Societies," *American Anthropologist*, 43 (1941), p. 376. Similarly, he defines the correlative term *exogamy* as: "marriage into a class of which I am not a member."

An article by Robert K. Merton, covering much of the same ground as the article by Davis, appeared almost at the same time. Merton is perceptive as usual when he relates intermarriage functionally to social structure. However, it seems to me that in this article his definitions of terms, and his proliferation of them, are not so helpful or appropriate to the subject as are the definitions given by Davis. Robert K. Merton, "Intermarriage and the Social Structure: Fact and Theory," *Psychiatry*, 4 (1941), pp. 361-74.

3. Alvin M. Katz and Reuben Hill, "Residential Propinquity and Marital Selection: A Review of Theory, Method, and Fact," *Marriage and Family Living*, 20 (1958), p. 29.

These writers credit Davie and Reeves with being the first to present the substance of this theory and to put it to an empirical test. Cf. Maurice R. Davie and Ruby Jo Reeves, "Propinquity Before Marriage," *American Journal of Sociology*, 44 (1939), pp. 510-17.

4. Julius Drachsler, *Democracy and Assimilation* (New York: Macmillan, 1920), p. 87.

5. Ruby Jo Kennedy, "Single or Triple Melting Pot? Intermarriage Trends in New Haven, 1870-1940," *American Journal of Sociology*, 49 (1944), pp. 331-39.

6. C. Arnold Anderson, "Our Present Knowledge of Assortative Mating," *Rural Sociology*, 3 (1938), p. 298.

7. Elin L. Anderson, *We Americans: A Study of Cleavage in an American City* (Cambridge: Harvard University Press, 1937), p. 165.

8. *Ibid.*, p. 88.

9. Lowry Nelson, "Intermarriage among Nationality Groups in a Rural Area of Minnesota," *American Journal of Sociology*, 48 (1943), p. 590.

10. Kennedy, *op. cit.*, pp. 331-39. See also her "Single or Triple Melting-Pot? Intermarriage in New Haven, 1870-1950," *American Journal of Sociology*, 58 (1952), pp. 56-59.

11. Milton L. Barron, *People Who Intermarry* (Syracuse: Syracuse University Press, 1946). Stern's article on intermarriage is short, but it has the merit of treating the subject historically and cross-culturally. Bernhard Stern, "Intermarriage," in *Encyclopedia of the Social Sciences*, ed. Edwin R. Seligman (New York: Macmillan, 1930-1935), vol. 8, pp. 151-54.

12. Albert I. Gordon, *Intermarriage: Interfaith, Interracial, Interethnic* (Boston: Beacon Press, 1964).

13. Charles Wagley and Marvin Harris, *Minorities in the New*

World: Six Case Studies (New York: Columbia University Press, 1958), p. xvi.

14. Joseph Golden, "Social Control of Negro-White Intermarriage," *Social Forces*, 36 (1958), p. 268. In 1967, the following sixteen states still retained such laws: Alabama, Arkansas, Delaware, Florida, Georgia, Kentucky, Louisiana, Mississippi, Missouri, North Carolina, Oklahoma, South Carolina, Tennessee, Texas, Virginia and West Virginia. "Loving vs. Commonwealth of Virginia," *Supreme Court Reporter*, 87 (1967), pp. 1817-24.

15. Louis Wirth and H. Goldhamer, "The Hybrid and the Problem of Miscegenation," *Characteristics of the American Negro*, ed. Otto Klineberg (New York: Harper & Bros., 1944), p. 281. It seems desirable to warn the reader at this point that it is very easy to misread the reported rates of intermarriage because two people and at least two groups are always involved. For example, the proportion of Negroes (individual persons) who have intermarried may be reported instead of the proportion of Negro marriages (acts involving two persons), thereby lowering the magnitude of the rate. Similarly, the rate may have as its base each 100 marriages involving Negroes *or* each 100 marriages involving whites *or* each 100 in the sum total of *all* marriages, *or* each 1,000 marriages on any of these bases. The same caution should be used in reading the reported rates for ethnic and religious intermarriage.

16. Drachsler, *op. cit.*, p. 121.

17. Joseph Golden, "Patterns of Negro-White Intermarriage," *American Sociological Review*, 19 (1954), pp. 144-47.

18. Todd H. Pavela, "An Exploratory Study of Negro-White Intermarriage in Indiana," *Journal of Marriage and the Family*, 26 (1964), pp. 209-11.

19. Annella Lynn, R.S.M., *Interracial Marriages in Washington, D.C., 1940-1947*, Catholic University Studies in Sociology #37 (Washington: Catholic University Press, 1953).

20. John H. Burma, "Interethnic Marriage in Los Angeles, 1948-1959," *Social Forces*, 42 (1963), pp. 157 and 160. A rate based on the number of Negro marriages would be considerably larger. It should also be noted that these low rates of intermarriage between Negroes and whites in this country tell only part of the story, leaving out illegal miscegenation over the years. Even in 1928, Melville Herskovits found that, of 1,551 American Negroes whose genealogies he investigated, only 22 per cent were unmixed Negro. The percentage of unmixed Negro Americans is estimated to have dropped considerably since then. *The American Negro: A Study in Racial Crossing* (New York: Alfred Knopf, 1928), p. 9.

21. Constantine Panunzio, "Intermarriage in Los Angeles, 1924-33," *American Journal of Sociology*, 47 (1942), p. 690.

22. Burma, *op. cit.*, pp. 156-59.

23. Lynn, *op. cit.*, p. 20.

24. Joseph P. Fitzpatrick, S.J., "Intermarriage of Puerto Ricans in New York City," *American Journal of Sociology*, 71 (1966), p. 396.

25. Edward T. Price, "A Geographic Analysis of White-Negro-Indian Racial Mixtures in the Eastern United States," *Annals of the Association of American Geographers*, 43 (1953), pp. 138-55.

26. Vernon J. Parenton and Roland J. Pellegrin, "The 'Sabines': A Study of Racial Hybrids in a Louisiana Coastal Parish," *Social Forces*, 29 (1950), pp. 148-54.

27. Thomas J. Harte, C.SS.R. "Social Origins of the Brandywine Population," *Phylon*, 24 (1963), p. 377.

28. Thomas J. Harte, C.SS.R., "Trends in Mate Selection in a Tri-Racial Isolate," *Social Forces*, 37 (1959), p. 220.

29. Romanzo Adams, *Interracial Marriage in Hawaii* (New York: Macmillan, 1937).

30. Andrew W. Lind, *Hawaii's People* (Honolulu: University of Hawaii Press, 1955).

31. C. K. Cheng and Douglas S. Yamamura, "Interracial Marriage and Divorce in Hawaii," *Social Forces*, 36 (1957), p. 82. A survey in the Honolulu Standard Metropolitan Area in January, 1961, confirmed these tendencies. Robert C. Schmitt and Robert A. Souza, "Social and Economic Characteristics of Interracial Households in Honolulu," *Social Problems*, 10 (1963), p. 265.

32. John Biesanz, "Inter-American Marriages on the Isthmus of Panama," *Social Forces*, 29 (1950), pp. 159-63.

33. Chester L. Hunt, "Cotabato: Melting Pot of the Philippines," *Philippine Social Sciences and Humanities Review*, 19 (1954), pp. 40-72; and Chester L. Hunt and Richard W. Coller, "Intermarriage and Cultural Change: A Study of Philippine-American Marriages," *Social Forces*, 35 (1957), pp. 223-30.

34. Roger Bastide, "Race Relations in Brazil," *International Social Science Bulletin*, 9 (1957), pp. 495-512.

35. Donald Pierson, *Negroes in Brazil* (Chicago: University of Chicago Press, 1942), p. 147.

36. Samuel A. Lowrie, "Racial and National Intermarriage in a Brazilian City," *American Journal of Sociology*, 44 (1939), p. 688.

37. Cheng and Yamamura, *op. cit.*, p. 77.

38. B. T. Catapusan, "Filipino Intermarriage Problems in the United States," *Sociology and Social Research*, 22 (1938), p. 265.

39. Burma, *op. cit.*, pp. 158-59.

40. John H. Burma, "Research Note on the Measurement of Interracial Marriage," *American Journal of Sociology*, 57 (1952), p. 589. Also Robert C. Schmitt, "Age Differences in Marriage in Hawaii," *Journal of Marriage and the Family*, 28 (1966), p. 58.

41. Larry D. Barnett, "Research on International and Inter-racial Marriages," *Marriage and Family Living*, 25 (1963), pp. 106-7. See also Joseph Golden, "Facilitating Factors in Negro-White Inter-marriage," *Phylon*, 6 (1945), pp. 273-84.

42. Davis, *op. cit.*, p. 389; and Merton, *op. cit.*, p. 367. Later we will consider the relationship of this situation to class endogamy and hypergamy.

43. A recent survey of over 5,000 college students across the country showed that 91 per cent do not favor marriage to a person of an-other color, that the overwhelming majority in the most "liberal" universities would be unwilling to marry a Negro, and that even in the University of Hawaii 75 per cent of the students would find it "hardest" or "next hardest" to marry someone outside their own *color* group (compared to religious, economic, educational, and national in-termarriage). See Gordon, *op. cit.*, pp. 33-36, 390.

44. John Harding, Bernard Kutner, Harold Proshansky, and Isidor Chein, "Prejudice and Ethnic Relations," *Handbook of Social Psychology*, ed. Gardner Lindzey (Reading, Mass.: Addison-Wesley, 1954), p. 1022.

45. Both Drachsler and Wessel, two of the most careful scholars on this subject, define "intermarriage" in such a way as to maximize somewhat the rate of its occurrence. The differences between them are not great, but it will illustrate the complexities of the problem of operational definitions here if we compare the two of them.

DRACHSLER: In general, "an intermarriage is a marriage between two persons of distinct national, religious or racial descent (the nation-ality of the father being taken as the nationality of the child)." A strict interpretation would exclude a case in which either father or mother were of the same nationality. He follows a "liberal interpreta-tion" by including as intermarriages those in which "either the fathers or the mothers of the parties of the intermarriage were of the same nationality," so long as the other parents were of different nationalities. However, if both fathers were of one national-ity (e.g., Polish) and both mothers were of a second nationality (e.g., French), it seems that the marriage of their son and daughter would not be counted as an "intermarriage." This is rather reasonable since no new element is added in the combination from what was present in either set of parents. So, operationally, the comparison which establishes that a union is an intermarriage is between husband's father and wife's father *or* between husband's mother and wife's mother, *not* between husband's father and wife's mother nor between husband's mother and wife's father. Drachsler does not ask questions about the nationality of the grandparents. *Op. cit.*, p. 251.

WESSEL: This researcher did ask questions about the grandparents, having given questionnaires to school children to be filled out by their parents. This definition of hers tends to include more marriages as intermarriages than did the definition just cited from Drachsler: "*Mixed* refers to any child all four of whose grandparents are not of the same ethnic origin and who is therefore the product of fusion. The grandparents may or may not be of the same geographic origin." But the following definition would, in a sense, underestimate the intermarriages: "*Old American* applies to any child all four of whose grandparents were born in this country. Old Americans may be of homogeneous or of mixed descent." *Intermarriage,* on the other hand, "is a term describing any union that results in bringing into the family line more than one racial strain." Somewhat later she introduces this "refinement" into the last definition: "kindred crossings" in marriage are classified as *intra*marriages, not *inter*marriages. In other words, the total British strain includes English, Scotch, Scotch-Irish, Canadian English, Canadian Scotch, Canadian unspecified, British mixed, and British-others. Jews in this study come from nine different countries, but predominantly from Russia. And so on. . . . In all these cases, reported ethnic derivation was preferred to the reported regional derivation. Bessie B. Wessel, *An Ethnic Survey of Woonsocket, R.I.* (Chicago: University of Chicago Press, 1931), pp. 21-22, 56-57.

Realizing these differences should make the reader cautious about interpreting rates of ethnic intermarriage reported by different researchers using the same terms.

46. *Ibid.,* pp. 23-24.

47. James H. Bossard, *Marriage and the Child* (Philadelphia: University of Pennsylvania Press, 1940), p. 100.

48. C. A. Price and J. Zubrzycki have done an excellent job of analyzing these problems in assessing the "extent to which an immigrant group is becoming assimilated through intermarriage." The lack of agreement between researchers is particularly noticeable regarding data for marriages of the first generation. "The Use of Inter-Marriage Statistics as an Index of Assimilation," *Population Studies,* 16 (1962), pp. 58-69.

49. Barron, *op. cit.,* p. 319.

50. Barron and others have noted that "the larger the group, the lower its rate." *Op. cit.,* p. 191. This is certainly true in general. The discussion of "residential propinquity" in the preceding chapter is not independent of this factor of group size. As a sociological factor or explanation, it leaves much to be desired—as will be brought out when we come to interfaith marriages.

51. The importance of the factor of a high sex ratio (male to female) in the first generation is called into question, however, by this information from Australia:

The survey of Griffith Italians, for instance, showed that during the years 1921-40 some 38 per cent of all male (immigrants) settling in Australia as single men married some years later either by proxy or else by returning to Italy to marry and bring back their brides.

Hence these marriages are not recorded in the land of settlement. Price and Zubrzycki, *op. cit.*, p. 65.

52. One of the most recent studies of this topic concerns the Puerto Ricans in New York City, a large and new immigrant group. Here some comparisons could be made with Drachsler's earlier study of the same city. Cf. Fitzpatrick, *op. cit.*, pp. 395-406.

53. Davis, *op. cit.*, p. 376.

54. Bernard Barber, *Social Stratification* (New York: Harcourt, Brace, 1957), p. 2.

55. Kingsley Davis, *Human Society* (New York: Macmillan, 1949), p. 364.

56. Davis, "Intermarriage in Caste Societies," *op. cit.*, p. 378.

57. In this case, "the couple usually have at least a partial membership of whichever is the lowest of the castes concerned, and their children are accepted into that caste. . . . No one has attempted to measure the frequency of these marriages." Frederick G. Bailey, "Closed Social Stratification in India," *European Journal of Sociology,* 4 (1963), p. 112.

58. Pierre L. Van den Berghe, "Hypergamy, Hypergenation, and Miscegenation," *Human Relations,* 13 (1960), p. 86.

59. August B. Hollingshead, "Class and Kinship in a Middle Western Community," *American Sociological Review,* 14 (1949), p. 475.

60. Simon Dinitz, Franklin Banks, and Benjamin Pasamanick, "Mate Selection and Social Class: Changes during the Past Century," *Marriage and Family Living,* 22 (1960), p. 351.

61. Thomas Hunt, "Occupational Status and Marriage Selection," *American Sociological Review,* 5 (1940), p. 504.

62. Richard Centers, "Marital Selection and Occupational Strata," *American Journal of Sociology,* 54 (1948), pp. 530-35.

63. Paul H. Landis and Katherine H. Day, "Education as a Factor in Mate Selection," *American Sociological Review,* 10 (1945), p. 559.

64. Gordon, *op. cit.*, pp. 33-36. Of course, for college students, marrying outside one's educational group would generally imply marrying one who has not studied in college, although it could refer to one who has gone on to graduate or professional studies.

65. John F. Scott, "The American College Sorority: Its Role in Class and Ethnic Endogamy," *American Sociological Review,* 30 (1965), pp. 514-27.

66. Davis, "Intermarriage in Caste Societies," *op. cit.*, p. 389. Melville J. Herskovits observed long ago that the same color distinction

is present in mate selection among Negroes. Of 380 students at Howard University, 56.5 per cent said their mother was lighter than their father, 13.2 per cent that she was about the same. "Social Selection in a Mixed Population," *Proceedings of the National Academy of Sciences*, 12 (1926), p. 588.

67. M. W. Gordon, "Race Patterns and Prejudice in Puerto Rico," *American Sociological Review*, 14 (1949), p. 299.

68. There is a correlative disadvantage for the upper-class female, which Scott aptly calls the "Brahmin problem." She cannot bargain in the marriage market with her high social status because she is relatively unable to confer it on her family (including her husband). *Op. cit.*, p. 519.

Chapter IV

1. Bernard Van Leeuwen, O.F.M., "Le mariage mixte, facteur de déchristianisation en Hollande," *Lumen Vitae*, 4 (1949), pp. 425-38.

2. Victor J. Traynor, S.J., "Urban and Rural Mixed Marriages," *Social Order*, 6 (1956), pp. 154-58.

3. Loren E. Chancellor and Thomas P. Monahan, "Religious Preference and Interreligious Mixtures in Marriages and Divorces in Iowa," *American Journal of Sociology*, 61 (1955), pp. 233-39. Lee G. Burchinal and Loren E. Chancellor, "Catholics, Urbanism, and Mixed-Catholic Marriage Rates," *Social Problems*, 9 (1962), pp. 359-65. Lee G. Burchinal, William F. Kenkel, and Loren E. Chancellor, "Comparison of State- and Diocese-Reported Marriage Data for Iowa, 1953-57," *American Catholic Sociological Review*, 23 (1962), pp. 21-29.

4. Erich Rosenthal, "Studies of Jewish Intermarriage in the United States," *American Jewish Year Book*, 64 (1963), p. 39.

5. New York: P. J. Kenedy & Sons.

6. Paul J. Reiss, "The Trend in Interfaith Marriages," *Journal for the Scientific Study of Religion*, 5 (1965), pp. 64-67. The author states that, "These data are now available for almost the entire country over a period of 20 years (1943-1962)." *Ibid.*, p. 64.

7. See John L. Thomas, S.J., *The American Catholic Family* (Englewood Cliffs, N.J.: Prentice-Hall, 1956), pp. 165-67.

8. See Murray H. Leiffer, "Interfaith Marriages and Their Effect on the Religious Training of Children," *Lumen Vitae*, 4 (1949), pp. 442-52. Also Michael E. Kolivosky, "Intermarriage Between Two Divergent Ethnic Groups as an Index of Assimilation" (unpublished Ph.D. dissertation, Michigan State University, 1953).

9. Some examples are: Dubius, "New Light on Mixed Marriages," *American Ecclesiastical Review*, 82 (1930), pp. 412-17. Perplexus, "Some Revelations of a Recent Parish Census," *American Ecclesiastical Review*, 82 (1930), pp. 312-14. Gerald J. Schnepp, S.M., "Mixed

Marriage," in *The Family Today: A Catholic Appraisal* (Washington: Family Life Bureau, National Catholic Welfare Conference, 1944), Vol. 1, pp. 107-15. Joseph H. Fichter, S.J., *Parochial School: A Sociological Study* (Notre Dame, Ind.: University of Notre Dame Press, 1958).

10. Paul C. Glick, "Intermarriage and Fertility Patterns Among Persons in Major Religious Groups," *Eugenics Quarterly*, 7 (1960), pp. 31-38.

11. Jerold S. Heiss, "Premarital Characteristics of the Religiously Intermarried in an Urban Area," *American Sociological Review*, 25 (1960), pp. 47-55.

12. Stanley K. Bigman, *The Jewish Population of Greater Washington in 1956* (Washington: Jewish Community Council, 1957).

13. Paul H. Besanceney, S.J., "Unbroken Protestant-Catholic Marriages Among Whites in the Detroit Area," *American Catholic Sociological Review*, 23 (1962), pp. 3-20.

14. Bigman, *op. cit.*, p. 140. A recent sample of Jewish households in Providence, R.I., is drawn from membership lists. See Sidney Goldstein and Calvin Goldscheider, "Social and Demographic Aspects of Jewish Intermarriage," *Social Problems*, 13 (1966), p. 388.

15. See Ray E. Baber, "A Study of 325 Mixed Marriages," *American Sociological Review*, 2 (1937), pp. 705-16; also Alfred J. Prince, "A Study of 194 Cross-Religion Marriages," *The Family Life Coordinator*, 11 (1962), pp. 3-7. Even though the author warns against generalizing, the reader will sometimes not be so cautious.

16. Some examples of this type of misinterpretation have been cited in Besanceney, *op. cit.*, p. 11, and in Hyman Rodman, "Essay-Review: The Textbook World of Family Sociology," *Social Problems*, 12 (1965), pp. 452-53.

17. Examples of the latter are: Arthur Ruppin, *The Jewish Fate and Future*, trans. E. W. Dickes (London: Macmillan, 1940), p. 108; Van Leeuwen, *op. cit.*, p. 429; David M. Heer, "The Trend of Interfaith Marriages in Canada: 1922-1957," *American Sociological Review*, 27 (1962), pp. 246-47; Louis Rosenberg, "Intermarriage in Canada, 1921-1960," in Werner J. Cahnman (ed.), *Intermarriage and Jewish Life: A Symposium* (New York: Herzl Press and Jewish Reconstructionist Press, 1963), p. 61. Rosenberg here describes the two alternative rates.

Maurice Fishberg also reports from civil registrations but handles the data differently. Instead of dividing the number of mixed marriages by the *total number* of marriages, he divides the mixed marriages by the *unmixed* marriages. Without having access to the raw data, it seems to be impossible to transform his ratio into a standard percentage of the whole class. See *The Jews: A Study of*

Race and Environment (New York: Charles Scribner's Sons, 1911), p. 196.

18. Hyman Rodman, "Technical Note on Two Rates of Mixed Marriage," *American Sociological Review*, 30 (1965), pp. 776-78. The formulas for transforming the mixed marriage rate for marriages into the mixed marriage rate for individuals and vice versa are:

$$y = \frac{100x}{200 - x} \quad \text{and} \quad x = \frac{200y}{100 + y}$$

where x is the mixed marriage rate for marriages and y is the mixed marriage rate for individuals.

19. For example, Jacques David, "Mariages mixtes et mariages religieusement homogènes en Suisse," *Lumen Vitae*, 4 (1949), p. 464.

20. "Religion Reported by the Civilian Population of the United States: March, 1957," *Current Population Reports: Population Characteristics*, Series P-20, No. 79 (Feb. 2, 1958), p. 8.

21. Milton L. Barron, *People Who Intermarry: Intermarriage in a New England Industrial Community* (Syracuse: Syracuse University Press, 1946), p. 318.

22. John L. Thomas, S.J., "The Factor of Religion in the Selection of Marriage Mates," *American Sociological Review*, 16 (1951), p. 489.

23. Traynor, *op. cit.*, p. 156. A perfect negative rank order correlation was found between these two variables for the Catholic population in the ten provinces of Canada in 1951, as reported in Harvey J. Locke, Georges Sabagh, and Mary M. Thomas, "Interfaith Marriages," *Social Problems*, 4 (1957), pp. 330-31.

24. Burchinal and Chancellor, *op. cit.*, pp. 362-63.

25. Rosenthal, *op. cit.*, p. 7.

26. The procedure is explained in a research note, "On Reporting Rates of Intermarriage," *American Journal of Sociology*, 70 (1965), p. 720. One must assume in such a case that the sex ratios of the several categories are not out of line with each other. As we saw in Chapter III, this sometimes becomes an important consideration if there are new and large immigrant groups in the community.

27. Glick, *op. cit.*, p. 35.

28. Heer, *op. cit.*, p. 249.

29. Leonard Broom, "Intermarriage and Mobility in Hawaii," *Transactions of the Third World Congress of Sociology*, 3 (1956), p. 279. Broom computes the percentage *differences* between observed and expected marriages, rather than the *ratio* of one to the other.

30. Stanley Lieberson uses an "index of homogamy" for ethnic intermarriages and cites some earlier uses of the same in: "The

Old-New Distinction and Immigrants in Australia," *American Socio-logical Review*, 28 (1963), p. 561. Roberto Bachi applies an "attraction index" according to religion and national origin in Israel and traces measures of this type back beyond 1924 in: "Statistical Research on Immigrants in the State of Israel," *Population Studies*, Supplement (March, 1950), p. 51.

31. Undoubtedly this is one of the principal reasons for the rather low rates of intermarriage discovered in the 1957 national survey by the Bureau of the Census. See "Religion Reported by the Civilian Population of the United States: March, 1957," *op. cit.*, p. 8.

32. For instance, the Catholic rate of intermarriage in Iowa in 1953 was 30 per cent according to ecclesiastical records, 42 per cent according to civil records. See Chancellor and Monahan, *op. cit.*, p. 237.

33. Prince, *op. cit.*, p. 4. Also Joseph B. Schuyler, S.J., *Northern Parish: A Sociological and Pastoral Study* (Chicago: Loyola University Press, 1960), p. 211.

34. For example, see Heiss, *op. cit.*, p. 48. Of course, Rosenthal is correct in saying that we must distinguish between the *formation* of intermarriages (which is the focus of this book) and the *status* of families (which is more relevant to religious behavior and attitudes after marriage). The questions a researcher asks will depend on which of these he is mainly interested in. *Op. cit.*, p. 7.

35. Joseph H. Fichter, S.J., *Social Relations in the Urban Parish* (Chicago: University of Chicago Press, 1954), p. 76.

36. David M. Eichhorn, "Conversions to Judaism by Reform and Conservative Rabbis," *Jewish Social Studies*, 16 (1954), p. 310.

37. Leiffer, *op. cit.*, p. 446.

38. Goldstein and Goldscheider, *op. cit.*, p. 390. Because of the nature of their sample they were unable to estimate what percentage of Jewish partners had converted to another religion or simply lost their identification with the Jewish community through intermarriage.

39. Gerhard Lenski, *The Religious Factor* (Garden City, N.Y.: Doubleday, 1961), p. 49.

40. Paul H. Besanceney, S.J., "Interfaith Marriages of Catholics in the Detroit Area," *Sociological Analysis*, 26 (1965), p. 39.

41. Ruby Jo Kennedy, "Single or Triple Melting-Pot? Intermarriage Trends in New Haven, 1870-1940," *American Journal of Sociology*, 49 (1944), pp. 331-39.

42. For a further statement of the same opinion, see my research note, "On Reporting Rates of Intermarriage," *op. cit.*, p. 719.

43. Rosenthal, *op. cit.*, p. 41.

44. Burchinal, Kenkel, and Chancellor, *op. cit.*, p. 26.

45. Catholics constitute about 5 per cent of the Negroes in the Detroit area. Cf. Albert J. Mayer and Harry Sharp, "Religious Pref-

erence and Worldly Success," *American Sociological Review,* 27 (1962), pp. 218-27.

46. Glick, *op. cit.,* p. 35.

47. See Jacob Baar and Werner J. Cahnman, "Interfaith Marriage in Switzerland," in Werner J. Cahnman (ed.), *Intermarriage and Jewish Life: A Symposium, op. cit.,* p. 55.

48. The first number in each pair was computed by Rodman's formula on the basis of the number in parentheses (which is taken from Ruppin's table and represents the number of intermarriages for each 100 *individual* Jews who were married). See Ruppin, *op. cit.,* p. 108.

49. A few other comments may be in order concerning these studies. The New York rate refers to second-generation Americans resident in Manhattan and the Bronx, whose Jewish-Gentile marriages Drachsler felt sure he had identified. How the Jews were identified from marriage records in the Kennedy studies also is not clear. Furthermore, Hollingshead's sample is restricted to those who were residents of New Haven in February of the year after their marriage, so that they could be interviewed. Still, these studies do meet the criteria considered most important for estimating the rates of intermarriage according to early religious preferences, and the other published rates not included in the table do not meet these criteria.

50. Rosenthal, *op. cit.,* pp. 34-35.

51. Kendall's *tau* was positive in all three provinces for which data were shown: .64 in Ontario, .69 in Manitoba, and .88 in Quebec. In fact, for these three provinces the rate of Jewish intermarriage increased by 126 per cent from 1927 to 1957, i.e., from 3.0 per cent to 6.8 per cent. Heer, *op. cit.,* pp. 246-49.

52. Barron, *op. cit.,* pp. 178 and 193. The two rates given were based on the exceedingly small total of 13 Jewish marriages.

53. "Religion Reported by the Civilian Population of the United States: March, 1957," *op. cit.,* p. 8. This rate was based on present religious identification only.

54. Rosenthal, *op. cit.,* p. 16. Only present religious identification was counted, and the sample was drawn mainly from membership lists of Jewish organizations (thereby undercounting mixed marriages).

55. Goldstein and Goldscheider, *op. cit.,* p. 389. Only present religious identification was counted, and the sample was drawn from membership lists of Jewish organizations.

56. Charles F. Westoff, Robert G. Potter, Jr., Philip C. Sagi, and Elliot G. Mishler, *Family Growth in Metropolitan America* (Princeton: Princeton University Press, 1961), p. 180. The intermarriage rate for individuals is stated in this volume as 4 per cent for Jews. Only present religious identification was counted, and the sample (being a study of fertility) was restricted not only to the largest

metropolitan areas but to those couples who had two children only, the second child being born in September, 1956.

57. Translated into intermarriage rates for *marriages,* this would be an increase from 33 per cent to 65 per cent. *Op. cit.,* pp. 428-30.

58. Thomas, "The Factor of Religion in the Selection of Marriage Mates," *op. cit.,* p. 489. Hyman Rodman noted that, in quoting Hollingshead's 6.2 rate for *individuals* and contrasting it with his 40.2 rate for *marriages,* Father Thomas exaggerated the difference here. See Rodman, "Textbook World of Family Sociology," *Social Problems,* 12 (1965), p. 452.

59. Heer, *op. cit.,* pp. 246-47. The values of Kendall's *tau* for the province trends vary from +.52 to +.91; for all of Canada it is +.88.

60. Reiss, *op. cit.,* p. 65.

61. Kennedy, *op. cit.,* pp. 333, 336.

62. Westoff *et al., op. cit.,* p. 180.

63. One reason that might help to explain the imbalance of this sample is that it was drawn from registrations of marriages contracted in July and October. The latter seems to be an unusually popular month for Catholic brides, as it was in this case. Also practicing Catholics must select some day outside of the seasons of Lent (March) and Advent (December) if they want to have a wedding in church.

64. "Religion Reported by the Civilian Population of the United States: March, 1957," *op. cit.,* p. 8.

65. Heer, *op. cit.,* p. 246. The values of Kendall's *tau* for the province trends vary from +.86 to +1.00; for all of Canada it is +1.00.

66. Thomas P. Monahan and Loren E. Chancellor, "Statistical Aspects of Marriage and Divorce by Religious Denomination in Iowa," *Eugenics Quarterly,* 2 (1955), pp. 162-73.

67. James H. Bossard and Harold C. Letts, "Mixed Marriages Involving Lutherans," *Marriage and Family Living,* 18 (1956), p. 308.

68. Leiffer, "Interfaith Marriages and Their Effect on the Religious Training of Children," *op. cit.,* pp. 442-54; also "Mixed Marriages and Church Loyalties," *Christian Century,* 66 (1949), pp. 78-80.

69. For example, see his "A Study of 194 Cross-Religion Marriages," *op. cit.,* pp. 3-7.

70. Westoff *et al., op. cit.,* p. 180. Respondents identified only their present religious preference, and only those couples were included who had just two children.

71. Arthur J. Vidich and Joseph Bensman, *Small Town in Mass Society: Class, Power and Religion in a Rural Community* (Princeton: Princeton University Press, 1958), p. 230.

72. Baar and Cahnman, *op. cit.,* pp. 54-55.

73. Rosenberg, *op. cit.,* p. 71.

74. "Religion Reported by the Civilian Population of the United States: March, 1957," *op. cit.*, p. 8.

75. Heiss, *op. cit.*, p. 49.

76. Rosenthal, *op. cit.*, pp. 50-51.

77. "Religion Reported by the Civilian Population of the United States: March, 1957," *op. cit.*, p. 8.

78. Heiss, *op. cit.*, p. 49.

79. "Religion Reported by the Civilian Population of the United

80. Heiss, *op. cit.*, p. 49.

81. Besanceney, "On Reporting Rates of Intermarriage," *op. cit.*, p. 720. A value of 1.00 would indicate the absence of endogamy. A look at part of the data suggested a very low rate of intermarriage for the Jews in Detroit, but their representation in the sample (about 3 per cent) seemed to be too small to justify separate analysis.

82. Glick, *op. cit.*, p. 35.

83. Heer, *op. cit.*, p. 247.

84. Ruppin, *op. cit.*, pp. 208-9.

85. David, *op. cit.*, p. 464.

86. Heer, *op. cit.*, p. 246. The value of Kendall's *tau* for the whole of Canada was +.90; for Quebec it was +.49.

87. J. Milton Yinger, *Journal for the Scientific Study of Religion*, 7 (Spring, 1968), pp. 97-103.

Chapter V

1. Milton Barron, *People Who Intermarry: Intermarriage in a New England Industrial Community* (Syracuse: Syracuse University Press, 1946), p. 194.

2. Maurice Fishberg, *The Jews: A Study of Race and Environment* (New York: Charles Scribner's Sons, 1911), p. 197.

3. Arthur Ruppin, *The Jewish Fate and Future*, trans. E. W. Dickes (London: Macmillan, 1940), p. 108.

4. Ruby Jo Reeves Kennedy, "Single or Triple Melting-Pot? Intermarriage Trends in New Haven, 1870-1940," *American Journal of Sociology*, 49 (1944), p. 333.

5. Erich Rosenthal, "Studies of Jewish Intermarriage in the United States," *American Jewish Year Book*, 64 (1963), p. 16.

6. *Ibid.*, p. 37.

7. Louis Rosenberg, "The Demography of the Jewish Community in Canada," *Jewish Journal of Sociology*, 1 (1959), p. 231.

8. John E. Mayer, "Jewish-Gentile Intermarriage Patterns: A Hypothesis," *Sociology and Social Research*, 45 (1961), pp. 191-93.

9. Barron, *op. cit.*, p. 171.

10. John L. Thomas, S.J., *The American Catholic Family* (Englewood Cliffs, N.J.: Prentice-Hall, 1956), p. 154.

11. Andrew M. Greeley, "Some Aspects of Interaction Between

Religious Groups in an Upper Middle Class Roman Catholic Parish," *Social Compass*, 9 (1962), p. 47.

12. Joseph H. Fichter, S.J., *Southern Parish, Vol. I; Dynamics of a City Church* (Chicago: University of Chicago Press, 1951), p. 107.

13. Bernard Van Leeuwen, O.F.M., "Le mariage mixte, facteur de déchristianisation en Hollande," *Lumen Vitae*, 4 (1949), p. 431.

14. Victor J. Traynor, S.J., "Urban and Rural Mixed Marriages," *Social Order*, 6 (1956), p. 156. Until there is more evidence available on the subject, it seems advisable to refrain from speculating about this difference in urban and rural patterns.

15. Charles F. Westoff *et al.*, *Family Growth in Metropolitan America* (Princeton: Princeton University Press, 1961), p. 180.

16. Alfred J. Prince, "A Study of 194 Cross-Religion Marriages," *Family Life Coordinator*, 11 (1962), p. 4.

17. Barron, *op. cit.*, p. 174.

18. James H. Bossard and Harold C. Letts, "Mixed Marriages Involving Lutherans," *Marriage and Family Living*, 18 (1956), p. 309.

19. For the ages 15 to 49, the ratio in the Detroit Standard Metropolitan Statistical Area was 94 men to 100 women in 1960; for the ages 50 to 69 it was 102 men to 100 women. After that age, female longevity took command. These ratios for whites only are derived from: U. S. Bureau of the Census, *U. S. Censuses of Population and Housing: 1960, Census Tracts, Detroit, Mich., Standard Metropolitan Statistical Area*, Final Report PHC (1)-40 (Washington: Government Printing Office, 1962), p. 79.

20. Milton Barron, "The Incidence of Jewish Intermarriage in Europe and America," *American Sociological Review*, 11 (1946), p. 13.

21. For Catholics in the income category $7,000-7,999, the rate was 56 per cent (N=72); and in the category $8,000 and over, it was 51 per cent (N=148)—compared to a rate of 42 per cent for all Catholics in this sample (N=776). These figures represent income of the family head only.

22. John L. Thomas, "Premarital Characteristics of the Religiously Intermarried in an Urban Area," *American Sociological Review*, 25 (1960), p. 53.

23. Jerold S. Heiss, "The Factor of Religion in the Selection of Marriage Mates," *American Sociological Review*, 16 (1951), p. 490.

24. August B. Hollingshead, "Cultural Factors in the Selection of Marriage Mates," *American Sociological Review*, 15 (1950), p. 626.

25. Rosenthal, *op. cit.*, p. 28.

26. Thomas P. Monahan and Loren E. Chancellor, "Statistical Aspects of Marriage and Divorce by Religious Denomination in Iowa," *Eugenics Quarterly*, 2 (1955), p. 164.

27. Traynor, *op. cit.*, p. 157.

28. Since the criterion here is the occupation of the husband's father, this means that young Catholic men and women whose fathers are in the higher occupations would be more likely to contract a religiously mixed marriage if they held to class endogamy (simply because Catholic marriage prospects are more scarce at this level). Furthermore, Catholic wives of Protestant husbands whose fathers were in these occupations would also appear in the 50.6 per cent of mixed marriages at that level. However, these would be cases of hypergamy, "marrying up." The same relationships persist when we look at the occupations of the husbands.

29. Rosenthal, *op. cit.*, pp. 25-27, 36, 43-44.

30. *Ibid.*, p. 22.

31. Hollingshead, *op. cit.*, p. 626.

32. *American Sociological Review*, 30 (1965), pp. 514-27.

33. Hollingshead, *op. cit.*, p. 624. Kennedy, *op. cit.*, p. 333.

34. Jerold S. Heiss, "Interfaith Marriage in an Urban Area" (unpublished Ph.D. dissertation, Indiana University, 1958), p. 107.

35. *Ibid.*

36. Julius Drachsler, *Democracy and Assimilation* (New York: Macmillan, 1920), pp. 121-22.

37. Rosenthal, *op. cit.*, p. 19.

38. Thomas, *op. cit.*, p. 490.

39. Lee G. Burchinal and Loren E. Chancellor, "Proportions of Catholics, Urbanism, and Mixed-Catholic Marriage Rates among Iowa Counties," *Social Problems*, 9 (1962), pp. 363, 365.

40. Rosenthal, *op. cit.*, p. 40.

41. *Ibid.*, p. 18.

Chapter VI

1. Loren E. Chancellor and Thomas P. Monahan, "Religious Preference and Interreligious Mixtures in Marriages and Divorces in Iowa," *American Journal of Sociology*, 61 (1955), p. 259.

2. Jerold S. Heiss, "Pre-marital Characteristics of the Religiously Intermarried in an Urban Area," *American Sociological Review*, 25 (1960), p. 48.

3. *Ibid.*, p. 53.

4. *Ibid.*, p. 50.

5. Gerald J. Schnepp, "Three Mixed Marriage Questions Answered," *Catholic World*, 156 (1942), p. 204. Also: Paul H. Besanceney, "Unbroken Protestant-Catholic Marriages among Whites in the Detroit Area," *American Catholic Sociological Review*, 23 (1962), p. 15.

6. Heiss, *op. cit.*, p. 50.

7. Milton L. Barron, "The Incidence of Jewish Intermarriage in Europe and America," *American Sociological Review*, 11 (1946), p. 13.

8. John L. Thomas, *The American Catholic Family* (Englewood Cliffs, N.J.: Prentice-Hall, 1956), p. 50.

9. David M. Heer, "The Trend of Interfaith Marriages in Canada: 1922-1957," *American Sociological Review*, 27 (1962), p. 250.

10. Heiss, *op. cit.*, p. 50.

11. Carleton S. Coon, "Have the Jews a Racial Identity?" in Isacque Graeber and Steuart H. Britt (eds.), *Jews in the Gentile World* (New York: Macmillan, 1942), Chapter 1.

12. Bernard Van Leeuwen, O.F.M., "Le mariage mixte, facteur de déchristianisation en Hollande," *Lumen Vitae*, 4 (1949), p. 430.

13. Lee G. Burchinal and Loren E. Chancellor, "Catholics, Urbanism, and Mixed-Catholic Marriage Rates," *Social Problems*, 9 (1962), p. 363.

14. Thomas P. Monahan and Loren E. Chancellor, "Statistical Aspects of Marriage and Divorce by Religious Denominations in Iowa," *Eugenics Quarterly*, 2 (1955), p. 164.

15. Heiss, *op. cit.*, p. 51.

16. Thomas F. Coakley, "Mixed Marriages, Their Causes, Their Effects, Their Prevention," *Lumen Vitae*, 4 (1949), p. 456.

17. John L. Thomas, S.J., "The Factor of Religion in the Selection of Marriage Mates," *American Sociological Review*, 16 (1951), p. 489.

18. Victor J. Traynor, S.J., "Urban and Rural Mixed Marriages," *Social Order*, 6 (1956), p. 157.

19. Heiss, *op. cit.*, p. 51.

20. Auguste Comte, *The Positive Philosophy of Auguste Comte*, trans. Harriet Martineau (New York: Calvin Blanchard, 1858), p. 46.

21. Emile Durkheim, *The Rules of Sociological Method*, trans. Sarah A. Solovay and John H. Mueller, ed. George E. Catlin (8th ed.; Glencoe, Ill.: Free Press, 1958), p. 3.

22. William G. Sumner, *Folkways: A Study of the Sociological Importance of Usages, Manners, Customs, Mores, and Morals* (New York: Mentor Book, 1960), p. 49.

23. Ralph Linton, *The Study of Man: An Introduction* (New York: Appleton-Century-Crofts, 1936), p. 105.

. 24. George C. Homans, *The Human Group* (New York: Harcourt, Brace, 1950), p. 123.

25. *Ibid.*, p. 125.

26. Talcott Parsons, *The Social System* (Glencoe, Ill.: Free Press, 1951), pp. 13-14.

27. Robin Williams, *American Society: A Sociological Interpretation* (New York: Alfred A. Knopf, 1959), p. 25.

28. For example, Ronald Freedman *et al.*, *Principles of Sociology*

(rev.; New York: Henry Holt, 1956), pp. 122-24; Tamotsu Shibutani, *Society and Personality* (Englewood Cliffs, N.J.: Prentice-Hall, 1961), pp. 40-46; Muzafer and Carolyn W. Sherif, *An Outline of Social Psychology* (rev. ed.; New York: Harper, 1956), pp. 237-79.

29. Dorwin Cartwright and Alvin Zander review the work of Sherif, Asch, and others in their editorial comments in *Group Dynamics: Research and Theory* (2nd ed.; Evanston, Ill.: Row, Peterson, 1960), pp. 165-88. Two good examples of recent research using this concept are found in the same volume: Leon Festinger, Stanley Schacter, and Kurt Back, "The Operation of Group Standards," pp. 241-59; and Stanley Schacter, "Deviation, Rejection, and Communications," pp. 260-85.

30. See, for example, *Society and Self: A Reader in Social Psychology*, ed. Bartlett H. Stoodley (New York: Free Press of Glencoe, 1962), pp. 203-15, "Normative Attitudes of Filipino Youth Compared with German and American Youth." Also: Ephraim H. Mizruchi and Robert Perucci, "Norm Qualities and Differential Effects of Deviant Behavior: An Exploratory Analysis," *American Sociological Review*, 27 (1962), pp. 391-99.

31. Homans, *op. cit.*, p. 269.

32. Florian Znaniecki, "Social Organizations and Institutions," *Twentieth Century Sociology*, ed. George Gurvitch and Wilbert E. Moore (New York: Philosophical Library, 1945), p. 199.

33. Robert M. MacIver and Charles H. Page, *Society: An Introductory Analysis* (New York: Rinehart, 1949), p. 15.

34. *Ibid.*

35. Williams, *op. cit.*, p. 29.

36. Cf. Sumner, *op. cit.*, p. 61; Robert C. Angell, *The Integration of American Society: A Study of Groups and Institutions* (New York: McGraw-Hill, 1941), p. 25; Joyce O. Hertzler, *American Social Institutions: A Sociological Analysis* (Boston: Allyn and Bacon, 1961), p. v; Constantine Panunzio, *Major Social Institutions: An Introduction* (New York: Macmillan, 1939), p. 546; Everett C. Hughes, "Institutions," *Principles of Sociology*, ed. Alfred M. Lee (2nd ed., rev.; New York: Barnes and Noble, 1959), p. 230.

37. Parsons, *op. cit.*, pp. 39-40.

38. *Ibid.*, p. 59.

39. *Ibid.*, p. 67.

40. *Ibid.*, p. 97.

41. Hertzler, *op. cit.*, p. 225.

42. Williams, *op. cit.*, p. 32.

43. Albion W. Small and George E. Vincent, *An Introduction to the Study of Society* (New York: American Book, 1894), p. 328.

44. Edward A. Ross, *Social Control: A Survey of the Foundations of Order* (New York: Macmillan, 1901).

45. *Papers and Proceedings of the American Sociological Society,* 12 (1917).

46. Luther L. Bernard, *Social Control in Its Sociological Aspects* (New York: Macmillan, 1939); Jerome Dowd, *Control in Human Societies* (New York: D. Appleton-Century, 1936); Paul H. Landis, *Social Control: Social Organization and Disorganization in Process* (rev.; Philadelphia: Lippincott, 1956); Richard T. LaPiere, *A Theory of Control* (New York: McGraw-Hill, 1954); Frederick E. Lumley, *The Means of Social Control* (New York: Century, 1925); *Social Control,* ed. Joseph S. Roucek (New York: D. Van Nostrand, 1947); somewhat revised in 1956.

47. Georges Gurvitch, "Social Control," *Twentieth Century Sociology,* ed. Georges Gurvitch and Wilbert E. Moore (New York: Philosophical Library, 1945), pp. 267-96. See also: August B. Hollingshead, "The Concept of Social Control," *American Sociological Review,* 6 (1941), pp. 217-24; Joseph S. Roucek, "The Development and Status of Social Control in American Sociology," *American Sociological Review,* 20 (1959), pp. 107-23.

48. For instance, Homans, *op. cit.;* Parsons, *op. cit.;* Shibutani, *op. cit.*

49. For example, Roscoe Pound, *Social Control Through Law* (New Haven: Yale University Press, 1942); Gordon C. Zahn, *German Catholics and Hitler's Wars: A Study in Social Control* (New York: Sheed and Ward, 1962).

50. Charles Loomis, *Social Systems* (Princeton: Van Nostrand, 1960), p. 35.

51. Hollingshead, *op. cit.,* p. 221.

52. Homans, *op. cit.,* p. 301.

53. William T. Liu and Frank Fahey, "Delinquency, Self-Esteem, and Social Controls: A Retroductive Analysis," *American Catholic Sociological Review,* 24 (1963), pp. 3-12.

54. Landis, *op. cit.,* p. 8.

55. For a good review of such studies, see: Irvin L. Child, "Socialization," *Handbook of Social Psychology,* ed. Gardner Lindzey (Reading, Mass.: 1954), pp. 655-92.

56. Parsons, *op. cit.,* p. 298.

57. *Ibid.,* p. 301.

58. Talcott Parsons and Robert F. Bales, *Family, Socialization and Interaction Process* (Glencoe, Ill.: Free Press, 1955), p. 39.

59. Landis, *op. cit.,* p. 148.

60. Homans, *op. cit.,* p. 290.

61. William R. Catton, "The Functions and Dysfunctions of Ethnocentrism: A Theory," *Social Problems,* 8 (1960-61), p. 204.

62. Parsons, *op. cit.,* p. 250.

63. Emile Durkheim, *The Division of Labor,* trans. George Simpson (Glencoe, Ill.: Free Press, 1947), pp. 102-3.

64. Homans, *op. cit.,* p. 310. For a fuller discussion of the same point, see Kaï T. Erikson, "Notes on the Sociology of Deviance," *Social Problems,* 9 (1962), pp. 307-14.

65. Robert K. Merton, *Social Theory and Social Structure* (rev.; Glencoe, Ill.: Free Press, 1957), pp. 360-63.

66. Durkheim, *The Division of Labor in Society, op. cit.,* p. 368; *Suicide: A Study in Sociology,* trans. John A. Spaulding and George Simpson, ed. George Simpson (Glencoe, Ill.: Free Press, 1951), pp. 241-76.

67. Isabel Cary-Lundberg, "On Durkheim, Suicide, and Anomie," *American Sociological Review,* 24 (1959) p. 250.

68. Loomis, *op. cit.,* p. 36.

69. Merton, *op. cit.,* p. 163.

70. *Ibid.,* p. 162.

71. Leo Srole, "Social Integration and Certain Corollaries: An Exploratory Study," *American Sociological Review,* 21 (1956), pp. 710-12.

72. Melvin Seeman, "On the Meaning of Alienation," *American Sociological Review,* 24 (1959), pp. 783-91.

73. Charles J. Browning, Malcolm F. Farmer, H. David Kirk, and G. Duncan Mitchell, "On the Meaning of Alienation," *American Sociological Review,* 26 (1961), pp. 780-81.

74. Srole, *op. cit.,* p. 711.

75. Gwynn Nettler, "A Measure of Alienation," *American Sociological Review,* 22 (1957), pp. 670-77.

76. Dwight G. Dean, "Alienation: Its Meaning and Measurement," *American Sociological Review,* 26 (1961), pp. 753-58.

77. Durkheim, *Suicide, op. cit.,* p. 260.

78. Dorothy L. Meier and Wendell Bell, "Anomia and Differential Access to the Achievement of Life Goals," *American Sociological Review,* 24 (1959), p. 200.

79. Dwight Dean and Jon A. Reeves, "Anomie: A Comparison of a Catholic and a Protestant Sample," *Sociometry,* 25 (1962), p. 211.

80. Merton, *op. cit.,* p. 157.

81. Durkheim, *op. cit.,* pp. 257-58.

82. Merton, *op. cit.,* p. 144.

83. Ephraim H. Mizruchi, "Social Structure and Anomia in a Small City," *American Sociological Review,* 25 (1960), p. 647.

84. Merton, *op. cit.,* pp. 139 ff.

85. Parsons, *op. cit.,* pp. 256 ff.

86. Robert Dubin, "Deviant Behavior and Social Structure," *American Sociological Review,* 24 (1959), pp. 147-64. Merton gives his reactions in the same issue of the *Review:* "Social Conformity,

Deviation and Opportunity-Structures: A Comment on the Contributions of Dubin and Cloward," pp. 177-89.

87. Festinger, Schacter, and Back, "The Operation of Group Standards," *op. cit.*; and Schacter, "Deviation, Rejection, and Communication," *op. cit.*

88. Howard Becker, "Normative Reactions to Normlessness," *American Sociological Review*, 25 (1960), pp. 803-10.

89. Alexander L. Clark and Jack P. Gibbs, "Social Control: A Reformulation," *Social Problems*, 12 (1965), pp. 401-2. These writers go on to construct an intelligent classification of actual and normative reactions, as well as actual and normative reactors.

90. Jack P. Gibbs, "Norms: The Problem of Definition and Classification," *American Journal of Sociology*, 70 (1965), pp. 588-89.

Chapter VII

1. Exodus 34:16. Translation by the Confraternity of Christian Doctrine (Washington, D. C.: Confraternity of Christian Doctrine, 1952).

2. Stanislaus Woywood, O.F.M., "Marriages between Catholics and Non-Catholics," *Homiletic and Pastoral Review*, 40 (1940), p. 411.

3. *Ibid.*, pp. 412-14.

4. *Ibid.*, p. 416.

5. Algernon D. Black, *If I Marry Outside My Religion* (New York: Public Affairs Pamphlets, 1954), p. 14.

6. Woywood, *op. cit.*, pp. 417-18.

7. Stanislaus Woywood, O.F.M., "Marriage Impediment of Mixed Religion," *Homiletic and Pastoral Review*, 40 (1940), p. 634.

8. Black, *op. cit.*, p. 15.

9. James A. Pike, *If You Marry Outside Your Faith* (New York: Harper, 1954), pp. 93-98.

10. *Toledo Catholic Chronicle*, March 25, 1966, p. 3.

11. *Toledo Catholic Chronicle*, March 3, 1967, p. 5.

12. Walter M. Abbott, S.J. (ed.), *The Documents of Vatican II* (New York: Guild Press, 1966), p. 381.

13. James H. Bossard and Eleanor S. Boll, *One Marriage, Two Faiths: Guidance on Interfaith Marriage* (New York: Ronald Press, 1957), p. 84.

14. M. Evodine McGrath, O.S.F., *The Role of the Catholic College in Preparing for Marriage and Family Life* (Washington: Catholic University Press, 1952), Table 2, p. 22.

15. Edgar Schmiedeler, O.S.B., *Looking Toward Marriage* (Washington: Family Life Bureau, National Catholic Welfare Conference, 1948); and *Marriage and the Family* (New York: McGraw-Hill, 1946). See also: Alphonse H. Clemens, *Marriage and the Family: An*

Integrated Approach for Catholics (Englewood Cliffs, N. J.: Prentice-Hall, 1957); Clement S. Mihanovich, Gerald J. Schnepp, and John L. Thomas, *A Guide to Catholic Marriage* (Milwaukee: Bruce, 1955).

16. For example, Henry A. Bowman, *Marriage for Moderns* (4th ed.; New York: McGraw-Hill, 1960), pp. 171-205.

17. John C. Wynn, *How Christian Parents Face Family Problems* (Philadelphia: Westminster Press, 1955).

18. Mario Colacci, *Christian Marriage Today* (Minneapolis: Augsburg Press, 1958).

19. George A. Kelly, *The Catholic Marriage Manual* (New York: Random House, 1958); and *The Catholic Family Handbook* (New York: Dell Publishing, 1962). See also: John A. O'Brien, *Happy Marriage* (New York: Popular Library, 1957).

20. Alfred M. Lee, "Socialization of the Individual," *Principles of Sociology*, ed. Alfred M. Lee (New York: Barnes and Noble, 1959); p. 309; J. O. Hertzler, *American Social Institutions: A Sociological Analysis* (Boston: Allyn and Bacon, 1961), p. 228; George Simpson and J. Milton Yinger, *Racial and Cultural Minorities* (rev.; New York: Harper, 1958), p. 568.

21. Glenn M. Vernon, "Interfaith Marriages—Bias in Professional Publications," *Religious Education*, 55 (1960), pp. 261-64.

22. For example, see: Anonymous, "What it Means to Marry A Catholic," *The Forum*, 81 (1929), pp. 339-45; Thomas W. Beesley, "What It Means to Marry a Protestant," *The Forum*, 82 (1929), pp. 226-30; A Catholic Husband and a Protestant Wife, "I Love You, But . . .," *Sign*, 31 (1952), pp. 12-15, 74-76; Maxwell Hamilton, "We Wouldn't Marry Each Other Again," *Catholic Digest*, 19 (1955), pp. 8-11; Carl Bakal, "The Risks You Take in Interfaith Marriage," *Good Housekeeping*, 149 (1959), p. 62.

23. Alfred Prince, "Attitudes of College Students toward Inter-Faith Marriages," *Marriage and Family Living*, 19 (1957), p. 120, abstract from *The Coordinator*, 5 (1956), pp. 11-23.

24. Harry E. Hoover, *Attitudes of High-School Students toward Mixed Marriages* (Washington: Catholic University Press, 1950), p. 51.

25. *Ibid.*, p. 58.

26. Gerhard Lenski, *The Religious Factor: A Sociological Study of Religion's Impact on Politics, Economics, and Family Life* (Garden City, N.Y.: Doubleday, 1961), pp. 48-49.

27. Albert I. Gordon, *Intermarriage: Interfaith, Interracial, Inter-ethnic* (Boston: Beacon Press, 1964), pp. 15-37.

28. Robert M. MacIver and Charles H. Page, *Society: An Introductory Analysis* (New York: Rinehart, 1949), p. 199.

29. Georg Simmel, *The Web of Group-Affiliations*, trans. Reinhard Bendix (Glencoe, Ill.: Free Press, 1955).

30. H. B. and Ava C. English, *A Comprehensive Dictionary of Psychological and Psychoanalytic Terms* (New York: Longmans, Green, 1958), p. 232.

31. Robert K. Merton, *Social Theory and Social Structure* (rev. ed.; Glencoe, Ill.: Free Press, 1957), p. 290.

32. Everett V. Stonequist, *The Marginal Man: A Study in Personality and Culture Conflict* (New York: Charles Scribner's Sons, 1937), p. 3.

33. Lenski, *op. cit.*, p. 9.

34. Even if we were to focus on secularism as a characteristic of a society, it would not be so much in terms of Lenski's "religious neutralism" as in the sense employed by J. Anthony Samenfink: "At the present writing the word 'secular' is used to denote a society whose morality is 'based solely upon regard to the well-being of mankind in the present life, to the exclusion of all considerations drawn from belief in God or in a future state.'" In "A Study of Some Aspects of Marital Behavior as Related to Religious Control," *Marriage and Family Living*, 20 (1958), p. 164.

35. Paul Landis, *Social Control: Social Organization and Disorganization in Process* (rev.; Philadelphia: Lippincott, 1956), p. 14. For a criticism of this "commitment to a belief in '*the total* historical process,'" see Christopher B. Becker's introduction to his father's posthumous Presidential address to the American Sociological Association, Howard Becker, "Normative Reactions to Normlessness," *American Sociological Review*, 25 (1960), p. 804.

36. Will Herberg, *Protestant—Catholic—Jew: An Essay in American Religious Sociology* (New York: Doubleday, 1955), p. 96.

37. *Ibid.*, p. 288.

38. Mabel A. Elliot and Francis E. Merrill, *Social Disorganization* (3rd ed.; New York: Harper, 1950), pp. 357-58.

39. James H. Bossard and Eleanor Boll, *Ritual in Family Living* (Philadelphia: University of Pennsylvania Press, 1950), p. 22.

40. Bossard and Boll, *One Marriage, Two Faiths, op. cit.*, p. 91.

41. Samenfink, *op. cit.*, p. 169.

42. Joseph Maier and William Spinrad, "Comparison of Religious Beliefs and Practices of Jewish, Catholic, and Protestant Students," *Phylon*, 18 (1958), pp. 356-58.

43. Lenski, *op. cit.*, p. 86.

44. *Ibid.*, p. 219.

45. Albert J. Mayer and Harry Sharp, "Religious Preference and Worldly Success," *American Sociological Review*, 27 (1962), p. 226.

46. Lee G. Burchinal and William F. Kenkel, "Religious Identification and Occupational Status of Grooms," *American Sociological Review*, 27 (1962), p. 531.

47. Joseph Veroff, Sheila Feld, and Gerald Gurin, "Achievement Motivation and Religious Background," *American Sociological Review*, 27 (1962), pp. 205-17.

48. Mayer and Sharp, *op. cit.*, p. 218. See Chapter III, above, for the ways in which striving for status shows itself in mate selection in general.

49. Landis, *op. cit.*, p. 898.

50. Hertzler, *op. cit.*, p. 241. For a similar statement, see James H. Tufts, *America's Social Morality* (New York: Henry Holt, 1953), p. 94.

51. Robin Williams, *American Society: A Sociological Interpretation* (New York: Alfred A. Knopf), 1959, p. 74.

52. Pike, *op. cit.*, p. 63.

53. One of the most consistent expressions of this theme is found in Ernest Burgess and Harvey Locke, *The Family: From Institution to Companionship* (2nd ed.; New York: American Book Co., 1960).

54. Robert O. Blood, Jr., and Donald M. Wolfe, *Husbands and Wives: The Dynamics of Married Living* (Glencoe, Ill.: Free Press, 1960), p. 257.

55. Lenski, *op. cit.*, p. 49.

Chapter VIII

1. Stanley K. Bigman, *The Jewish Population of Greater Washington in 1956* (Washington: Jewish Community Council, 1957), p. 141.

2. Alfred J. Prince, "A Study of 194 Cross-Religion Marriages," *The Family Life Coordinator*, 11 (1962), p. 6.

3. Harry M. Johnson, *Sociology: A Systematic Introduction* (New York: Harcourt, Brace, and World, 1960), p. 168.

4. Georg Karlsson, "On Mate Selection," *International Journal of Comparative Sociology*, 3 (1962), p. 92.

5. Ray E. Baber, "Some Mate Selection Standards of College Students and Their Parents," *Journal of Social Hygiene*, 22 (1936), pp. 123-24. Alfred J. Prince, "Factors in Mate Selection," *The Family Life Coordinator*, 10 (1960), p. 57.

6. Peter I. Rose, "Small-town Jews and Their Neighbors in the United States," *Jewish Journal of Sociology*, 3 (1962), p. 183. Hershel Shanks, "Jewish-Gentile Intermarriage: Facts and Trends," *Commentary*, 16 (1953), p. 374. Marshall Sklare and Marc Vosk, *The Riverton Study: How Jews Look at Themselves and Their Neighbors* (New York: American Jewish Committee, 1957), pp. 32-37.

7. Reuben R. Resnik, "Some Sociological Aspects of Intermarriage of Jew and Non-Jew," *Social Forces*, 12 (1933), p. 99.

8. John E. Mayer, *Jewish-Gentile Courtships: An Exploratory Study of a Social Process* (New York: Free Press of Glencoe, 1961), pp. 125-77.

9. *Ibid.*, p. 177.

10. Alan Bates, "Parental Roles in Courtship," *Social Forces*, 20 (1942), p. 483.

11. Marvin Sussman, "Parental Participation in Mate Selection and Its Effects upon Family Continuity," *Social Forces*, 32 (1953), pp. 78-79.

12. Bigman, *op. cit.*, p. 128.

13. Mayer, *op. cit.*, pp. 179-98.

14. Leonard Blumberg and Robert R. Bell, "Urban Migration and Kinship Ties," *Social Problems*, 6 (1959), pp. 328-33. Eugene Litwak, "The Use of Extended Family Groups in the Achievement of Social Goals: Some Policy Implications," *Social Problems*, 7 (1960), pp. 177-87. Eugene Litwak, "Geographic Mobility and Extended Family Cohesion," *American Sociological Review*, 25 (1960), pp. 385-94. Marvin B. Sussman, "The Isolated Nuclear Family: Fact or Fiction," *Social Problems*; 6 (1959), pp. 333-40.

15. Gerhard Lenski, *The Religious Factor* (Garden City, N.Y.: Doubleday, 1961), pp. 219-23.

16. *Ibid.*, p. 245.

17. Paul H. Besanceney, S.J., "Interfaith Marriages of Catholics in the Detroit Area," *Sociological Analysis*, 26 (1965), p. 41.

18. Gerald J. Schnepp, S.M., *The Family Today: A Catholic Appraisal* (Washington: National Catholic Welfare Conference, 1944), p. 110.

19. Peter H. and Alice S. Rossi, "Some Effects of Parochial School Education in America," *Daedalus*, 90 (1960), p. 314.

20. Andrew M. Greeley and Peter H. Rossi, *The Education of Catholic Americans* (Chicago: Aldine, 1966), p. 68.

21. Lee G. Burchinal, "Membership Groups and Attitudes Toward Cross-Religious Dating and Marriage," *Marriage and Family Living*, 22 (1960), p. 253.

22. Alfred J. Prince, "Attitudes of College Students Toward Inter-Faith Marriages," *Marriage and Family Living*, 19 (1957), p. 120.

23. Related aspects treated elsewhere in this book are as follows: Chapter III—"Ethnic Intermarriage"; Chapter IV—"The 'triple melting-pot hypothesis'"; Chapter V—"Religious Intermarriage and Nationality Groups"; Chapter VI—some illustrations before the reader was introduced to the whole set of our hypotheses.

24. Francis J. Brown and Joseph S. Roucek (ed.), *One America: The History, Contributions, and Present Problems of Our Racial and National Minorities* (rev.; New York: Prentice-Hall, 1945), p. 264.

25. Oscar Handlin, *The Uprooted* (New York: Grosset and Dunlap, 1951), p. 117.

26. William L. Warner and Leo Srole, *The Social Systems of*

American Ethnic Groups (New Haven: Yale University Press, 1945), p. 218.

27. William C. Smith, *Americans in the Making: The Natural History of the Assimilation of Immigrants* (New York: D. Appleton-Century, 1939), p. 362.

28. Will Herberg, *Protestant–Catholic–Jew* (New York: Doubleday, 1955), pp. 31, 42.

29. Lenski, *op. cit.*, pp. 41-43. Another apparent exception to this were the Southern-born white Protestant migrants to Detroit, who showed no more religious activity by his measures than first-generation foreign immigrants, even though the former were at least sixth-generation Americans.

30. Joseph P. Fitzpatrick, "Intermarriage of Puerto Ricans in New York City," *American Journal of Sociology*, 71 (1966), pp. 403-4.

31. Herberg, *op. cit.*, p. 43.

32. Bigman, *op. cit.*, p. 133.

33. Erich Rosenthal, "Studies of Jewish Intermarriage in the United States," *American Jewish Year Book*, 64 (1963), p. 19.

34. *Ibid.*, p. 39.

Chapter IX

1. Ernest R. Mowrer, "Social Crises and Social Disorganization," *American Sociological Review*, 15 (1950), p. 65.

2. Paul J. Reiss, "The Trend in Interfaith Marriages," *Journal for the Scientific Study of Religion*, 5 (1965), p. 65.

3. Lee G. Burchinal and Loren E. Chancellor, "Ages at Marriage, Occupations of Grooms, and Interreligious Marriage Rates," *Social Forces*, 40 (1962), p. 350.

4. John H. Burma, "Interethnic Marriage in Los Angeles, 1948-1959," *Social Forces*, 42 (1963), p. 165.

5. Loren E. Chancellor and Thomas P. Monahan, "Religious Preference and Interreligious Mixtures in Marriages and Divorces in Iowa," *American Journal of Sociology*, 61 (1955), p. 237. Harold T. Christensen and Kenneth E. Barber, "Interfaith Versus Intrafaith Marriage in Indiana," *Journal of Marriage and the Family*, 29 (1967), p. 465.

6. Niles Carpenter, *The Sociology of City Life* (New York: Longmans, Green, 1931), pp. 217-18.

7. If, for the moment, we assume that white Protestants and Catholics constitute the total population born in the Detroit area, we can compute a statistic such as we used for the overall intermarriage rates before (p. 56 and note 26 of Chapter IV). Then the "expected" intermarriage rate for Protestants born in Detroit would be .58 and for Catholics .42. The ratio of the actual to the expected rate of intermarriage then becomes the same for both Protestants

and Catholics—.69. When this rough method of controlling for the size of the group has been used, Protestant native Detroiters intermarry no more often than do the Catholic native Detroiters.

8. Emile Durkheim, *Suicide: A Study in Sociology*, trans. John A. Spaulding and George Simpson, ed. George Simpson (Glencoe, Ill.: Free Press, 1951), pp. 246-54.

9. Gerhard Lenski, *The Religious Factor: A Sociological Study of Religion's Impact on Politics, Economics, and Family Life* (Garden City, N.Y.: Doubleday, 1961), p. 110. Since we are including Lenski's data in this secondary analysis, a word of explanation regarding this hypothesis is called for. Religiously homogeneous marriage was one of the criteria he used for involvement in the religious community (together with the criterion of having all of almost all of one's relatives and friends in the same religious community). One might conclude that we are predicting what he has already demonstrated with the same data. We are, of course, reversing the order of prediction from his communal involvement leading to the lack of occupational mobility (for *daughters* as well as sons) to our predictive order of occupational mobility leading to interfaith marriage (comparing *sons* with their fathers). As Lenski would readily grant, there is no way at present to choose between these two orders of causality except to see how they fit into a broader theoretical scheme. A careful longitudinal study may some day clarify the situation. We must also call attention now to the fact that we are using not only Lenski's 1958 data in Table 11, but also Blood's 1955 data and Swanson's 1959 data. Actually, the number of cases from the 1955 survey is larger in this table than the other two surveys combined. So we are not simply restating old evidence in a new form.

10. For reasons supporting this assumption of ranks, see Seymour Lipset and Reinhard Bendix, *Social Mobility in Industrial Society* (Berkeley: University of California Press, 1959), pp. 14-16.

11. *Ibid.*, pp. 17, 88.

12. *Ibid.*, p. 56.

13. *Ibid.*, pp. 51-54.

14. Lenski, *op. cit.*, pp. 76-77.

15. Robert K. Merton, *Social Theory and Social Structure* (rev.; Glencoe, Ill.: Free Press, 1957), p. 265. However, the fact that Merton also finds this anticipation in a group's "isolates," who are not mobile, means that mobility does not necessarily follow from anticipatory socialization. *Ibid.*, p. 305.

16. "Occupational Mobility and Church Participation," *Social Forces*, 38 (1960), p. 316.

17. Lipset and Bendix, *op. cit.*, p. 65.

18. Eugene Litwak, "Occupational Mobility and Extended Family Cohesion," *American Sociological Review*, 25 (1960), pp. 9-21; "Geo-

graphic Mobility and Extended Family Cohesion," *American Sociological Review*, 25 (1960), pp. 385-94.

19. Richard L. Simpson and H. Max Miller, "Social Status and Anomia," *Social Problems*, 10 (1963), p. 262.

Chapter X

1. Further verification of this was found in the author's 1967 survey of all the students in four Jesuit high schools in the areas of Akron, Cleveland, Detroit, and Toledo. According to the answers these boys gave regarding their parents' religious preferences, only *one out of three* of those marriages which were mixed in religious background is still mixed (N=815).

2. Stanislaus Woywood, O.F.M., *Homilitic and Pastoral Review*, 28 (1928), pp. 703-11.

3. Bernard A. Sause, O.S.B., *Why Catholic Marriage is Different* (St. Louis: B. Herder, 1937), pp. 81-82.

4. John C. Heenan, *They Made Me Sign: A Series of Talks to a Non-Catholic about to Marry a Catholic* (New York: Sheed and Ward, 1949), p. 104.

5. George A. Kelly, *The Catholic Family Handbook* (New York: Random House and Dell Publishing, 1959), pp. 257-72.

6. George A. Kelly, *The Catholic Marriage Manual* (New York: Random House, 1958), pp. 167-74. See also: John A. O'Brien, *Happy Marriage* (New York: Popular Library, 1957), pp. 91-119.

7. O'Brien, *op. cit.*, Ch. 7: "Converting Mixed Courtships into Catholic Marriages," pp. 120-63.

8. Walter M. Abbott, S.J. (ed.), *The Documents of Vatican II* (New York: Guild Press, 1966).

9. Walter M. Abbott, S.J., "Two Council Fathers: Cardinal Leger and Cardinal Cushing," *America*, 108 (1963), p. 865. On proposed changes see also: Bertulf van Leeuwen, O.F.M., "Législation de mariages mixtes et rapports entre catholiques et protestants," *Social Compass*, 11 (1964), pp. 1-12.

10. "Mixed Marriage Question," *America*, 109 (1963), p. 8.

11. *Toledo Catholic Chronicle*, March 25, 1966, p. 3.

12. Ladislas M. Orsy, S.J., "Mixed Marriages," *America*, 117 (1967), p. 245.

13. William J. Sullivan *et al.*, *Mixed Marriage: An Honest Appraisal* (St. Meinrad, Ind.: Abbey Press, 1966). Also A. M. J. Kreykamp, O.P., *et al.*, *Protestant-Catholic Marriages: Interpreted by Pastors and Priests*, trans. Isaac C. Rottenberg (Philadelphia: Westminster Press, 1967).

14. "Joint Care of Mixed Marriages?," *Herder Correspondence*, 4

(1967), pp. 19-20. Also " 'Mixed Marriage' Retreat," *America,* 118 (June 29, 1968).

15. Paul and Jeanne Simon, *Protestant-Catholic Marriages Can Succeed* (New York: Association Press, 1967). Also: Mary Gregory Low, "I Mixed Our Unmixed Marriage," in Sullivan *et al., op. cit.,* pp. 92-108.

Appendix A

1. Most of the facts in this section are drawn from George B. Catlin, *The Story of Detroit* (Detroit: Evening News Association, 1923). This was recommended to the writer by a librarian of the Burton Historical Collection at the Detroit Public Library as "the best single-volume history of Detroit."

2. *Detroit Free Press,* December 8, 1874.

3. Lois Rankin, "Detroit Nationality Groups," *Michigan History Magazine,* 23 (1939), p. 177.

4. Donald J. Bogue, *Population Growth in Standard Metropolitan Areas, 1900-1950* (Washington: Government Printing Office, 1953), pp. 62-69.

5. *Detroit News,* January 10, 1926.

6. City Plan Commission, *Economic Base of Detroit* (Detroit: City Plan Commission, 1944), p. 7.

7. Derived from Albert J. Mayer and Harry Sharp, "Religious Preference and Worldly Success," *American Sociological Review,* 27 (1962), p. 221.

8. For a fuller description, see Ronald Freedman, "The Detroit Area Study: A Training and Research Laboratory in the Community," *American Journal of Sociology,* 59 (1953), pp. 30-33; and Harry Sharp, "Graduate Training Through the Detroit Area Study," *American Sociological Review,* 26 (1961), pp. 110-14. A complete bibliography of studies based on Detroit Area Study research since 1951 can be obtained from the Department of Sociology, Survey Research Center, University of Michigan.

The faculty participants whose data are being reanalyzed in this book are: 1955 — Robert O. Blood and Morris Axelrod; 1958 — Gerhard Lenski; 1959 — Guy E. Swanson and Harvey Brazer; 1962 — Ronald Freedman and David Goldberg. The Directors of the Detroit Area Study during this period were Harry Sharp (1954-61) and John C. Scott (1961-65).

9. To provide further details for those who are interested: After primary sampling units were determined and stratified according to size of population, geographic location, and economic values, selection from each stratum was based on a table of random numbers. Wherever possible, city directories were used (after checking for

completeness) for systematic sampling of pages and then of addresses, in clusters of three. A "block supplement" method was used to augment the city directory sample. Each dwelling unit was given the same probability of being selected for the sample, a sampling fraction of 1/1100 being used in 1958 and 1959. In fact, the clusters of three just referred to were meant to yield three subsamples, two of which were used in 1958 and 1959. For 1955 the sampling procedure was almost the same, except that the sampling fraction was 1/900. If requested, the Detroit Area Study will supply the following detailed descriptions of the sampling procedure for each of the three years: John Takeshita, "Selection of a Sample of Dwelling Units for the Detroit Area Study, 1954-55," #1070, mimeographed; "The Sample Design for the 1957-58 Detroit Area Study," #1443, mimeographed; "Selection of Sample: Detroit Area Study, 1958-59," #1458, mimeographed. The problem of combining these samples into one study has also been carefully investigated by C. Michael Lanphier, former research assistant for the Detroit Area Study.

10. Robert O. Blood, Jr., and Donald M. Wolfe, *Husbands and Wives: The Dynamics of Married Living* (Glencoe, Ill.: Free Press, 1960), pp. 276-80; Gerhard Lenski, *The Religious Factor: A Sociologist's Inquiry* (Garden City, N.Y.: Doubleday, 1961), pp. 331-40.

11. "Measures of Sampling Error," Project 855, Detroit Area Study, Survey Research Center, University of Michigan, April, 1959, mimeographed.

12. For a detailed evaluation of the surveys of 1956, 1957, and 1958, see Harry Sharp and Allan Feldt, "Some Factors in a Probability Sample Survey of a Metropolitan Community," *American Sociological Review*, 24 (1959), pp. 650-61.

13. Catholic wives are overrepresented in this small sample by about 10 per cent. The reason for this is that there are two penitential seasons in the year, the four weeks of Advent just before Christmas and the six weeks of Lent before Easter, in which Roman Catholics may not have a wedding in church. This means that the weddings of Catholics which might have taken place during this one-fifth of the year will be distributed over the other weeks. This is at least a partial explanation for the large number of Catholics in this sample.

14. State records in Iowa show that 63 per cent of all remarriages involving Catholics are mixed marriages, compared to 30 per cent of the first marriages; see Lee G. Burchinal, William F. Kenkel, and Loren E. Chancellor, "Comparisons of State- and Diocese-Reported Marriage Data for Iowa, 1953-57," *American Catholic Sociological Review*, 23 (1962), p. 25.

15. Lenski, *op. cit.*, p. 49.

16. David M. Eichhorn, "Conversions to Judaism by Reform and Conservative Rabbis," *Jewish Social Studies*, 16 (1954), p. 310.

17. In the 1962 sample the wives interviewed were asked regarding themselves (and similarly for their husbands): "And now, I want to ask you about your religious preference—that is, are you Protestant, Catholic, Jewish, or something else?" Then the question: "Have you always been [Protestant, Catholic, Jewish, etc.]?" Finally, "When did you make this change?" Since they were not asked to specify what their previous religious preference was, but only whether they had changed, we cannot know for certain in what religious group the changers were socialized. However, in view of the religious composition of the Detroit area population, we should make few errors if we make the following assumptions: A wife now Protestant, who says that she has changed religious preference, is assumed to have been Catholic before the change. One may say the equivalent to this for the husbands and for changes to Catholic. In the process of classifying marriages by religious types according to these criteria, just six marriages were found to include neither a Protestant nor a Catholic and therefore to be ineligible for our study. There were 185 marriages still meeting our requirements for analysis.

Index